Prayer Book Studies
Volume Three

Initial Pastoral Offices, Issues X-XV

Edited by
Derek A. Olsen

Copyright © 2026 The Domestic and Foreign Missionary Society of the Protestant Episcopal Church in the United States of America

The English text of the liturgies presented in this book is in the public domain and is freely available for quotation without restriction.

Unless otherwise noted, Scripture quotations are from The New Revised Standard Version Bible, copyright © 1989 National Council of the Churches of Christ in the United States of America. Used by permission. All rights reserved worldwide.

Seabury Books
19 East 34th Street
New York, NY 10016
www.churchpublishing.org

Seabury Books is an imprint of Church Publishing Incorporated.

Cover design by Newgen
Typeset by Integra Software Services Pvt. Ltd.

ISBN 978-1-64065-927-8 (paperback)
ISBN 978-1-64065-928-5 (hardback)
ISBN 978-1-64065-929-2 (eBook)

Library of Congress Control Number: 2025945259

CONTENTS

Introduction vii

Prayer Book Studies X: The Solemnization of Matrimony

Preface 3

History 6

Proposed Revisions 7
   The Introduction 7
   The Marriage 8
   The Benediction 9

Holy Matrimony 10
   The Form of Solemnization of Matrimony 10

Prayer Book Studies XI: A Thanksgiving for the Birth of a Child

Preface 17

The Need of Revision 19

Proposed Changes 20
   The Title 20
   Opening Rubrics 20
   Exhortation 21
   Psalms 21
   Lesson 21
   The Prayers 22

A Thanksgiving for the Birth of a Child 22
   Psalm cxxi. Levavi oculos 23

Prayer Book Studies XII:
The Propers for the Minor Holy Days

Preface 29

Part One: The Collects 32
New Materials in the Anglican Prayer Books 32
The Problem of Suitable Collects 34
Principles of Present Proposals 37
New Collects Proposed 41

Part Two: The Epistles and Gospels 56
Principles of Choice 58
Martyrs 60
Confessors 64
Ascetics 66
Missionaries 68
Doctors 69
Scriptural Saints 77
Events 82
Commons 83

Part Three: Movable Octaves and Seasons 84
The Easter and Whitsun Octaves 84
The Ember Days 86
Rogation Days 92
Weekdays of Lent 93

Part Four: The Proposed Propers 104
The Proposed Calendar 104
Proposed Collects, Epistles, and Gospels for the Lesser Feasts
and Fasts 116

Indices 157
Movable Days: Epistles and Gospels 157
Immovable Days: Epistles and Gospels 159
Interim Epistles and Gospels Proposed for the Week
Days of Lent 160
Immovable Days 161

Prayer Book Studies XIII: The Order for the Burial of the Dead

Preface 167

General Comments 169

The Revisions 170
At the Grave 170
At the Burial of a Child 171

The Order for the Burial of the Dead 172

At the Burial of a Child 184

Prayer Book Studies XIV: An Office of Institution of Rectors into Parishes

Preface 191

History 193
Origin and Development in Feudalism 193
In England 193
Induction in the Colonial Church 195
The American Office 196

Proposed Revision 198

An Office of Institution of Rectors into Parishes 200

Prayer Book Studies XV: The Problem and Method of Prayer Book Revision

Foreword 207

The Problem of Procedures 208

A New Method 211

A Specific Proposal 215

INTRODUCTION

The Series as a Whole

The *Prayer Book Studies* (PBS) series documents the 26-year process of study and conversation that led to the adoption of the American 1979 Book of Common Prayer. It falls broadly into two parts, distinguished by the use of Roman numerals and Arabic numerals. PBS I-XVII were published by the members of the Standing Liturgical Commission between 1950 and 1966 to communicate research and draft liturgies leading toward a revision process; PBS 18-29 were published by the various drafting committees between 1970 and 1976 once the revision process was formally begun and the earlier drafts were being transformed into new usable liturgies, leading up to the adoption of the new prayer book in 1979. Finally, PBS 30 and its commentary were added in 1989 to discuss inclusive and expansive language for God for further liturgical efforts.

Context of these Studies

The studies contained in this volume, PBS X-XV, hit the first major seam in the series. The first five studies (X-XIV) mostly deal with the pastoral offices, with the exception of PBS XII, which takes on the collects of the Church Year and should be seen within the broader context of PBS I-XIV. These fourteen studies that appeared in ten publications (four volumes contain two studies) systematically explore all of the liturgical materials within the 1928 Book of Common Prayer, incorporating scholarly research alongside input from clergy and congregations, concluding each study with a sample liturgy based on the study and reflection of the Commission.

Each of these fourteen studies begin with an identical preface laying out the guiding principles: to objectively and impartially inform the broader church on the principles and issues involved in the revision of each portion, not for the benefit of one theological party but to the education of all.

The overwhelming impression of these documents is of a committee, anchored by Bayard Jones, Morton Stone, and Massey Shepherd Jr.—the professors of the leading Episcopal seminaries of the day—that accomplished its work in a careful and thorough fashion. A great deal of thought, discussion, and argument has gone into these materials. The results are careful and fairly conservative modifications, assuming a retention of the "traditional" Elizabethan/Jacobean idiom of the English Prayer Book and the King James Bible.

The final study, PBS XV, is not properly a study of any particular liturgy. Rather, it is a plea directly from the Standing Liturgical Commission to the delegates of the 1961 General Convention for the adoption of the category of "trial use" in order that the liturgies produced by the Commission could be experienced by worshipping congregations and be tested in actual practice, rather than in theoretical read-throughs.

These Studies

PBS X/XI

This first study on marriage is a now-typical gentle revision of the 1928 rite, primarily concerned with altering rubrics and words that have changed meaning. Other changes, like both rings now being blessed before either is given, are relatively minor.

The second study, revising the former rite of the churching of women, makes some major changes. Here, the original prayer book logic for the rite—removing the ritual taint of childbirth from a new mother—is rejected, and the rite is rethought and restructured as a communal thanksgiving for the birth of a child. Like the studies on the visitation of the sick (PBS III) and the penitential office (PBS VII), this study demonstrates the way the revisers reinterpreted a rite no longer in step with modern beliefs and attitudes.

PBS XII

Far and away the longest study in this volume, the third study picks up where PBS IX on the sanctoral calendar left off. Taking the list of recommended feasts and fasts from there, this study provides the liturgical materials in terms of epistles, Gospels, and collects for their Eucharistic celebration. The new groupings of saints, such as pastors, missionaries, theologians, etc., are first found here, and most saints share collects with a small group of like-minded souls (biographical collects having been explicitly rejected).

PBS XIII/XIV

The fourth study on burial is remarkably terse in its initial material. There is only the briefest sketch of historical development, and barely a nod to the principles of revision. The vast majority of the content is simply the revised rites, which are lightly amended from their 1928 models.

The fifth study on the institution of a rector contains much more historical detail than burial, as well as principles of revision. There are few revisions from the 1928 rite, with the exception of one alteration that already points to a key shift in Episcopal public worship: whereas the institution in the 1928 rite could occur in the context of Morning Prayer, Evening Prayer, or Eucharist, this revised rite requires the celebration of the Eucharist by the newly instituted rector.

PBS XV

The fifth and final "study" in this volume is not a true liturgical study, but rather a plea to the delegates of the 1961 General Convention. It is a study in that it rehearses the history and failures of American prayer book revision based on the lapses of parliamentary procedure; it notes that the 1928 book was passed over a period of fifteen years and five successive conventions before all parts were ratified twice by both houses, and that only because the 1925 convention halted all new business until the prayer book matters were completed! Indeed, a resolution to initiate a formal process of prayer book revision was passed by the House of Deputies in 1958 but never taken up by the House of Bishops. Rather than making the same mistake or worse, this study calls for new solutions to old problems, chiefly the designation of "trial use."

PRAYER BOOK STUDIES X: THE SOLEMNIZATION OF MATRIMONY

The Standing Liturgical Commission
of the Protestant Episcopal Church in the
United States of America

1958

PREFACE

The last revision of our Prayer Book was brought to a rather abrupt conclusion in 1928. Consideration of it had preoccupied the time of General Convention ever since 1913. Everyone was weary of the long and ponderous legislative process, and desired to make the new Prayer Book available as soon as possible for the use of the Church.

But the work of revision, which sometimes has seemed difficult to start, in this case proved hard to stop. The years of debate had aroused widespread interest in the whole subject: and the mind of the Church was more receptive of suggestions for revision when the work was brought to an end than when it began. Moreover, the revision was actually closed to new action in 1925, in order that it might receive final adoption in 1928: so that it was not possible to give due consideration to a number of very desirable features in the English and Scottish revisions, which appeared simultaneously with our own. It was further realized that there were some rough edges in what had been done, as well as an unsatisfied demand for still further alterations.

The problem of defects in detail was met by continuing the Revision Commission, and giving it rather large 'editorial' powers (subject only to review by General Convention) to correct obvious errors in the text as adopted, in the publication of the new Prayer Book. Then, to deal with the constructive proposals for other changes which continued to be brought up in every General Convention, the Revision Commission was reconstituted as a Standing Liturgical Commission. To this body all matters concerning the Prayer Book were to be referred, for preservation in permanent files, and for continuing consideration, until such time as the accumulated matter was sufficient in amount and importance to justify proposing another Revision.

The number of such referrals by General Convention, of Memorials from Dioceses, and of suggestions made directly to the Commission from all regions and schools and parties in the Church, has now reached such a total that it is evident that there is a widespread and insistent demand for a general revision of the Prayer Book.

The Standing Liturgical Commission is not, however, proposing any immediate revision. On the contrary, we believe that there ought to be a period of study and discussion, to acquaint the Church at large with the principles and issues involved, in order that the eventual action may be taken intelligently, and if possible without consuming so much of the time of our supreme legislative synod.

Accordingly, the General Convention of 1949 signaled the Fourth Centennial Year of the First Book of Common Prayer in English by authorizing the Liturgical Commission to publish its findings, in the form of a series of *Prayer Book Studies*.

It must be emphasized that the liturgical forms presented in these *Studies* are not — and under our Constitution, cannot be — sanctioned for public use. They are submitted for free discussion. The Commission will be grateful for copies or articles, resolutions, and direct comment, for its consideration, that the mind of the Church may be fully known to the body charged with reporting it.

In this undertaking, we have endeavored to be objective and impartial. It is not possible to avoid every matter which may be thought by some to be controversial. Ideas which seem to be constructively valuable will be brought to the attention of the Church, without too much regard as to whether they may ultimately be judged to be expedient. We cannot undertake to eliminate every proposal to which anyone might conceivably object: to do so would be to admit that any constructive progress is impossible. What we can do is to be alert not to alter the present *balance* of expressed or implied doctrine of the Church. We can seek to counterbalance every proposal which might seem to favor some one party of opinion by some other change in the opposite direction. The goal we have constantly had in mind — however imperfectly we may have succeeded in attaining it — is the shaping of a future Prayer Book which *every* party might embrace with the well-founded conviction that therein its own position had been strengthened, its witness enhanced, and its devotions enriched.

The objective we have pursued is the same as that expressed by the Commission for the Revision of 1892: "*Resolved*, That this Committee, in all its suggestions and acts, be guided by those principles of liturgical construction and ritual use which have guided the compilation and amendments of the Book of Common Prayer, and have made it what it is."

THE STANDING LITURGICAL COMMISSION:

GOODRICH R. FENNER, *Chairman*
ARTHUR C. LICHTENBERGER
* BAYARD H. JONES, *Vice Chairman*
JOHN W. SUTER, *Custodian*
MASSEY H. SHEPHERD, JR.
CHARLES W. F. SMITH
FRANCIS B. SAYRE, JR.
BERTRAM L. SMITH
SPENCER ERVIN, *Secretary*
JOHN ASHTON
* Died, April 27, 1957

The chief preliminary work on the Marriage Service was in charge of two former members of the Commission, the Reverend Dr. Churchill J. Gibson and the Reverend Walter Williams. Preparation of the introduction to the Study was entrusted to the late Dr. Jones, to whom the Commission records its gratitude for the principal substance of the Study herewith published. Dr. Jones, however, should not be held accountable for the final draft of this Study in all its particular detail.

MASSEY H. SHEPHERD, JR.
Editor, for the Commission.

History

As in several European countries, the Marriage Service of the Church in England before the Reformation consisted of a prescribed tradition in the vernacular, rather than a fixed formula in Latin. This tradition has maintained its place in the use of the Roman Church in England and America to the present day; and this circumstance explains why the marriage ritual officially approved for Roman Catholics in these English-speaking countries is closer to that of the Book of Common Prayer than is the Latin form of the *Rituale Romanum*. For both services are alike descended from the English rite as it was in medieval times.

The form of Marriage Service adopted by the Church of England in the First Prayer Book of 1549 was basically that of the Sarum Manual, with a few features borrowed from the York Manual. The rite has remained thereafter in the English Prayer Book, through successive revisions, without material alteration, as follows:

1. An Introduction, embodying the so-called *Cautelae* or "Cautions," setting forth a eulogy of the holy estate of Matrimony, and emphasizing the necessity of the utmost carefulness and reverence in undertaking that relation.
2. The mutual contracts and avowals which constitute the Marriage. The essential "matter" of this sacrament consists of the reciprocal consents before witnesses — as the final proclamation says, "have consented together . . . and have witnessed the same before God and this company." It should be noted that the illustrative ceremonies — "having declared the same, by giving and receiving of a ring, and by joining Hands" — of whatever dramatic value, are none of them essential.

   The Marriage really consists of two passages, the Betrothal and the Espousal. The Betrothal survives as the residue of the original family ritual of solemn engagement, preparing the way for the (still future) contract. The manifest intention of this form is to establish the free will and accord of the parties making these promises. Immediately thereafter comes the actual Espousal, executing the marriage contract in the present tense. It will be noted that these two passages are said together continuously, without pause or interruption.
3. Then there was a processional Psalm, during which the wedding party proceeded from their original station at the choir gate to the altar rail.
4. The service concluded with summary prayers, and the Church's benediction of the action. A direction that the newly married couple receive the Holy Communion "the same day of their marriage" was slightly modified in the 1661 Book to provide "at the time of their marriage, or at the first opportunity after their marriage."

In America, in the early days, members of the Church were few and far between, and church buildings fewer still. Therefore the makers of the Prayer Book of 1789 gave sanction to one feature which has always remained unknown to every other branch of the Anglican Communion: namely, the home wedding held "in some proper house" instead of in the church building. Lacking the scenic setting of the sacred edifice, the processional Psalm was simply dropped from the service. Because of this, unfortunately, certain members of the Church of England in the nineteenth century accused the American Prayer Book of providing "a mere Betrothal Service." This criticism was quite without justification, since the only constituents of the English service which were eliminated by the American rite were the processional Psalm and the final Homily on the Holy Estate — neither one of which is in the slightest degree essential to the Espousals.

The proposed revision of the Marriage Service in the English Book of 1928 divided the rite into four parts: The Introduction, The Marriage, The Benediction, and The Communion. We consider that this order should be followed by the American rite; but the slight shortenings of the American order hitherto may properly be retained.

A majority of the Commission believe that it would be valuable to preface the Marriage Service in the Prayer Book with a page on which was printed the Declaration of Intention required of all parties to Holy Matrimony as now set forth in Canon 17, Section 3. This preface would be analogous to the present Prayer Book Preface to the Ordinal. A minority of the Commission consider it unwise to introduce into the Prayer Book matters that are of canonical, rather than of liturgical, regulation; but they readily accede to the majority opinion in proposing this suggestion to the Church for its critical comment and judgment, inasmuch as these Studies are not offered to the Church for legislative action by General Convention but solely for study and reflective consideration by individuals and groups within the Church concerned with the making of our Prayer Book as responsive as possible to the needs of our Church.

Proposed Revisions

The Introduction

The Commission proposes only two slight alterations in the present introduction of the Marriage Service, as contained on page 300 of the Prayer Book. In the opening rubric, it suggests that a qualifying clause be added — "if urgent cause require" — to the permission to hold the service "in some proper house." The original reason for this exception, allowing a home wedding, is not so urgent today as it was in the time of our Founding Fathers, after the American Revolution. We are more plentifully supplied with church buildings, and with easy transportation to them. And there is no good argument for the conduct of a Church rite in any place other than a church edifice when circumstances make it possible, although less than convenient. However, the Commission believes that there may still be causes of a weighty character that may demand some exception to the normative rule. There are still families that live in isolated areas, remote from settled communities where church buildings are available. There are conditions of physical illness or disability that make transportation from the home inadvisable. And there are peculiar circumstances of a pastoral nature where the officiating minister may judge it inexpedient to arrange for weddings in the church edifice.

In the charge to the couple, the word "dreadful" has been changed to "dread," to avoid the misunderstandings possible because of the popular associations with the former term.

The Marriage

The rubric on the top of page 301 has been shortened, in view of the present canonical requirements imposed upon the clergy with respect to pre-marital instructions and inquiries.

The giving away of the Bride has been made optional, rather than mandatory, since in many cases — especially those of older persons — this survival of medieval custom has become meaningless.

A new rubric, allowing the optional insertion of a Psalm, Hymn, or Anthem after the Betrothals, taking the wedding company to the altar for the Espousals and Benediction; is inserted after the giving away of the Bride. It should be emphasized that such a procession in the middle of the service is neither necessary nor, in all cases, convenient. The rubric merely recognizes a custom that has developed in modern times, especially in those churches where the sanctuary is separated from the nave by a chancel choir. There is certainly no ancient tradition for a break in the service at this point, and several members of the Commission have expressed a strong dissent from placing such a rubric at this place, rather than before the Lord's Prayer and after the giving of the Ring.[1]

A minor deletion from the first rubric at the top of page 302 is suggested: namely, the omission of "after the Minister." In many cases the bridal couple either reads the vows from the Prayer Book or recites them from memory. Hence it is not necessary for the Minister, in every case, to instruct them in the words of the vows phrase by phrase.

---

1. It is only fair to the late Dr. Jones of our Commission, to record his characteristically vigorous comment on this matter, especially in view of his being unable to present in person his dissent from the Commission's final vote on this rubric. In his draft introduction, he wrote: "It is hard to account for the custom which has grown up in the nineteenth century, of splitting asunder the Betrothals from the Espousals, and inserting the latter after the Giving of the Ring, and going up to the altar rail for that purpose: though the English order has no such shift of place here; and the American rite has no provision whatever by rubric or otherwise for such a shift. Although this ritual has made its way into 'Emily Post,' it is in fact completely unjustified; and it remains a mystery why our Anglophiles ever thought they were replacing the Espousals which the British critics had claimed to be missing."

The Giving of a Ring by the groom to the bride is one of the ancient survivals of Roman custom in our rite that has largely lost its original meaning of bestowal of a dowry. It is a symbol of something far deeper and more spiritual. And in modern times it has become increasingly customary for both parties to give rings to each other. The Commission believes that the time has come to accede to the widely expressed desire for some recognition in the service of the "double ring" ceremony. (There is precedent for this in the marriage rituals of a number of European countries.) Hence the formularies associated with the Giving of the Ring have been revamped to allow a blessing and giving of rings by both the man and the woman, when it may be so desired.

The Sarum Manual provided a form for the Blessing of the Ring. The American revision of 1928 was the only Anglican text providing for a prayer of this nature. But this Blessing was, not very happily, inserted after the bestowal of the Ring, which it was designed to precede. The present proposals are designed to correct this dislocation. And the form of Blessing has been worded in the hope that it will preserve the graceful, if fragile, rhetoric of the formulary, by avoiding either a banal pluralizing of the words or a tiresome repetition of them by shifting the pronouns "he" and "she" in a separate Blessing for each Ring.

The Benediction

No changes are proposed in the formularies that now complete the Marriage Service, beginning with the Lord's Prayer, except for a rewording of the rubric before the final Blessing. Instead of "the Minister," the words "a Priest" are substituted, to clarify a problem that often arises and make certain the unaltering tradition of the Church that only a Minister in priest's (or, of course, episcopal) Orders is qualified to pronounce such a Benediction.

It has also been proposed — and the Commission offers this suggestion for comment and criticism — that in many cases some form of dismissal of the congregation is desirable, after the wedding party have retired from the church. A permissive form is presented: the Salutation, the prayer "For a Blessing on the Families of the Land" (Prayer Book, page 598), and the Blessing from Numbers 6:24-26. This dismissal would in any case be omitted whenever a Nuptial Eucharist follows immediately upon the Marriage Rite. It is also proposed to introduce the proper Collect, Epistle and Gospel for a Nuptial celebration of Holy Communion as a conclusion — making it clear, however, that such a celebration, though highly desirable in proper circumstances, is nonetheless optional. But the Commission believes that in so placing these propers here, we shall not only be returning to the traditional teaching of the Prayer Book that such a celebration is a fitting climax of the nuptial rites, but we may thereby encourage a wider acceptance of the Nuptial Eucharist among our membership as a constituent part of a Church wedding in its fullness and perfection.

Holy Matrimony

¶ Before the Solemnization of any Marriage, the Minister shall have required that the parties sign the following Declaration:

We, A.B. and C.D., desiring to receive the blessing of Holy Matrimony in the Church, do solemnly declare that we hold marriage to be a lifelong union of husband and wife as it is set forth in the Form of Solemnization of Holy Matrimony in the Book of Common Prayer. We believe it is for the purpose of mutual fellowship, encouragement, and understanding, for the procreation (if it may be) of children, and their physical and spiritual nurture, for the safeguarding and benefit of society. And we do engage ourselves, so far as in us lies, to make our utmost effort to establish this relationship and to seek God's help thereto.

¶ And when the Banns are published, it shall be in the following form:

I publish the Banns of Marriage between N. of _____, and N. of _____. If any of you know cause, or just impediment, why these two persons should not be joined together in Holy Matrimony, ye are to declare it. This is the first [second or third] time of asking.

The Form of Solemnization of Matrimony

The Introduction

¶ At the day and time appointed for Solemnization of Matrimony, the Persons to be married shall come into the body of the Church, or if urgent cause require, shall be ready in some proper house, with their friends and neighbours; and there standing together, the Man on the right hand, and the Woman on the left, the Minister shall say,

DEARLY beloved, we are gathered together here in the sight of God, and in the face of this company, to join together this Man and this Woman in holy Matrimony; which is an honourable estate, instituted of God, signifying unto us the mystical union which is betwixt Christ and his Church: which holy estate Christ adorned and beautified with his presence and first miracle that he wrought in Cana of Galilee, and is commended of Saint Paul to be honourable among all men: and therefore is not by any to be entered into unadvisedly or lightly; but reverently, discreetly, advisedly, soberly, and in the fear of God. Into this holy estate these two persons present come now to be joined. If any man can show just cause why they may not lawfully be joined together, let him now speak, or else hereafter for ever hold his peace.

¶ And also speaking unto the Persons who are to be married, he shall say,

I REQUIRE and charge you both, as ye will answer at the dread day of judgment when the secrets of all hearts shall be disclosed, that if either of you know any impediment, why ye may not be lawfully joined together in Matrimony, ye do now confess it. For be ye well assured, that if any persons are joined together otherwise than as God's Word doth allow, their marriage is not lawful.

The Marriage

¶ *If no impediment be alleged or suspected, the Minister shall say to the Man,*

N WILT thou have this Woman to thy wedded wife, to live together after God's ordinance in the holy estate of Matrimony? Wilt thou love her, comfort her, honour, and keep her in sickness and in health; and, forsaking all others, keep thee only unto her, so long as ye both shall live?

¶ *The Man shall answer,*

I will.

¶ *Then shall the minister say unto the Woman,*

N WILT thou have this Man to thy wedded Husband, to live together after God's ordinance in the holy estate of Matrimony? Wilt thou love him, comfort him, honour, and keep him in sickness and in health; and, forsaking all others, keep thee only unto him, so long as ye both shall live?

¶ *The Woman shall answer,*

I will.

¶ *Then may the Minister say,*

Who giveth this Woman to be married to this Man?

¶ *Then the Minister, followed by the Man and the Woman, may go to the Lord's Table; while there may be sung a Psalm, Hymn, or Anthem.*

¶ *Then shall they give their troth to each other in this manner. The Minister, receiving the Woman at her father's or friend's hands, shall cause the Man with his right hand to take the Woman by her right hand, and to say as followeth,*

I N. take thee N. to my wedded wife, to have and to hold from this day forward, for better for worse, for richer for poorer, in sickness and in health, to love and to cherish, till death us do part, according to God's holy ordinance; and thereto I plight thee my troth.

¶ *Then shall they loose their hands; and the Woman with her right hand taking the Man by his right hand, shall likewise say after the Minister*

I *N.* take thee *N.* to my wedded Husband, to have and to hold from this day forward, for better for worse, for richer for poorer, in sickness and in health, to love and to cherish, till death us do part, according to God's holy ordinance; and thereto I give thee my troth.

¶ Then shall they loose their hands; and the Woman with her right hand taking the Man by his right hand, shall likewise say,

I *N.* take thee *N.* to my wedded Husband, to have and to hold from this day forward, for better for worse, for richer for poorer, in sickness and in health, to love and to cherish, till death us do part, according to God's holy ordinance; and thereto I give thee my troth.

¶ Then shall they again loose their hands; and the Man shall give unto the Woman a Ring; and the Woman may likewise give a Ring unto the Man. And the Minister, receiving the Ring or Rings, may say,

BLESS, O Lord, this Ring (these Rings), that both giver and wearer may abide in thy peace and continue in thy favour, unto their life's end; through Jesus Christ our Lord, Amen.

¶ Then, the giver of the Ring shall take the same, and put it upon the fourth finger of the left hand of the other party; and holding it there, and taught by the Minister, shall say,

WITH this Ring I thee wed: In the Name of the Father and of the Son, and of the Holy Ghost. Amen.

The Benediction

Minister. Let us pray.

¶ Then shall the Minister and the People, still standing, say the Lord's Prayer.

OUR Father, who art in heaven, Hallowed be thy Name. Thy kingdom come. Thy will be done, On earth as it is in heaven. Give us this day our daily bread. And forgive us our trespasses, As we forgive those who trespass against us. And lead us not into temptation, But deliver us from evil. For thine is the kingdom, and the power, and the glory, For ever and ever. Amen.

¶ Then shall the Minister say,

O ETERNAL God, Creator and Preserver of all mankind, Giver of all spiritual grace, the Author of everlasting life; Send thy blessing upon these thy servants, this man and this woman, whom we bless in thy Name; that they, living faithfully together, may surely perform and keep the vow and covenant betwixt them made, (whereof *this Ring* given and received is a token and pledge,) and may ever remain in perfect love and peace together, and live according to thy laws; through Jesus Christ our Lord. *Amen.*

¶ *The Minister may add one or both of the following prayers.*

O ALMIGHTY God, Creator of mankind, who only art the well-spring of life: Bestow upon these thy servants, if it be thy will, the gift and heritage of children; and grant that they may see their children brought up in thy faith and fear, to the honour and glory of thy Name; through Jesus Christ our Lord. *Amen.*

O GOD, who hast so consecrated the state of Matrimony that in it is represented the spiritual marriage and unity betwixt Christ and his Church; Look mercifully upon these thy servants, that they may love, honour, and cherish each other, and so live together in faithfulness and patience, in wisdom and true godliness, that their home may be a haven of blessing and of peace; through the same Jesus Christ our Lord, who liveth and reigneth with thee and the Holy Spirit ever, one God, world without end. *Amen.*

¶ *Then shall the Minister join their right hands together, and say,*

Those whom God hath joined together let no man put asunder.

¶ *Then shall the Minister speak unto the company.*

FORASMUCH as *N.* and *N.* have consented together in holy wedlock, and have witnessed the same before God and this company, and thereto have given and pledged their troth, each to the other, and have declared the same by giving and receiving *a Ring*, and by joining hands; I pronounce that they are Man and Wife, In the Name of the Father, and of the Son, and of the Holy Ghost. *Amen.*

¶ *The Husband and Wife kneeling, a Priest shall add this Blessing.*

GOD the Father, God the Son, God the Holy Ghost, bless, preserve, and keep you; the Lord mercifully with his favour look upon you, and fill you with all spiritual benediction and grace; that ye may so live together in this life, that in the world to come ye may have life everlasting. *Amen.*

¶ *Here, except when there is a Communion, the Minister may dismiss the Congregation as follows, saying,*

The Lord be with you.
Answer. And with thy spirit.
Minister. Let us pray.

ALMIGHTY God, our heavenly Father, who settest the solitary in families; We commend to thy continual care the homes in which thy people dwell. Put far from them, we beseech thee, every root of bitterness, the desire of vain-glory, and the pride of life. Fill them with faith, virtue, knowledge, temperance, patience, godliness. Knit together in constant affection those who, in holy wedlock, have been made one flesh; turn the heart of the fathers to the children, and the heart of the children to the fathers; and so enkindle fervent charity among us all, that we be evermore kindly affectioned with brotherly love; through Jesus Christ our Lord. *Amen.*

THE LORD bless you, and keep you. The LORD make his face to shine upon you, and be gracious unto you. The LORD lift up his countenance upon you, and give you peace, both now and evermore. *Amen.*

The Communion

The Collect

O ETERNAL God, we humbly beseech thee, favourably to behold these thy servants now (*or* about to be) joined in wedlock according to thy holy ordinance; and grant that they, seeking first thy kingdom and thy righteousness, may obtain the manifold blessings of thy grace; through Jesus Christ our Lord. *Amen.*

The Epistle. Ephesians v.20.

GIVE thanks always for all things unto God and the Father in the name of our Lord Jesus Christ; submitting yourselves one to another in the fear of God. Wives, submit yourselves unto your own husbands, as unto the Lord. For the husband is the head of the wife, even as Christ is the head of the church: and he is the saviour of the body. Therefore as the church is subject unto Christ, so let the wives be to their own husbands in every thing. Husbands, love your wives, even as Christ also loved the church, and gave himself for it; that he might sanctify and cleanse it with the washing of water by the word, that he might present it to himself a glorious church, not having spot, or wrinkle, or any such thing; but that it should be holy and without blemish. So ought men to love their wives as their own bodies. He that loveth his wife loveth himself. For no man ever yet hated his own flesh; but nourisheth and cherisheth it, even as the Lord the church: for we are members of his body, of his flesh, and of his bones. For this cause shall a man leave his father and mother, and shall be joined unto his wife, and they two shall be one flesh. This is a great mystery: but I speak concerning Christ and the church. Nevertheless let every one of you in particular so love his wife even as himself; and the wife see that she reverence her husband.

The Gospel. St. Matthew xix. 4.

JESUS answered and said unto them, Have ye not read, that he which made them at the beginning made them male and female, and said, For this cause shall a man leave father and mother, and shall cleave to his wife: and they twain shall be one flesh? Wherefore they are no more twain, but one flesh? What therefore God hath joined together, let not man put asunder.

PRAYER BOOK STUDIES XI: A THANKSGIVING FOR THE BIRTH OF A CHILD

The Standing Liturgical Commission
of the Protestant Episcopal Church in the
United States of America

1958

PREFACE

The last revision of our Prayer Book was brought to a rather abrupt conclusion in 1928. Consideration of it had preoccupied the time of General Convention ever since 1913. Everyone was weary of the long and ponderous legislative process, and desired to make the new Prayer Book available as soon as possible for the use of the Church.

But the work of revision, which sometimes has seemed difficult to start, in this case proved hard to stop. The years of debate had aroused widespread interest in the whole subject: and the mind of the Church was more receptive of suggestions for revision when the work was brought to an end than when it began. Moreover, the revision was actually closed to new action in 1925, in order that it might receive final adoption in 1928: so that it was not possible to give due consideration to a number of very desirable features in the English and Scottish revisions, which appeared simultaneously with our own. It was further realized that there were some rough edges in what had been done, as well as an unsatisfied demand for still further alterations.

The problem of defects in detail was met by continuing the Revision Commission, and giving it rather large 'editorial' powers (subject only to review by General Convention) to correct obvious errors in the text as adopted, in the publication of the new Prayer Book. Then, to deal with the constructive proposals for other changes which continued to be brought up in every General Convention, the Revision Commission was reconstituted as a Standing Liturgical Commission. To this body all matters concerning the Prayer Book were to be referred, for preservation in permanent files, and for continuing consideration, until such time as the accumulated matter was sufficient in amount and importance to justify proposing another Revision.

The number of such referrals by General Convention, of Memorials from Dioceses, and of suggestions made directly to the Commission from all regions and schools and parties in the Church, has now reached such a total that it is evident that there is a widespread and insistent demand for a general revision of the Prayer Book.

The Standing Liturgical Commission is not, however, proposing any immediate revision. On the contrary, we believe that there ought to be a period of study and discussion, to acquaint the Church at large with the principles and issues involved, in order that the eventual action may be taken intelligently, and if possible without consuming so much of the time of our supreme legislative synod.

Accordingly, the General Convention of 1949 signalized the Fourth Centennial Year of the First Book of Common Prayer in English by authorizing the Liturgical Commission to publish its findings, in the form of a series of *Prayer Book Studies*.

It must be emphasized that the liturgical forms presented in these *Studies* are not — and under our Constitution, cannot be — sanctioned for public use. They are submitted for free discussion. The Commission will be grateful for copies or articles, resolutions, and direct comment, for its consideration, that the mind of the Church may be fully known to the body charged with reporting it.

In this undertaking, we have endeavored to be objective and impartial. It is not possible to avoid every matter which may be thought by some to be controversial. Ideas which seem to be constructively valuable will be brought to the attention of the Church, without too much regard as to whether they may ultimately be judged to be expedient. We cannot undertake to eliminate every proposal to which anyone might conceivably object: to do so would be to admit that any constructive progress is impossible. What we can do is to be alert not to alter the present *balance* of expressed or implied doctrine of the Church. We can seek to counterbalance every proposal which might seem to favor some one party of opinion by some other change in the opposite direction. The goal we have constantly had in mind — however imperfectly we may have succeeded in attaining it — is the shaping of a future Prayer Book which *every* party might embrace with the well-founded conviction that therein its own position had been strengthened, its witness enhanced, and its devotions enriched.

The objective we have pursued is the same as that expressed by the Commission for the Revision of 1892: "*Resolved*, That this Committee, in all its suggestions and acts, be guided by those principles of liturgical construction and ritual use which have guided the compilation and amendments of the Book of Common Prayer, and have made it what it is."

THE STANDING LITURGICAL COMMISSION:

GOODRICH R. FENNER, *Chairman*
ARTHUR C. LICHTENBERGER
* BAYARD H. JONES, *Vice Chairman*
JOHN W. SUTER, *Custodian*
MASSEY H. SHEPHERD, JR.
CHARLES W. F. SMITH
FRANCIS B. SAYRE, JR.
BERTRAM L. SMITH
SPENCER ERVIN, *Secretary*
JOHN ASHTON

* Died, April 27, 1957

The proposals for revision of the Churching Office were first prepared by a sub-committee headed by the Reverend Walter Williams. The final draft of this Study has been in charge of Bishop Lichtenberger and Dr. Shepherd.

MASSEY H. SHEPHERD, JR.
Editor, for the Commission.

The Need of Revision

The infrequent use of the Churching of Women Office in the Prayer Book has been the occasion of considerable comment and suggestion in the correspondence filed with the Liturgical Commission. Reactions to the service have been either negative — that the Office ought to be eliminated altogether from the Prayer Book — or positive in their proposals for a radical reconstruction of its materials.

On the negative side, it has been pointed out that despite the careful revisions that the Office has undergone in successive editions of the Prayer Book, the ancient taboo of uncleanness associated with childbirth, with the concomitant notion that the rite is some kind of purification, has lingered about the service. Though it cannot be fairly stated that the present Prayer Book Office either suggests or encourages such an outworn, not to say un-Christian, viewpoint with respect to childbirth, it cannot be denied that such prejudice still exists with respect to the service. It may be that this association of ideas is kept alive — unconsciously perhaps — by suggestions from the Prayer Book feast of the Presentation of our Lord in the Temple, with its popular title, still preserved in the heading of the Prayer Book (pages 231–32), of "The Purification."

More reasonable is the insistence that the Office suffers today from an exaggerated emphasis upon the dangers of childbirth, since modern medicine has so greatly reduced, at least in America, as also in many other "Western" countries, the mortality-rate of both mothers and newborn infants. It would be foolish, of course, to deny the seriousness of "great pain and peril of childbirth" as mentioned in the Office, or to overlook the plain facts of tragic loss of life and health that do occur. A Prayer Book service that avoided all reference to these hard realities would lack relevance to basic human situations and experience. What the objectors to the Office maintain, however, is the unreality of building an entire service about this theme, in the light of present-day conditions where the normative expectancy of the family is hopeful of a happy and successful birth of a new life. All that is needed in the Prayer Book, from this point of view, are one or two prayers in the section "Thanksgivings" that may be used when desired, either privately with the family or publicly in the course of the regular offices of corporate worship of the Church.

On the other hand, there are those who believe that the birth of a child in a Christian family is of such high significance that the Church's liturgy should give it due and proper recognition by a suitable service of thanksgiving. They would revamp the present Churching Office to make it a corporate act of the entire family concerned, or at least of both parents, rather than of the mother alone, and set it normally within the context of the public worship of the whole "household of faith." Such a service would include not only a thanksgiving for the safe deliverance of the mother, but also — and more importantly — for the birth of a child, with additional prayers, when the occasion seems appropriate, for the home and for the Christian nurture of the newborn member of the family.

The Liturgical Commission shares this latter point of view, which it believes to be in line with trends in other Anglican Prayer Books. By altering the title of the service, it has attempted to place a right emphasis upon the primary nature and purpose of the Office. But the Commission has felt that the contents of the service have not needed so radical a reconstruction as many have supposed. The changes herewith proposed have not materially altered the simple structure of the present Prayer Book service; and though there has been a slight lengthening of the Office, if it is said in its entirety, an attempt has been made to make its contents more flexible so that it might be adapted to varying family situations. The rubrics have been carefully revised, to eliminate archaic survivals and references, and to adapt them to modern conditions.

The Commission also believes that this Office should be maintained in its present location in the sequence of Prayer Book services, following as it does logically the marriage service. We would also wish to call attention to the need of including within the Prayer Book itself, at the next revision of our liturgy, the form of service for the Adoption of a Child that now appears in the *Book of Offices for Special Occasions* authorized by General Convention. This latter service was prepared by the Commission several years ago at the specific request of the General Convention, and has found a most cordial reception in the Church. We believe that it should not be left ultimately in a separate, although official, book of special Offices, but should find a place in the Prayer Book directly following the present service of Thanksgiving for the Birth of a Child.

Proposed Changes

The Title

The new title, as stated above, gives the primary emphasis that the Office should have. It should also have a greater psychological appeal to our Church people than does the title of the present Office, and thus encourage and develop a more widespread use.

Opening Rubrics

The four rubrics contain the principal substance of what is directed in the present Office both by its opening rubrics and by the rubric at the end of the service. They give the Minister clear indications of the varied ways and places where the Office can be appropriately used. And they make specific the intention that wherever feasible the entire family, and not just the mother alone, have a part in the service.

Exhortation

The present Exhortation of the Office is retained, but with the significant addition of the phrase: "and to bless thy home with the gift and heritage of this child." (Obviously, if twins are born, the Minister will say "these children.") The pronouns have been changed from the plural "you" to the singular "thee" since the Office will normally be used for a single family. But there is no inherent reason why several families might not participate together in a service, in which case the plurals "you" and "your" may be employed. The Exhortation has also been revamped so that the entire family is bidden to join in the psalm with the Minister. This avoids the awkwardness of the present service, where the mother alone is bidden to say the psalm, but the directive is corrected by a rubric. No reference is made to the posture of those reciting the psalm, as this may be left to the choice of the persons concerned; but the rubric before the Exhortation suggests in any case that standing would be the normative posture, for the psalm is said as an act of thanksgiving.

Psalms

A choice of Psalms is offered. The Commission recommends the restoration of Psalm 121, the one traditionally associated with the Office both in the Sarum Use and in the First and Second Prayer Books of 1549 and 1552. Psalm 116 was introduced into the Office in the revision of 1661, and is particularly appropriate when the Office is followed immediately by the Holy Communion. It will be noted that the Commission recommends the entire psalm, not the shortened version that has characterized the American Prayer Book since 1789. The verses omitted hitherto in the American Book are all fitting to the occasion.

Lesson

The principal new feature of the proposed Office is the addition of a lesson from Deuteronomy 6:4-9; but the rubric makes the lesson optional, not mandatory. When the Office is used separately, the lesson services in filling it out with helpful instruction in God's Word to the families of His people. It gives the Office a general similarity of structure with that of the Daily Offices. If used before the Holy Communion, the lesson of this Office adds to the total rite salient Old Testament material, and in particular gives a specific application to the Summary of the Law contained in the Eucharist.

The Prayers

The pattern of the prayers follows that of the present service. The Lord's Prayer has the doxology, since in this service it is not preceded by the Kyrie and it has no penitential context. The versicles remain the same, but the wording is restored to a general application rather than to "this woman." The first Collect has been considerably revised to include not merely thanksgiving for deliverance in childbirth, but also for the child; and the petition is directed to the thought of the Christian nurture of the child rather than to the continuing Christian life of the mother alone. The phrase "with her husband" is placed in parentheses to provide for those occasions when the father has either died before the birth of the child, or for some tragic circumstance has no direct responsibility for the upbringing of the child.

In place of the present concluding Collect (which is only permissive), the Commission recommends the addition at this place of two prayers now appearing in the Family Prayer section of the Prayer Book: "For the Children," and "For a Blessing on the Families of the Land." The appropriateness of these prayers in this context does not need to be argued. But the Commission believes that there is value in placing together in the Prayer Book related prayers, in contexts where they fit. Their inclusion here would be convenient to the Minister, and provide him with all that is needful to a proper ending of the service. But the printing of these prayers in this place would in no way necessitate their exclusion from other parts of the Prayer Book, whether in the occasional Prayers and Thanksgivings, or in Family Prayer. What these latter sections of the Prayer Book should contain will be the subject of other Studies by the Commission.

A Thanksgiving for the Birth of a Child

¶ *This Service, or the Collect named* The Thanksgiving of Women after Childbirth, *as it stands among the Occasional Prayers and Thanksgivings, may be used before the Holy Communion or separately.*

¶ *The Woman, as soon as may be after her delivery, shall come into the Church, with such other members of her family as may be convenient.*

¶ *This Service may be used in the hospital or in the home.*

¶ *The Minister shall say unto the Family, all standing,*

FORASMUCH as it hath pleased Almighty God, of his goodness, to give thee safe deliverance, to preserve thee in the great danger of Child-birth, and to bless thy home with the gift and heritage of this child; let us therefore give hearty thanks unto God, and say,

Psalm cxxi. Levavi oculos

I WILL lift up mine eyes unto the hills; from whence cometh my help?

My help cometh even from the LORD, who hath made heaven and earth.

He will not suffer thy foot to be moved; and he that keepeth thee will not sleep.

Behold, he that keepeth Israel shall neither slumber nor sleep.

The LORD himself is thy keeper; the LORD is thy defence upon thy right hand;

So that the sun shall not burn thee by day, neither the moon by night.

The LORD shall preserve thee from all evil; yea, it is even he that shall keep thy soul.

The LORD shall preserve thy going out, and thy coming in, from this time forth for evermore

Glory be to the Father, and to the Son, and to the Holy Ghost;

As it was in the beginning, is now, and ever shall be, world without end. Amen.

¶ *Or this,*

MY delight is in the LORD; because he hath heard the voice of my prayer; Because he hath inclined his ear unto me; therefore will I call upon him as long as I live.

The snares of death compassed me round about, and the pains of hell gat hold upon me.

I found trouble and heaviness; then called I upon the Name of the LORD; O LORD, I beseech thee, deliver my soul.

Gracious is the LORD, and righteous; yea, our God is merciful.

The LORD preserveth the simple: I was in misery, and he helped me.

Turn again then unto thy rest, O my soul; for the LORD hath rewarded thee.

And why? thou hast delivered my soul from death, mine eyes from tears, and my feet from falling.

I will walk before the LORD in the land of the living.

I believed, and therefore will I speak; but I was sore troubled: I said in my haste, All men are liars.

What reward shall I give unto the LORD for all the benefits that he hath done unto me?

I will receive the cup of salvation, and call upon the Name of the LORD.

I will pay my vows now in the presence of all his people: right dear in the sight of the LORD is the death of his saints.

Behold, O Lord, how that I am thy servant; I am thy servant, and the son of thine handmaid; thou hast broken my bonds in sunder.

I will offer to thee the sacrifice of thanksgiving, and will call upon the Name of the Lord.

I will pay my vows unto the Lord, in the sight of all his people, in the courts of the Lord's house; even in the midst of thee, O Jerusalem. Praise the Lord.

Glory be to the Father, and to the Son, and to the Holy Ghost;

As it was in the beginning, is now, and ever shall be, world without end. Amen.

¶ *Then the Minister may read as a Lesson, Deuteronomy vi. 4-9.*

¶ *Then shall the Minister say,*

Let us pray.

OUR Father, who art in heaven, Hallowed be thy Name. Thy kingdom come. Thy will be done, On earth as it is in heaven. Give us this day our daily bread. And forgive us our trespasses, As we forgive those who trespass against us. And lead us not into temptation, But deliver us from evil. For thine is the kingdom, and the power, and the glory, for ever and ever. Amen.

Minister. O Lord, save thy servants;
Answer. Who put their trust in thee.
Minister. Be thou to them a strong tower;
Answer. From the face of our enemy.
Minister. Lord, hear our prayer.
Answer. And let our cry come unto thee.
Minister. Let us pray.

ALMIGHTY and most merciful Father, we give thee humble and hearty thanks that thou hast brought this thy servant through her travail to rejoice in the birth of a child. Continue, we beseech thee, thy goodness to her, that she, restored to health and strength, may (with her husband) lead this child in the way of truth and righteousness, to the glory of thy Name, and the blessing of their home; through Jesus Christ our Lord. *Amen.*

ALMIGHTY God, heavenly Father, who hast blessed us with the joy and care of children; Give us light and strength so to train them, that they may love whatsoever things are true and pure and lovely, and of good report, following the example of their Saviour Jesus Christ. Amen.

A Thanksgiving for the Birth of a Child

ALMIGHTY God, our heavenly Father, who settest the solitary in families; We commend to thy continual care the homes in which thy people dwell. Put far from them, we beseech thee, every root of bitterness, the desire of vainglory, and the pride of life. Fill them with faith, virtue, knowledge, temperance, patience, godliness. Knit together in constant affection those who, in holy wedlock, have been made one flesh; turn the heart of the parents to the children, and the heart of the children to the parents; and so enkindle fervent charity among us all, that we be evermore kindly affectioned with brotherly love; through Jesus Christ our Lord. *Amen.*

PRAYER BOOK STUDIES XII: THE PROPERS FOR THE MINOR HOLY DAYS

The Standing Liturgical Commission
of the Protestant Episcopal Church in the
United States of America

1958

PREFACE

The last revision of our Prayer Book was brought to a rather abrupt conclusion in 1928. Consideration of it had preoccupied the time of General Convention ever since 1913. Everyone was weary of the long and ponderous legislative process, and desired to make the new Prayer Book available as soon as possible for the use of the Church.

But the work of revision, which sometimes has seemed difficult to start, in this case proved hard to stop. The years of debate had aroused widespread interest in the whole subject; and the mind of the Church was more receptive of suggestions for revision when the work was brought to an end than when it began. Moreover, the revision was actually closed to new action in 1925, in order that it might receive final adoption in 1928: so that it was not possible to give the consideration to a number of very desirable features in the English and Scottish revisions, which appeared simultaneously with our own. It was further realized that there were some rough edges in what had been done, as well as an unsatisfied demand for still further alterations.

The problems of defects in detail were met by continuing the Revision Commission, and giving it rather large editorial powers (subject only to review by General Convention) to correct obvious errors in the text as adopted, in the publication of the new Prayer Book. Then, to deal with the constructive proposals for other changes which continued to be brought up in every General Convention, the Revision Commission was reconstituted as a Standing Liturgical Commission. To this body all matters concerning the Prayer Book were to be referred, for preservation in permanent files, and for continuing consideration, until such time as the accumulated matter was sufficient in amount and importance to justify proposing another Revision.

The number of such referrals by General Convention, of Memorials from Dioceses, and of suggestions made directly tothe Commission from all regions and schools and parties in the Church, has now reached such a total that it is evident that there is a widespread and insistent demand for a general revision of the Prayer Book.

The Standing Liturgical Commission is not, however, proposing any immediate revision. On the contrary, we believe that there ought to be a period of study and discussion, to acquaint the Church at large with the principles and issues involved, in order that the eventual action may be taken intelligently, and if possible without consuming so much of the time of our supreme legislative synod.

Accordingly, the General Convention of 1949 signalized the Fourth Centennial Year of the First Book of Common Prayer in English by authorizing the Liturgical Commission to publish its findings, in the form of a series of Prayer Book Studies.

It must be emphasized that the liturgical forms presented in these Studies are not — and under our Constitution, cannot be — sanctioned for public use. They are submitted for free discussion. The Commission will be grateful for copies or articles, resolutions, and direct comment, for its consideration, that the mind of the Church may be fully known to the body charged with reporting it.

In this undertaking, we have endeavored to be objective and impartial. It is not possible to avoid every matter which may be thought by some to be controversial. Ideas which seem to be constructively valuable will be brought to the attention of the Church, without too much regard as to whether they may ultimately be judged to be expedient. We cannot undertake to eliminate every proposal to which anyone might conceivably object: to do so would be to admit that any constructive progress is impossible. What we can do is to be alert not to alter the present balance of expressed or implied doctrine of the Church. We can seek to counterbalance every proposal which might seem to favor some one party of opinion by some other change in the opposite direction. The goal we have constantly had in mind however imperfectly we may have succeeded in attaining it — is the shaping of a future Prayer Book which every party might embrace with the well-founded conviction that therein its own position had been strengthened, its witness enhanced, and its devotions enriched.

The objective we have pursued is the same as that expressed by the Commission for the Revision of 1892: "Resolved, That this Committee, in all its suggestions and acts, be guided by those principles of liturgical construction and ritual use which have guided the compilation and amendments of the Book of Common Prayer, and have made it what it is."

THE STANDING LITURGICAL COMMISSION:

GOODRICH R. FENNER, *Chairman*
ARTHUR C. LICHTENBERGER
JOHN W. SUTER, *Custodian*
MASSEY H. SHEPHERD, JR., *Vice Chairman*
CHARLES W. F. SMITH
FRANCIS B. SAYRE, JR.
BERTRAM L. SMITH
SPENCER ERVIN, *Secretary*
JOHN W. ASHTON
FRANK STEPHEN CELLIER

The major preliminary work for this Study was made by the late Dr. Bayard H. Jones, whose indefatigable labors were ably seconded by the Reverend Morton C. Stone, former Secretary of the Commission. It is therefore with profound gratitude that the Commission dedicates this Study to Dr. Jones' memory.

Although both Dr. Jones and Mr. Stone did much of the groundwork for Part One, on the Collects, this section of the Study has been prepared in its present form by Dr. Shepherd with the assistance of Dr. Suter. Part Two is substantially the work of Dr. Jones, representing a manuscript which he left in the Commission's hands before his untimely death. It has only required a slight editing to bring it into line with final decisions made by the Commission after Dr. Jones had completed his draft. Part Three is also taken from Dr. Jones' draft manuscript, except for the section on the Lenten weekday propers, which has been in the charge of Dr. Shepherd.

This Study is a sequel to Prayer Book Studies No. IX on the Calendar. While every effort has been made to bring the two Studies into harmony one with the other, it will be obvious that the organization of the material in the parts herewith prepared by Dr. Jones represents a slightly different arrangement of the material from that finally approved by the Commission. The variation, however, is not one that is likely to cause confusion. And the Commission has felt that it was best to leave the draft prepared by Dr. Jones with as little alteration as was absolutely necessary.

Attention is called to the re-printing here of the Proposed Calendar, in which certain errors in the format of this Calendar have been corrected. There have been, however, no changes made in the names or events listed in the Proposed Calendar.

MASSEY H. SHEPHERD, JR.
Editor, for the Commission

Part One: The Collects

New Materials in the Anglican Prayer Books

The traditional pattern of propers for the celebration of Holy Communion on Holy Days, established in the Book of Common Prayer since its second edition of 1552, consists of a Collect, Epistle, and Gospel. The First Prayer Book of 1549 had included also an Introit Psalm. But no succeeding revision of the English liturgy since that time, in any province of the Anglican Communion, has extended the appointed propers beyond the three formulae provided by the 1552 Book, with the exception, of course, of a few additional Proper Prefaces.

It is well known that the English Reformers dealt very gently with the time-honored propers for Sundays and Holy Days that they retained for the Prayer Book from the Sarum Missal. In most cases they translated, with some occasional alterations, the Collects, Epistles and Gospels of their inherited Latin rite. But a number of new Collects were prepared for the fixed Holy Days. Of the six feasts in the Christmas-Epiphany cycle, two — Christmas Day and Circumcision — received new Collects; three — St. Stephen, St. John, and Holy Innocents had their traditional Collects much revised; and only one, the Collect for the Epiphany, remained virtually unaltered. In the Sanctorale, beginning with St. Andrew's Day, thirteen of the eighteen Holy Days were provided with new Collects. Translations of the older Latin Collects were made only for Purification, Annunciation, and Michaelmas, and modified versions of the Latin forms were kept for the Conversion of St. Paul and for St. Bartholomew.

The reason for this sizable change in the Collects for Saints' Days is not far to seek. The Latin prayers for such days usually made reference to the merits, intercession, or protection of the saints. Such notions were rejected by the Reformers as alien to the doctrine of the New Testament. They were not prepared, and wisely so, to admit into the liturgy any suggestion of mediation between God and man other than through our Lord Jesus Christ, "our only Mediator and Advocate." In place of the rejected Latin formulae, the Reformers composed their new Collects out of the themes provided by the Scriptural lessons of the day. A few of the new Collects were of a general nature; most of them were biographical — that is, some salient aspect of the saint's life was taken as the basis for petition and supplication. The two types are easily illustrated by reference to the new prayers for the four Evangelists. The Collects for St. John and St. Mark, being based upon the Epistles for these days, make no specific allusion to the lives of these gospel writers.[1] But the Collects for St. Matthew and St. Luke have a definite biographical basis.[2]

No addition to the "Reformation settlement" of the Calendar and propers for Holy Days has been made in the Prayer Book until the recent revisions of this century. Neither in Queen Elizabeth's Calendar of 1561 nor in the English Book of 1661 were the Black Letter Days provided with or intended to have any liturgical observance. It was the American revision of 1892, with its cautious addition of the Transfiguration as a Red Letter Day, with its own Collect, Epistle, and Gospel, that started a trend, which has been taken up with increasing momentum in each successive revision of Anglican Prayer Books. To date, however, no Prayer Book of the Anglican Communion has attempted to draw up for each Black Letter Day admitted to its Calendar, with approval of liturgical observance, a full and distinct set of propers. In particular, the number of new Collects has been relatively small, and not nearly so extensive as the provision for new Epistles and Gospels.

The Canadian Book of 1922 had an extensive list of Black Letter commemorations, but made no provision for propers to go with them. The Irish Book of 1926 contented itself with the addition of two new Red Letter Days, St. Patrick and Transfiguration, each with its own propers, but gave no suggestion of other Holy Days beyond the traditional ones of the Prayer Book. The American Church, on the other hand, turned down a proposed list of Black Letter Days, but inserted in its 1928 Book a set of propers for "A Saint's Day," with alternative Collects. It was the English Proposed Book of 1927-28, and the Scottish and South African Books of 1929 that really opened the way to a more adequate provision for Black Letter Days; and the Indian Book of 1951 and the Canadian Draft Book of 1955 have followed their example. Even so, these books rely in the main upon a set of "Commons" for most of the additional observances. Special Collects are provided for relatively few days, chiefly additional feasts of our Lord or the Blessed Virgin, or of national Patron Saints.

---

1. Ed. Note: These are the collects for the Apostles John and Mark referred to by the text:

MERCYFULL Lorde, we beseche thee to caste thy bryght beames of lyght upon thy Churche: that it beeyng lyghtened by the doctryne of thy blessed Apostle and Euangelyste John may attayne to thy euerlastyng gyftes; Through Jesus Christe our Lorde.

ALMYGHTIE God, whiche haste instructed thy holy Church with the heavenly doctrine of thy Evangelist Sainct Marke: Geve us grace so to be established by thy holy Gospell, that we be not, lyke chyldren, caried away with every blast of vaine Doctrine; through Jesus Christ our Lorde.

2. Ed. Note: These are the collects for the Apostles Matthew and Luke referred to by the text:

ALMIGHTIE God, whiche by thy blessed sonne dyddest call Mathewe from the receipte of custome [tax office.] to be an Apostle and Evangelist; Graunt us grace to forsake all covetous desires, and inordinate love of riches, and to folowe thy sayed sonne Jesus Christ; who lyveth and reigneth, &c.

ALMIGHTIE God whiche calledst Luke the phisicion, whose prayse is in the gospell, to be a phisicion of the soule ; it may please thee, by the holsome medicines of his doctryne, to heale all the diseases of our soules; through thy sonne Jesus Christe our Lorde.

Meanwhile a fair number of private devotional manuals and of unauthorized Missals in English made their appearance in England and America, with their own Calendar and propers for extra Holy Days, drawn up according to the tastes and interests of their several editors. Bishop John Wordsworth of Salisbury (1885-1911) was a pioneer in such efforts. Many of his Collects were taken up into *The English Liturgy*, published in 1903 by Percy Dearmer, W. H. Frere, and Bishop S. M. Taylor of Kingston. After the appearance of the English 1928 Book, Dr. Frere (now Bishop of Truro) put forth in 1935 (revised, 1938) for his diocese *Collects, Epistles and Gospels For the Lesser Feasts According to the Calendar Set Out in 1928*. Another work that has been widely used, having gone through many editions, has been *The Priest's Book of Private Devotion*, compiled by J. Oldknow and A. D. Crake, from which was excerpted a smaller manual, *Prime and Hours according to the use of the Church of England*. Among the more popular Missals has been that of the Rev. E. A. L. Clarke, *The People's Missal* (1916; revised, 1919). The first edition of *The American Missal* appeared in 1931.

Needless to say these manuals and missals have been extensively used, even though they are illegal, not only by religious communities but at many parish altars. In England a number of dioceses have issued diocesan Service Books with supplementary material. But the only book of this kind put forth in America has been the *Service Book for the Diocese of New Jersey*, authorized by the Bishop, and published in 1940. This last work contains propers for five Holy Days and for five Commons; most of its materials are drawn from other Anglican Prayer Books or represent reworkings and adaptations of formulae in the American Prayer Book.[3] It may be said of this work also, as of the books issued by Bishops Wordsworth and Frere, that its doctrinal content is completely in harmony with the theological perspectives of the Church's official liturgy. The same cannot be said for many of the Collects to be found in the missals, especially when they have translated or paraphrased prayers from the Latin rite.

The Problem of Suitable Collects

As stated in the Study on the Calendar, there has been no lack of widespread interest in the American Church for a larger and richer Calendar of Holy Days with greater variety of propers. But though the Commission has had no trouble in receiving a host of names and observances for consideration in extending the Calendar, there has come into its hands almost nothing in the way of suggestion for suitable propers. If it has found the task of screening the names to be added to the

---

3. Ed. Note: The *Service Book for the Diocese of New Jersey* contains a Common of Martyrs, a Common of Confessors and Doctors (with separate collects for Confessors, Evangelists, and Doctors), a Common of Bishops, a Common of Abbots, and a Common for Holy Women. It also includes propers for The Visitation of the Blessed Virgin Mary, St. Mary Magdalene, the Nativity of the Blessed Virgin Mary, Holy Cross Day, and the Feast of Christ the King.

Calendar a difficult and delicate labor, it has discovered an even greater perplexity in the selection of adequate propers to go with them. It makes no claim to special competence in this matter, and sincerely begs those who are concerned with the problem to lend it every constructive aid. The writing of Collects for liturgical use is a most exacting discipline. One is tempted to say that it is an art possible only to a literary genius, who at the same time has a profound knowledge of theology and a rich experience of prayer. In any case, the best Collects are generally the work of individuals; they are rarely effective when produced by a committee.

The original purpose of the Commission was to follow the lead of other Anglican Prayer Books and suggest in the main the use of a relatively few Commons. We naturally turned to the other Prayer Books of our sister Anglican provinces for guidance. But the total material available from these sources proved to be not only slender in scope, but also of very unequal merit, including those Collects that were common to several of the Prayer Books. Only eleven commemorations in our proposed list of ninety-four had special Collects in one or more of the other Prayer Books. The distribution may be tabulated as follows:

Feast	English 1928	Scottish	Irish	South African	Indian	Canadian 1955
Name of Jesus	X	X		X	X	X
Patrick		X	X			
Joseph				X	X	X
Columba		X				
Peter and Paul				X	X	X
Visitation B.V.M.	X	X		X	X	X
Mary Magdalene	X	X		X	X	X
Falling Asleep B.V.M.				X	X	
Augustine of Hippo				X		
Holy Cross	X			X	X	X
Margaret		X				

The Scottish Book contained a different Collect for the Name of Jesus from that of the other Books; and it used the same Collect for Patrick and Columba, albeit another formulary than the one for Patrick in the Irish Book. The Indian and Canadian Books gave two Collects for Peter and Paul, one for each Apostle — the one for St. Peter being the same as that of the older Prayer Book tradition. The Collect for Holy Cross was different in the English, South African, and Canadian Books, while the Scottish Book directed the use of the Collect for Palm Sunday on this feast. Only the Collects for the Visitation and for St. Mary Magdalene were the same in the several Books that provided them.

A comparable situation with respect to the Common Collects was evident upon analysis. In particular, the Collects for use on feasts of the Blessed Virgin varied considerably, depending upon the number of such feasts admitted to the several Calendars. The following table gives a synopsis of the various classifications of Commons (showing the number of formularies in each category):

	English 1928	Scottish	South African	Indian	Canadian 1955
Vigil				1	
Martyr	1	1	3	3	1
Doctor or Confessor	1	1	2	1	(Uses St. John Evangelist Collect)
Bishop	1		3	1	1
Abbot or Abbess	1		1	1	
Missionaries	1			2	1
Virgins: Martyr	1	1	1	1	
Virgins: Not a Martyr			1	1	
Matron	1		1	1	
Holy Women					1
Blessed Virgin Mary					
Falling Asleep			1	1	
Nativity	1	1	1	1	1
Conception	1		1	1	
Votive				1	
A Saint	1	1	3	1	2
Saints					
Anglican Communion	1				
National Martyrs or Missionaries			1	1	

It will be seen at once from the foregoing tabulation that the South African and Indian Books contain the largest selection, and for the most part subsume the material in the other Books. The eighteen Common Collects in the Indian Book — in the main superior in quality to those of the others — include four that are of no use to our list: the Vigil of a Saint, and three feasts of the Blessed Virgin. The end result, therefore, is a meagre selection to distribute among our ninety-four entries.

Our next procedure was an attempt to work out a special Collect for each one of our Black Letter commemorations. Two of our former Commission members worked diligently for a number of years at this monumental undertaking. The Missals were of little use, for the theological reasons already stated. The Collects of Dr. Frere's book and some of those in Fr. Clarke's Missal provided useful ideas, but were seldom drawn upon without considerable modifications. The aim of our subcommittee was to provide Collects of a biographical character, comparable to those of the Apostles and Evangelists in the Prayer Book. A complete schedule of Collects was finally prepared and sent to a number of persons skilled in these matters for criticism; and the results of these endeavors were used experimentally in a few of our seminaries and in certain private chapels. The ensuing comments after this trial use were not encouraging. Too many of these Collects gave the effect of being overly contrived and erudite. To place them in the Prayer Book would demand an annotated commentary for the benefit of those lay people who did not have an extensive knowledge of Church History and were therefore unable to appreciate the subtle allusions in these Collects. However admirable most of these Collects might be for personal, devotional use, they lacked that quality of universal application that is needed in a formulary for corporate, liturgical use.

Principles of Present Proposals

The present proposals of new Collects for the minor Holy Days are an endeavor to strike the happy mean between two kinds of monotony: one, the over-working of a few, constantly repeated Common Collects; the other, an overstraining after originality by attempting to bring out singular lessons for the commemoration of each and every individual saint. For the two renamed Red Letter feasts and the ninety-two proposed Black Letter commemorations, we are offering a total of thirty-six Collects of which seventeen are appointed for one occasion only, the others for two or more occasions. But none of them are listed for more than six commemorations; and of these, an effort has been made to avoid using the same Collect twice over within the space of one month. However, there are one or two exceptions to this latter usage. By such a distribution of the Collects, it is hoped that tedium may be lessened, and thus the devout attention of the worshippers encouraged.

After careful consideration, we have found it inexpedient to use the traditional classifications of saints and therefore of Collects, as they have been appointed both in the Latin Missals and in the other Anglican Prayer Books. The difficulty with these classifications is mainly due to the fact that they overlap. For example, Saint Boniface was a Martyr, a Bishop, a Doctor, and a Missionary. Saint Chrysostom was a Bishop, a Confessor and a Doctor — some would even account him as a Martyr; but in the devotion and memory of the Church, he is actually accounted the Church's greatest Preacher. Pope Gregory the Great was a Bishop, Confessor, and Doctor; but our Church remembers him primarily as the "Apostle of the English People." There is also a problem posed by the traditional class known as Virgins. Our Church holds without question the monastic life in high esteem; but it has never, since the Reformation, viewed the celibate life as a higher gift of grace worthy of special distinction in the common devotion of its liturgical life. It does not question the propriety of recognizing this grace of virginity in the common life of monastic communities. But it does not seem fitting or realistic to ask parish congregations to accord an especial emphasis to this state of life in its regular offices of worship.

The criterion by which the Church today evaluates the record of those whom it commemorates is *service* — service of God and of one's fellow men, irrespective of the position, rank, or state of the individual concerned. We remember a Bishop not so much because he was a bishop, but because he was, by God's grace in this office, a teacher, a witness, a missionary, or, it may be, a writer of profound devotional works or of hymns and prayers, or a humble ministrant to the poor and needy. The charismata of the Holy Ghost are manifold, and in God's providence either a single one of them or many of them may be given to an individual, whether he be in Holy Orders or in the ranks of the laity, whether he be a celibate living within or without a monastic community or a married Christian living a family life of exemplary honesty and good report.

In our Proposed Calendar (published in *Prayer Book Studies* No. IX) we have entered the various worthies to be commemorated with titles of their office and rank in the Church as a method of identification. Thus we have used the categories of Bishop, Priest, Deacon, King, Abbot, Friar, and Monk. But we have also frequently employed a title not found in the traditional classifications, namely, that of Missionary, especially where the individual so described has been the first evangelist or "apostle" of a people or territory. We believe that this title is fully justified, since the primary purpose of the Church's existence is to be missionary. And, it may be added, in our own Episcopal Church, the singular executive agency of our American Communion (i.e., the National Council) is empowered with authority to promote the missionary work of the Church in all its many phases and facets.

It will be readily noted, however, in the Collects which are herewith proposed, that little attention is given to these more traditional titles. Indeed, most of the worthies are described under the single noun "servant." We have preserved where fitting the title of "martyr," even where the prayer makes clear that the individual commemorated gave witness unto death, for the sake of the Christian faith. Otherwise, we have allowed the Collects to be distributed in such a way that the primary service of the individual saint is noted — be it missionary work, teaching and preaching, charitable endeavor — or some outstanding quality of Christian character — courage, zeal, purity, faithfulness, steadfastness, joy, etc.

In all these Collects, however, the aim has been, in so far as they point a lesson, to select certain universal qualities and duties that are properly applicable to all Christians in their several vocations. A few of the Collects contain more particular petitions for the Church's Ministry, but these are always so framed as to bring out the implications of ministerial vocation for all the people of God. In a very small number of cases, the perceptive and knowledgable worshipper may recognize phrases that are peculiarly associated with the saint commemorated. (These will be noted in the commentary on the several Collects as presented below.)

Single Collects, without provision for use more than once, are provided for all the New Testament saints added to our Proposed Calendar, for certain eminent Fathers of the early Church, and for commemorations of historical events. These include:

> The Holy Name of our Lord Jesus Christ
> St. Timothy
> St. Cornelius
> St. Titus
> Gregory the Great
> St. Joseph
> The First Book of Common Prayer
> Irenaeus
> SS. Peter and Paul
> The Visitation of the B.V.M.
> St. Mary Magdalene
> St. Mary the Virgin
> Augustine of Hippo
> The Exaltation of the Holy Cross
> Jerome
> Francis of Assisi
> Consecration of Samuel Seabury

Four Collects are used for the Martyrs, in the following groups:

	Agnes
(1)	Perpetua and Felicitas
	Martyrs of Lyons
	Ignatius
(2)	Alban
	Laurence
	Polycarp
(3)	Justin
	Cyprian
	Boniface
(4)	Patteson
	Hannington

The last of these groups has an additional theme, in view of the missionary labors to heathen lands of the worthies commemorated. Another Collect, for those who gave their lives, but whose deaths might not be viewed by all Churchmen as in the same class of "martyrdom" for the Christian faith, as are the names of the foregoing, contain the memorials of

| William Laud |
| William Tyndale |
| Latimer and Ridley. |

The missionaries provide two other groups, beyond the three martyr-names already noted. They are:

(1)	Ansgarius
	Gregory the Illuminator
	George Augustus Selwyn
	Cyril and Methodius
	Jackson Kemper
	Channing Moore Williams
(2)	David
	Patrick
	Augustine of Canterbury
	Columba
	Aidan
	Willibrord

Other missionaries might well have been included in these groups — such men as Theodore of Tarsus and Bishop Schereschewsky. But they find their place in Collects recalling different, though equally notable gifts of service.

We have attempted not to be arbitrary in the use of Collects for more than one worthy, and to find what might be termed obvious or natural groupings. The three monarchs: Louis, Alfred, and Margaret, share the same Collect; as do five early Fathers who gave great contributions to the shaping of the dogma of the Incarnation — Hilary, Athanasius, Gregory Nazianzen, Basil, and Leo. It was readily evident that modern leaders in Christian humanitarianism such as Maurice and Wilberforce could be classed under the same Collect, but their predecessors of earlier times, such as Nicholas and Elizabeth of Hungary, were better served by other memorials. We believe, however, that a close study of the groupings, while they avoid rigid classifications, will bring out no less valid associations according to certain common qualities of life and service.

New Collects Proposed

With each Collect as suggested, we shall append a brief commentary, noting the primary sources drawn upon for the formulary, and, where it may seem useful, some brief remarks as to its appropriateness for the saint or occasion to which it is assigned. The Commission states once more that it does not consider these Collects incapable of improvement, and requests readers of this Study to send it concrete suggestions for their improvement or replacement.

A. *Collects to be Used only Once*

The Greater Holy Days

1. THE HOLY NAME OF OUR LORD JESUS CHRIST (January 1).

> Eternal Father, who didst give thine incarnate Son a Name, betokening not his majesty but our salvation: We pray thee to set the Name of Jesus high above every name, and to plant in every heart the love of our only Saviour; who liveth and reigneth with thee and the Holy Ghost, one God, world without end. *Amen.*

This Collect has been taken from *Daily Prayer*, compiled by Eric Milner-White and G. W. Briggs (Oxford, 1941), page 38. An alteration has been made in the opening address; the original reads: "who didst give thine only Son the Name most dear to thee and needful for mankind, betokening not his majesty, but our salvation." Also we have made a verbal change from "the only Saviour" to "our only Saviour." The Collect fits the Epistle for the Day, but finely utilizes other Biblical allusions, such as Matthew 1:21 and Ephesians 1:21.

2. SAINT PETER AND SAINT PAUL, APOSTLES (June 29).

> Almighty God, whose blessed Apostles Peter and Paul hallowed this day by their martyrdom: Grant that thy household the Church, being instructed by their doctrine and example, and knit together in unity by thy Spirit, may ever stand firm upon the one foundation, which is Jesus Christ our Lord, who liveth and reigneth with thee and the same Spirit, one God, world without end. *Amen.*

The reasons for the Commission's proposal to restore the commemoration of St. Paul to June 29 in association with St. Peter have been given in our Study on the Calendar. To provide a Collect for the observance of the two chief apostles together, the Commission had several possibilities before it. It might have continued to utilize the present Prayer Book Collect, one that is peculiarly fitting to St. Peter alone, but add an additional clause with a specific mention of St. Paul. This was the solution adopted in *The People's Anglican Missal*. Or it might have adopted the less desirable expedient of the Lutheran liturgy and merely change the phrase "thy Apostle Saint Peter" of the present Collect to "thy holy Apostles." Another possibility — that chosen by the Indian Prayer Book, the Canadian Draft Book of 1955, and *The American Missal* — would have been to provide two Collects for the day, one for each of the apostles. A fourth solution was suggested by the South African Book, which follows the lead of the ancient Missals, namely, a single new Collect for both Apostles together. This way of handling the problem is also provided, as an alternative, in the Canadian Draft Book and *The American Missal*. The Commission decided upon this last way of meeting the problem.

The ancient Latin Collect of the feast afforded a primary basis for the construction of the new prayer. However, the free paraphrases of it found in the South African and the Canadian Books did not seem either felicitous or incisive to the ear. Nor could we adopt a literal translation of the Latin Collect, such as that given in *The American Missal*. For the truth is, the Collect is a peculiarly "Roman" one in its reference to the foundation of the Church in Rome by the two apostles.

The difficulty of a suitable rendering of this Latin Collect lies in its petition clause,

> Da ecclesiae tuae, eorum in omnibus sequi praeceptum, per quos religionis sumpsit exordium.
> Grant to thy Church in all things to follow the precepts of those through whom it received the beginning of religion.

"To receive the beginning of religion" would certainly mean something very different to a modern American than what either the Latin means or what it meant to an ancient Roman Christian. Yet there are packed into five Latin words some magnificent ideas: the pre-eminent position of Peter and Paul among the apostles, their extensive missionary labors that took them finally to martyrdom in the capital of the ancient world, and the primary significance of their testimony to the faith and the implications of its teaching. Our problem therefore was to re-capture the spirit of this ancient Collect in a version apt for congregations using the Prayer Book.

The Commission does not claim to have succeeded altogether in its adaptation, and would welcome other suggestions of a suitable paraphrase. The basis of its reconstruction has been Corinthians 3:10-11, with allusions to Colossians 2:2, 19, and Ephesians 2:20. An attempt has been made to hold fast to the doctrine of our Lord as the one true foundation of the Church, but to leave in the mind a suggestion of both the Lord's saying to Peter ("upon this rock I will build my Church" — *cf.* the Gospel for the day) and the favorite Pauline metaphor of the Church as a building on the foundation of the apostles and prophets' labors. At the same time, an effort has been made to stress the essential unity of faith and life which marked the relationship of the two chief apostles.

The Lesser Holy Days

3. SAINT TIMOTHY (January 24).

> Almighty and merciful God, who didst call Saint Timothy to endure hardship for the sake of thy dear Son: Strengthen us in like manner to stand firm in adversity, through the grace of Christ Jesus, that we may obtain salvation with eternal glory, who livest and reignest with the same thy Son Jesus Christ and the Holy Ghost ever, one God, world without end. *Amen.*

Phrases from 2 Timothy 2:1, 3, 10 (King James Version) have been employed for the framing of this Collect by the members of the Commission. The Epistle appointed for the day is 2 Timothy 1:1-7.

4. CORNELIUS, THE CENTURION (February 4).

> O God, who by thy Spirit didst call Cornelius the Centurion to be the first Christian among the Gentiles: Grant to thy Church in every nation a ready mind and will to proclaim thy love to all who turn to thee with unfeigned hope and faith; for the sake of Jesus Christ our Lord, who liveth and reigneth with thee and the same Spirit ever, one God, world without end. *Amen.*

The model of this Collect, prepared by the Commission, has been Cranmer's biographical collects based upon the Scriptural lesson of the day — in this case, the Epistle (Acts 11:1-8). The moral application of the story has applied the theme that God is "no respecter of persons."

5. SAINT TITUS (February 6).

> Blessed Lord, who didst charge Saint Titus to speak the things that accord with sound doctrine and to offer himself a pattern of good works: Grant to all thy people to live soberly, righteously, and godly in this present age, that they may with sure confidence look for the blessed hope and glorious appearing of our great God and Saviour Jesus Christ, who liveth and reigneth with thee and the Holy Spirit ever, one God, world without end. *Amen.*

As in the case of the Collect for St. Timothy, this Collect is based upon phrases in the Pastoral Epistles, in the present instance Titus 2:1, 7, 12-13. (The Epistle appointed for the day is Titus 1:1-5.) Several words and phrases in the exordium were adopted from the version of the late Reverend Dr. B. S. Easton, *The Pastoral Epistles* (Scribner's, 1947), page 89; for they seemed to make better sense for the modern worshipper than either the King James or Revised Standard Versions' renderings.

6. GREGORY THE GREAT (March 12).

> Almighty and merciful God, who didst raise up in Gregory the Great a servant of the servants of God, by whose labour the people of England were brought into the knowledge of the Catholic and Apostolic faith: Preserve in thy Church evermore a thankful remembrance of his devotion, that thy people, being zealous in every good work, may receive with him and thy servants everywhere the crown of glory that fadeth not away; through Jesus Christ our Lord. *Amen.*

This Collect, prepared by the Commission, is designed to bring out the singular instance, among his many virtues, whereby Gregory is particularly memorable in the tradition, of the English Church and its daughter provinces. The Venerable Bede, in his *Ecclesiastical History of the English People* (ii.1), said with justice that "though he is not an apostle to others, yet he is so to us; for we are the seal of his apostleship in our Lord." In the exordium of the Collect, the phrase "servant of the servants of God" will be recognized as the peculiar title which Gregory adopted for his exalted office. Yet it is a phrase that is full of meaning, whether or not one is conscious of its historical associations and occasion.

7. SAINT JOSEPH (March 19).

> O God, who didst call blessed Joseph to be the faithful guardian of thine only-begotten Son, and the spouse of his virgin Mother: Give us grace to follow his example in constant worship of thee and obedience to thy commands, that our homes may be sanctified by thy presence, and our children nurtured in thy fear and love; through the same Jesus Christ our Lord. *Amen.*

This gracious Collect with its petition for the Christian family and home has been drawn by the Commission from the Indian Prayer Book.

8. THE FIRST BOOK OF COMMON PRAYER (June 9).

> Almighty and everliving God, who didst guide thy servant Thomas Cranmer, with others, to render the worship of thy Church in a language understanded of the people: Make us ever thankful for this our heritage, and help us so to pray in the Spirit and with the understanding also, that we may worthily magnify thy holy Name; through Jesus Christ our Lord, who liveth and reigneth with thee and the same Holy Spirit ever, one God, world without end. *Amen.*

An adaptation has been made in this Collect from one put forth at the time of the 400th anniversary of the First Prayer Book, celebrated in 1949. The main inspiration of the Collect is 1 Corinthians 14:15. It has been suggested to the Commission that a possible alternative to this Collect might be the Collect "For the Spirit of Prayer" (Prayer Book, page 594). But the Commission believes that this Collect, or one similar to it, serves better as a commemoration of the historical event that is observed on this day.

9. IRENAEUS (June 28).

> Almighty God, who didst uphold thy servant Irenaeus with strength to maintain the truth against every wind of vain doctrine: We beseech thee to keep us steadfast in thy true religion, that we may walk in constancy and in peace the way that leadeth to eternal life; through Jesus Christ our Lord. *Amen.*

The Collect is a free rendering of the one for Irenaeus' feast in the Roman Missal. An attempt has been made to avoid too much play upon the word "peace," which is the meaning of Irenaeus' name. The opening address contains an allusion, as does the Collect for St. Mark's Day, to Ephesians 4:14. It recalls the valiant work of Irenaeus against the Gnostic heresies of his time that came so near to overwhelming the Church Catholic.

10. THE VISITATION OF THE BLESSED VIRGIN MARY (July 2).

> O Christ, our God Incarnate, whose virgin Mother was blessed in bearing thee, but still more blessed in keeping thy word: Grant us, who honour the exaltation of her lowliness, to follow the example of her devotion to thy will, who livest and reignest with the Father and the Holy Ghost ever, one God, world without end. *Amen.*

Based upon Luke 11:27-28, this Collect is one of the finest of William Bright (see his *Ancient Collects*, p. 236). The Commission considered this prayer far superior to the Collect for this feast used in the other Anglican Prayer Books. The phrase "exaltation of her lowliness" also admirably fits with the Gospel appointed for the day, Luke 1:39-56, a lection that contains the *Magnificat*.

11. MARY MAGDALENE (July 22).

> O Almighty God, whose blessed Son did sanctify Mary Magdalene, and called her to be a witness to his Resurrection: Mercifully grant that by thy grace we may be healed of all our infirmities, and alway serve thee in the power of his endless life, who with thee and the Holy Ghost liveth and reigneth, one God, world without end. *Amen.*

The form of this Collect is basically that of the Scottish Prayer Book. It is found, with slight variation, also in the other modern Anglican Prayer Books of England, Canada, South Africa, and India. Unlike the Collect for this feast in the 1549 Prayer Book, this prayer avoids identifying Mary Magdalene with the sinful woman of Luke 7:36 ff. It stresses rather her role in the Resurrection, with a passing allusion to Mark 16:9.

12. SAINT MARY THE VIRGIN (August 15).

> O God, who on this day didst take to thyself the blessed Virgin Mary, mother of thine only Son: Grant that we who have been redeemed by his blood may share her glory in thine eternal kingdom; through the same Jesus Christ our Lord, who liveth and reigneth with thee and the Holy Ghost ever, one God, world without end. *Amen.*

The Commission has drawn this Collect, with minor alterations, from the South African Prayer Book, where it occurs as the Collect for this feast.

13. AUGUSTINE OF HIPPO (August 28).

> O Lord God, who art the light of the minds that know thee, the life of the souls that love thee, and the strength of the hearts that serve thee: Help us, after the example of thy servant Saint Augustine, so to know thee that we may truly love thee, so to love thee that we may fully serve thee, whom to serve is perfect freedom; through Jesus Christ our Lord. *Amen.*

This prayer occurs in slightly variant forms in many modern anthologies. The version given here is based upon the form in the Reverend W. E. Orchard's *Divine Service* (Oxford, 1919). A very similar rendering is familiar to our people who have used the Forward Movement's *Prayers New and Old* (Cincinnati, 1937, page 45). Dr. Orchard drew his form from Selina F. Fox's well-known collection, *A Chain of Prayer Across the Ages*, first published in 1916, where it is attributed to the Gelasian Sacramentary. A careful search of the Gelasian by the Commission, however, has failed to produce a Latin original, although the prayer is quite similar in some ways to the Collect for Peace in Morning Prayer, which is derived from the Gelasian Sacramentary. The Commission would be grateful for any help in tracking down the source of this Collect.

The phrases have a distinct Augustinian ring, and are thus eminently suitable for use on the saint's feast day. They recall the opening passages of his *Confessions*. But again, it has been impossible for the Commission to produce an exact equivalent from Augustine's writings. The phrase "whom to serve is perfect freedom" — that recalls a similar line in the Morning Prayer Collect for Peace — may be found in Augustine's *De Quantitate Animae*, 34: *in cuius servitio placere perfecta et sola libertas est.*

14. EXALTATION OF THE HOLY CROSS (September 14).

> Almighty God, whose beloved Son for our sake willingly offered himself to endure the agony and shame of the Cross: Remove from us all cowardice of heart, and give us courage to take up our cross and bear it patiently in his service; through the same thy Son, Jesus Christ our Lord, who liveth and reigneth with thee and the Holy Ghost ever, one God, world without end. *Amen.*

This Collect is adapted from one in Milner-White and Briggs, *Daily Prayer*, page 32 (see above under No. 1, p. 14). But one phrase, "that we may bear it patiently in his service," has been suggested by one of the Collects for this feast in the Sarum Missal. The Collect for Holy Cross employed in the English 1928 and the Indian Prayer Books did not seem to the Commission to be theologically sound. The Scottish Book directs the use of the Collect for Palm Sunday. Both the South African and Canadian Draft Books have individual Collects for the feast; but neither of them seemed to the Commission to be as suggestive as the one taken and adapted from Dean Milner-White and Dr. Briggs' collection.

15. JEROME (September 30).

O God, who hast given us the holy Scriptures for a light to shine upon our path: Grant us, after the example of thy servant Jerome, so to learn of thee and of thy truth according to that Word, that we may find in it the light that shineth more and more unto the perfect day; through Jesus Christ our Lord. *Amen.*

This Collect is adapted from one in Bishop W. H. Frere's book of propers for the English Calendar of 1928 (see above, p. 3). It is based upon Psalm 119:105 and Proverbs 4:18. It seemed wise to emphasize this particular aspect of Jerome's life and work. And the Collect might well have a special usefulness as an additional one on the Holy Scriptures, comparable to the one for the Second Sunday in Advent.

16. FRANCIS OF ASSISI (October 4).

Most high, almighty, and good Lord: Grant thy people grace to renounce gladly the vanities of this world, that, after the example of blessed Francis, we may for love of thee delight in all thy creatures, with perfectness of joy; through Jesus Christ our Lord. *Amen.*

The great popularity, and one might say singularity, of St. Francis is perhaps justification enough for providing him with a separate Collect of his own. The Commission has prepared the above from phrases familiar in early Franciscan literature. The opening address recalls the saint's well-known *Canticle of the Sun*. The final phrase, "with perfectness of joy," brings to mind one of the most appealing stories of the *Fioretti* — Francis' discussion with Brother Leo concerning "perfect joy." The Prayer Book contains only one other Collect similar in character and spirit to the above — "For Joy in God's Creation," page 596.[4] We believe

---

4. Ed. Note: O HEAVENLY Father, who hast filled the world with beauty; Open, we beseech thee, our eyes to behold thy gracious hand in all thy works; that rejoicing in thy whole creation, we may learn to serve thee with gladness; for the sake of him by whom all things were made, thy Son, Jesus Christ our Lord. Amen.

that the theme is one that needs strengthening in our corporate prayer, and that St. Francis is the best example for us of this exuberant joy in God's works even to the least of His creatures.

17. THE CONSECRATION OF SAMUEL SEABURY (November 14).

> Almighty God, who by thy divine providence hast appointed divers Orders of Ministers in thy Church, and by thy Son Jesus Christ didst give to thy holy Apostles many excellent gifts: Give grace, we beseech thee, to all Bishops of thy Church, and more especially to those who serve in that branch of the same planted by thee in this land; that, following the example of thy servant Samuel Seabury, they may diligently preach thy Word, and duly administer the godly Discipline thereof, to the glory of thy Name, and the edification of thy Church; through the same Jesus Christ our Lord. *Amen.*

The reader will recognize in this Collect an adaptation of prayers in the Prayer Book on pages 531 and 549 of the Ordinal.[5] It seemed to the Commission that such a "recalling" of the Ordinal on this occasion is eminently suitable as a reminder of Bishop Seabury's devotion to the maintenance of the episcopal succession in our Church.

B. *Collects for the Martyrs*

18. AGNES (January 21).
PERPETUA AND HER COMPANIONS (March 7).
THE MARTYRS OF LYONS (June 2).

> Almighty and everlasting God, with whom thy meek ones go forth as the mighty: Grant us so to cherish the memory of thy blessed martyr(s) _____, that we may share her pure and steadfast faith in thee; through Jesus Christ our Lord. *Amen.*

---

5. † Ed. Note: ALMIGHTY God, who by thy divine providence hast appointed divers Orders of Ministers in thy Church, and didst inspire thine Apostles to choose into the Order of Deacons the first Martyr Saint Stephen, with others; Mercifully behold these thy servants now called to the like Office and Administration: so replenish them with the truth of thy Doctrine, and adorn them with innocency of life, that, both by word and good example, they may faithfully serve thee in this Office, to the glory of thy Name, and the edification of thy Church; through the merits of our Saviour Jesus Christ, who liveth and reigneth with thee and the Holy Ghost, now and for ever. Amen.

ALMIGHTY God, giver of all good things, who by thy Holy Spirit hast appointed divers Orders of Ministers in thy Church; Mercifully behold these thy servants now called to the Office of Priesthood; and so replenish them with the truth of thy Doctrine, and adorn them with innocency of life, that, both by word and good example, they may faithfully serve thee in this Office, to the glory of thy Name, and the edification of thy Church; through the merits of our Saviour Jesus Christ, who liveth and reigneth with thee and the same Holy Spirit, world without end. Amen.

The Collect is based upon one for St. Agnes' feast in the Gregorian Sacramentary. But in place of the original clause "who dost choose the weak things of the world to confound the things which are mighty," the Commission has drawn from a phrase used by William Bright in his Collect "For all who do the Work of the Church" (*Ancient Collects*, p. 237): "with whom thy little ones go forth as the mighty." Both phrases are well-suited to describe the heroines who are the chief subjects of these commemorations. However, the Pauline expression, "weak things of the world" might not convey to the modern congregation the exact notion that is desired, hence the change of the word "weak" to "meek."

19. VINCENT (January 22).
IGNATIUS (February 1).
ALBAN (June 22).
LAURENCE (August 10).

> Almighty God, by whose grace and power thy holy Deacon and martyr _____ triumphed over suffering and despised death: Grant, we beseech thee, that enduring hardness and waxing valiant in fight, we may with the noble army of martyrs receive the crown of everlasting life; through Jesus Christ our Lord. *Amen.*

This Collect is taken from the English 1928, South African, and Indian Prayer Books, where it is used as a Common of Martyrs. The words "Deacon and" would in this case only be used in the feasts of Vincent and Laurence.

20. POLYCARP (January 26).
JUSTIN (April 4).
CYPRIAN (September 13).

> Almighty God, who didst give thy servant _____ boldness to confess the Name of our Saviour Jesus Christ before the rulers of this world, and courage to die for this faith: Grant that we likewise may ever be ready to give a reason for the hope that is in us, and to suffer gladly for his sake; through the same Jesus Christ our Lord. *Amen.*

In the case of these three martyrs, we possess authentic accounts of their confession before magistrates and governors. The Collect has been prepared by the Commission, on the basis of 1 Peter 3:15 and 4:16.

21. BONIFACE (June 5).
JOHN COLERIDGE PATTESON (September 20).
JAMES HANNINGTON (October 29).

> Almighty God, who didst call thy faithful servant to be a witness and martyr in the land of _____, and by his labours and suffering didst raise

up a people for thine own possession: Shed forth, we beseech thee, thy Holy Spirit upon thy Church in all lands, that by the sacrifice and service of many, thy holy Name may be glorified and thy blessed kingdom enlarged; through Jesus Christ our Lord, who liveth and reigneth with thee and the same Spirit ever, one God, world without end. *Amen.*

The Commission adapted this Collect from one in the South African Prayer Book for a commemoration of "African Missionaries and Martyrs" (February 20).

22. WILLIAM LAUD (January 10).
WILLIAM TYNDALE (October 6).
HUGH LATIMER AND NICHOLAS RIDLEY (October 16).

Accept, O Lord, our thanksgiving this day for thy servant(s) _____, and grant unto us in like manner such constancy and zeal in thy service, that we may obtain with him and thy servants everywhere a good confession and the crown of everlasting life; through Jesus Christ our Lord. *Amen.*

Not every churchman would account these men "martyrs" in the same sense as those commemorated in the Collects of Nos. 18-21. Hence the Commission sought a Collect that would not commit the Church as a whole definitely to this term, but which would nonetheless recognize the life-given testimony of these worthies for their convictions. The present Collect has been taken, with slight alteration, from a Common for Departed Christians in the Indian Prayer Book.

C. *Other Missionaries*

23. ANSGARIUS (February 3).
GREGORY THE ILLUMINATOR (March 23).
GEORGE AUGUSTUS SELWYN (April 12).
CYRIL AND METHODIUS (May 11).
JACKSON KEMPER (May 24).
CHANNING MOORE WILLIAMS (December 2).

Almighty and everlasting God, we thank thee for thy servant _____, whom thou didst call to preach the Gospel to the people of _____; Raise up, we pray thee, in this and every land, heralds and evangelists of thy kingdom, that thy Church may make known the unsearchable riches of Christ, and may increase with the increase of God; through the same thy Son, Jesus Christ our Lord. *Amen.*

This Collect from the Indian Prayer Book, adapted from one in the English 1928 Book, has a fine ending by its use of Ephesians 3:8 and Colossians 2:19. In using it for Jackson Kemper a slight adaptation will be needed, namely: "in *this our land*" and "raise up in every land."

24. DAVID (March 1).
  PATRICK (March 17).
  AUGUSTINE OF CANTERBURY (May 26).
  COLUMBA (June 10).
  AIDAN (August 31).
  WILLIBRORD (November 7).

> O Almighty God, who in thy providence didst choose thy servant _____ to be an apostle to the people of to bring those who were wandering in darkness and error to the true light and knowledge of thee: Grant us so to walk in that light, that we may come at last to the light of everlasting life; through the merits of Jesus Christ thy Son our Lord. *Amen.*

The Commission felt it appropriate to extend the use of this Collect, appointed in the Irish Prayer Book for St. Patrick, to other "apostles" of pagan peoples associated with the early days of the Christian mission among the Celtic and Anglo-Saxon tribes. Patrick, a Romano-Briton, evangelized Ireland. Augustine, an Italian, and Aidan, an Irishman, inaugurated the missions to the English. Columba, another Irishman, is the patron-apostle of Scotland; and Willibrord, an Englishman, holds the same remembrance among the people of the Netherlands.

D. *Christian Rulers*

25. LOUIS, KING OF FRANCE (August 25).
  ALFRED THE GREAT (October 26).
  MARGARET, QUEEN OF SCOTLAND (November 16).

> O God, who didst call thy servant _____ to an earthly throne that *he* might advance thy heavenly kingdom, and didst endue *him* with zeal for thy Church and charity towards thy people: Mercifully grant that we who commemorate *his* example may be fruitful in good works, and attain to the glorious fellowship of thy saints; through Jesus Christ our Lord. *Amen.*

The Collect is taken from the Scottish Prayer Book's commemoration of Queen Margaret. It fits equally well the other two medieval monarchs on our Calendar list, Louis and Alfred.

E. *Early Fathers, Theologians, Scholars*

26. HILARY (January 14).
   LEO THE GREAT (April 11).
   ATHANASIUS (May 2).
   GREGORY NAZIANZEN (May 9).
   BASIL THE GREAT (June 14).

>   Almighty, everlasting God, whose servant _____ steadfastly confessed the true faith of thy Son our Saviour Jesus Christ to be Very God and Very Man: Grant that we may hold fast to this faith, and evermore magnify his holy Name; through the same thy Son Jesus Christ our Lord, who liveth and reigneth with thee and the Holy Spirit ever, one God, world without end. *Amen.*

A Collect of the Gregorian Sacramentary, as translated by William Bright (*Ancient Collects*, p. 75), suggested the text of this Collect for use in commemorations of several of the great Fathers of the early Church who gave valiant service in the formation of the ecumenical Creeds.

27. JOHN CHRYSOSTOM (January 27).
   AMBROSE (April 4).

>   O God, who didst give grace to thy servant _____ eloquently to declare thy righteousness in the great congregation, and fearlessly to bear reproach for the honour of thy Name: Mercifully grant unto all bishops and pastors such excellency in preaching, and fidelity in ministering thy Word, that thy people may be partakers with them of the glory that shall be revealed; through Jesus Christ our Lord. *Amen.*

Chrysostom and Ambrose were the greatest preachers of the ancient Church, if not of all ages of the Church's history to the present time. Both of them suffered from the consequences of their bold witness to the truth, though with quite differing results so far as their earthly fate was concerned. This Collect has been prepared by the Commission, utilizing phrases from Psalm 40:11 (Prayer Book version) and Romans 8:18.

28. THOMAS AQUINAS (March 8).
   JOHN OF DAMASCUS (May 6).
   BEDE THE VENERABLE (May 27).
   EPHREM (June 18).
   JEREMY TAYLOR (August 14).
   SAMUEL I. J. SCHERESCHEWSKY (October 15).

>   Almighty God, who hast enriched thy Church with the singular learning and holiness of thy servant _____: Grant us to hold fast the true doctrine of thy Son our Saviour Jesus Christ, and to fashion our lives

according to the same, to the glory of thy great Name, and the benefit of thy holy Church; through the same Jesus Christ our Lord. *Amen.*

The Commission has prepared this Collect for a group of worthies who combined in extraordinary manner the gifts cited in the Collect: learning and holiness. The concluding phrases have been borrowed from an Ember prayer in the Prayer Book, page 39.[6]

29. ANSELM (April 21).
    JOSEPH BUTLER (June 16).
    HIPPOLYTUS (August 13).
    CLEMENT OF ROME (November 23).
    CLEMENT OF ALEXANDRIA (December 4).

> O God, who hast enlightened thy Church by the teaching of thy servant _____: Enrich us evermore, we beseech thee, with thy heavenly grace, and raise up faithful witnesses who by their life and doctrine will set forth the truth of thy salvation; through Jesus Christ our Lord. *Amen.*

This Collect, with slight modification, has been taken from a Common for Doctors or Confessors in the English 1928, Scottish, South African, and Indian Prayer Books.

F. Others

30. ANTONY (January 17).
    MARTIN (November 11).

> O God, who by thy Holy Spirit didst enable thy servant _____ to withstand the temptations of the world, the flesh, and the devil: Grant that we, in the same Spirit, may with pure hearts and minds follow thee, the only God; through Jesus Christ our Lord. *Amen.*

These two early monks, the "Fathers" of the monastic movement in the East and the West, respectively, fall naturally under the use of one and the same Collect. The Commission has adapted for the purpose the Collect for the Eighteenth Sunday after Trinity.

---

6. Ed. Note: ALMIGHTY God, the giver of all good gifts, who of thy divine providence hast appointed divers Orders in thy Church; Give thy grace, we humbly beseech thee, to all those who are to be called to any office and administration in the same; and so replenish them with the truth of thy doctrine, and endue them with innocency of life, that they may faithfully serve before thee, to the glory of thy great Name, and the benefit of thy holy Church; through Jesus Christ our Lord. Amen.

31. PHILLIPS BROOKS (January 23).
    WILLIAM REED HUNTINGTON (July 27).

>   Almighty and everlasting God, the source and perfection of all virtues, who didst inspire thy servant _____ both to do what is right and to preach what is true: Grant that all ministers and stewards of thy mysteries may afford to thy faithful people, by word and example, the instruction which is of thy grace; through Jesus Christ our Lord. *Amen.*

The Collect is adapted from one translated by William Bright from the Leonine Sacramentary (*Ancient Collects*, p. 190).

32. THOMAS BRAY (February 15).
    DUNSTAN (May 19).
    WILLIAM WHITE (July 17).
    JOHN HENRY HOBART (September 12).
    THEODORE OF TARSUS (September 19).

>   O God, who dost ever hallow and protect thy Church: Raise up therein, through thy Spirit, good and faithful stewards of the mysteries of Christ, as thou didst in thy servant _____; that by their ministry and example thy people may abide in thy favour and walk in the way of truth; through Jesus Christ our Lord, who liveth and reigneth with thee in the unity of the same Spirit ever, one God, world without end. *Amen.*

The Commission has here adapted the Collect now in the Prayer Book, page 562, at the conclusion of the Litany for Ordinations.

33. GEORGE HERBERT (February 27).
    JOHN KEBLE (March 29).
    ALCUIN (May 20).
    THOMAS A KEMPIS (July 26).
    LANCELOT ANDREWES (September 27).
    CHARLES SIMEON (November 12).

>   O eternal Lord God, who holdest all souls in life: We beseech thee to shed forth upon thy whole Church in paradise and on earth the bright beams of thy light and thy peace; and grant that we, following the good examples of thy servant _____, and of all those who loved and served thee here, may at the last enter with them into thine unending joy; through Jesus Christ our Lord. *Amen.*

This Collect is an adaptation of the Collect appointed in the Prayer Book, page 268, "At the Burial of the Dead."

34. THOMAS KEN (March 20).
    WILLIAM LAW (April 6).
    BENEDICT (July 11).
    DOMINIC (August 4).
    SERGIUS (September 25).
    HILDA (November 17).

> Almighty and everlasting God, we give thee thanks for the purity and strength with which thou didst endow thy servant _____; and we pray that by thy grace we may have a like power to hallow and conform our souls and bodies to the purpose of thy most holy will; through Jesus Christ our Lord. *Amen.*

The basis of this Collect was taken by the Commission from the Reverend E. A. L. Clarke's *The People's Missal*, where it appears for the Common of a Virgin-Martyr. It seems to be admirably suited to the varied "ascetical" gifts of the group of worthies here listed from all periods of the Church's history.

35. JOHN FREDERICK DENISON MAURICE (April 1).
    WILLIAM WILBERFORCE (July 29).

> Let thy continual mercy, O Lord, enkindle in thy Church the never-failing gift of charity, that, following the example of thy servant _____, we may have grace to defend the children of the poor, and maintain the cause of them that have no helper; for the sake of him who gave his life for us, thy Son our Saviour Jesus Christ. *Amen.*

To point up the Christian humanitarianism of Maurice and Wilberforce, the Commission has prepared this Collect, based upon passages in 1 Corinthians 13:8 and Psalms 72:4, 12, and 140:12.

36. WILLIAM AUGUSTUS MUHLENBERG (April 8).
    MONNICA (May 4).
    BERNARD (August 20).
    ELIZABETH OF HUNGARY (November 19).
    NICHOLAS (December 6).

> Almighty and everlasting God, who didst enkindle the flame of thy love in the heart of thy servant _____: Grant to us, thy humble servants, the same faith and power of love; that, as we rejoice in his triumph, we may profit by his example; through Jesus Christ our Lord. *Amen.*

This Collect seems to have been made especially for these worthies of so great mystical and charitable energy and devotion. Our 1928 American revision took it as a Common for a Saint's Day from William Bright's *Ancient Collects* (p. 69). It is a translation of a Collect in the Gothic Missal.

37. COMMON COLLECTS OF A SAINT.

The Proposed Calendar does not and cannot provide all the names that may properly be commemorated, under certain conditions, in all our parishes and Church institutions. Many of them have patronal festivals in honor of saints not included in the Commission's list. Thus it has seemed advisable to make provision for such circumstances as may arise, when the Ordinary considers it proper to do so, for other Saints. This has been done in all the other recent Anglican Prayer Books. And our own American Book of 1928 would support this, presumably, by its propers for a Saint's Day. To this end the Commission has selected four Collects, not otherwise used, which may be adopted according to the discretion of the celebrant.

The Collect, "O almighty God, who hast called us to faith in thee," etc., is the alternative Collect for a Saint's Day in our present Prayer Book, page 258.

The second Collect, "Almighty and everlasting God, who didst strengthen thy servant," etc., has been taken from the "Common of a Martyr" in the South African and Indian Prayer Books. By the omission of the phrase "and blessed martyr" it may well serve for any other type of saint.

The third Collect, "O almighty God, who willest to be glorified in thy saints," etc., is also a Common in other Prayer Books: in the English 1928 and Indian Books "Of any Saint," in the South African Book a Common "Of a Bishop."

The final Collect proposed is one of the finest compositions of William Bright (*Ancient Collects*, p. 236). It is based upon Hebrews 12:22-23. The Commission was much tempted to use this Collect for several of the worthies in its proposed Calendar. But all efforts to insert into it a clause that would mention the name of the saint, seemed only to mar the literary quality and rhythmic beauty of the Collect.

Part Two: The Epistles and Gospels

One chief purpose of the enriching of the Calendar with the further commemorations known as the "Black Letter" days has been to permit the introduction of a judicious amount of variety in the use of Epistles and Gospels. At the present time a week which does not happen to contain a "Red Letter" day means that precisely the same service, identical in every word, must be used at the Holy Communion for seven days in a row, in any church which has a daily celebration. This does not encourage frequent attendance of the laity, and indeed has a distinctly damping effect at such occasions as summer conferences, where many of them make their first acquaintance with a daily service. Moreover, the monotony of such a routine bears down at least equally heavily upon the clergy who take the services. The ill-judged and rather unhappy use of a number of foreign Missals has undoubtedly been in very large part an attempt to get away from this monotony of scriptural provisions, far more than a blind yearning for a following of Rome. It is hoped that a discreet provision by the Church will make unnecessary such a use of alien lections which our examination has shown to be definitely out of harmony with the established standards of Anglican belief and worship.

For this purpose, we have appointed Epistles and Gospels for the outstanding commemorations, fixed and movable. We believed it to be highly undesirable to bring in the new observances in such a manner as to obscure the great outlines of the Christian Year, which is, always has been, and must always remain the main outline of the teaching of the Church through the ordered reading of Holy Scripture at the Liturgy. The Roman Calendar is so cluttered with all manner of commemorations of competing rank that even the Sunday cycle is often broken into: to the extent that such a thing as a "green mass," even on the Sundays after Epiphany and Pentecost, is the rarest of events. To this end, and to preserve a native Anglican simplicity which Cranmer rightly valued, we propose to direct that none of the new "Black Letter Days" shall ever supplant a Sunday service. This regulation would ensure that the new matter should serve for enrichment and variety on weekdays only, without occulting the Christian Year.

Moreover, only a relatively few of the more eminent Saints' Days should be entitled to these provisions of a proper Epistle and Gospel; the other entries being confined to a commemorative Collect. Only those days are to be dignified with the status of Minor Holy Days, and distinguished by italic type in the Calendar. And not to overload the Prayer Book, the Epistles and Gospels should not be printed out, but the citations of chapters and verses given in Lectionary form — with, if necessary, the precise beginning and ending of the lections noted. This is what has been done in the current English and Scottish revisions, and seems the most practicable method. It would not be difficult to expand the section of "The Holy Communion, with the Collects, Epistles, and Gospels" to dimensions very like those of our whole present Prayer Book — which of course is exactly the case with the Roman Missal. But if and as the added matter approved itself in use, it would be entirely possible to authorize an Altar Book which did print all the Epistles and Gospels in full.

Our list of Minor Holy Days comprises 40 fixed dates for the observance of principal personalities and events of Christian history with full propers. Of the Movable Days with the rank of Minor Holy Days, we propose to give proper Epistles and Gospels to each of the twelve Ember and the three Rogation Days, instead of the one in each class now provided; to provide for two days each week in Lent which have no proper service now, and similarly to round out the Octaves of Easter, and Whitsunday with the assignments respectively necessary to give each of the Octaves a service of its own. This makes a total of 28 added provisions for the Movable Days.

It is believed that the addition of these 68 proper Epistles and Gospels will be sufficient to secure a quite adequate variety for any purpose in the pattern of the year; and also, what is perhaps of nearly equal importance, to ensure that there should be a really representative and comprehensive coverage of the best of the Holy Scriptures in the Liturgical Lectionary. It does not appear necessary to explore further a proposition made by a member of the former Committee on the Revision of the Lectionary, that each week of the Christian Year might be provided with two sets of alternative Epistles and Gospels equivalent to or illustrative of the Sunday lections, drawn from the Office Lectionary, as that in turn had been derived from the liturgical list.[7]

Principles of Choice

It might be assumed that the simplest and best thing to do would be to copy the Roman assignments for these added Holy Days. But even a brief exploration of the Roman Missal throws considerable doubt on the advisability of putting much weight on the Roman method; and an exhaustive study brands a general adoption of the Roman provisions as a categorical impossibility.

It is probable that most people are under the general impression that the Epistles and Gospels designated for the Red Letter Days now in the Prayer Book are particularly chosen and specifically adapted to the personalities of the saints which they celebrate. Such cases as SS. Andrew, Thomas, John Evangelist, John Baptist, and Peter certainly fulfill the conditions. But in a surprising number of instances there was lacking in Scripture a specific reference by name to the saint in question, or such reference was passed over even if it is to be found; and therefore, instead of anything that could really be called a proper lection, we are provided with what is essentially a "Common," that is, a passage which would apply to any number of a rather extended class of persons. Thus in the Epistles for SS. Matthew, Mark, and Luke, none of them have anything which tie them to the saints to which they are assigned; all have some sort of reference to "Evangelists," which would qualify them to be a Common for any Evangelist: and in fact these assignments could be exchanged in any order without in the slightest affecting their appropriateness. The Gospels for SS. Paul, Matthias, Mark, Barnabas, Bartholomew, Luke, and Simon and Jude are just so many samples of a "Common of Apostles," and so used, quite indifferently. In fact, the use of this kind of "Common" in the case of St. Paul is distinctly unfortunate, since the allusion to the "twelve thrones," perfectly applicable to the twelve disciples to whom this passage was originally addressed, is completely inapplicable to St. Paul. The Prayer Book rightly lists him as one of fourteen Apostles; he was most certainly never one of the Twelve.

---

7. Bayard H. Jones, *The American Lectionary* (Morehouse-Gorham, 1944), 150-155.

This use of the method of "Commons" apparently disquieted the Reformers, as well as subsequent revisers of the Prayer Book. More specific Epistles have been adopted at or since the Reformation for SS. Thomas, Philip and James, Barnabas, James, Luke, and John Evangelist.

Now when we turn to the voluminous material in the Roman Missal for the restored commemorations for which we wish to provide, we find that it is all but exclusively built up of this kind of lections which would be applicable to any one of a given class of saints, rather than by a careful sifting of the available material to find the closest possible Scriptural presentation of the particular character and achievements of the personality in question. Only a relatively few outstanding figures succeed in obtaining really proper lections of their own. The Missal does however display an increasing tendency to search out a more specifically applicable reference for some of the more modern saints; and this is especially marked in the collection of local and national commemorations in the Appendix *pro aliquibus locis*. We came to the conclusion that all the "Commons," as well as the exceptional assignments, ought to be studied, and those lections adopted which were most nearly in correspondence with the nature of each case.

This characteristic Roman use of Commons may be all very well in a Calendar which is densely crowded with a great variety of commemorations, whose intricate permutations and combinations with the pattern of the Movables may suffice to mitigate the recurrence of the same Commons twenty times a year. But adopted, as we propose, in much smaller numbers into a much simpler scheme, the monotony would certainly be felt, precisely as our 1928 provision of a single Common for Ember Days becomes a burden if actually rehearsed a dozen times each year. A direct following of the Roman plan would therefore fall short of two of our main aims in advocating the inclusion of Minor Holy Days, namely the securing of a real variety in the liturgical provisions, and a more inclusive coverage of the riches of Holy Scripture.[8]

But it is the quality of this material that makes any wholesale adoption of it become unthinkable. Some of the selections are extremely good, and may be most thankfully adopted just as they stand. Some may be markedly improved by a slight, judicious lengthening or shortening, exactly as Cranmer found to be the case with the Sarum-Roman assignments which he adopted. Others, excellent in themselves, have been so unintelligently assigned as to be almost grotesquely inappropriate to their subjects; though they may do excellently in some other place. And then there are all gradations down to pericopes which are incredibly stupid, and worse, some mutilations of integral passages, and some tamperings with and even outright rewritings of the Vulgate text.

---

8. Ed. Note: This is an interesting sentence, and provides insight into the intentions of the working group behind this study.

Therefore our use of the Roman material will have to be critical and selective — "the dross to consume, and the gold to refine." The number of any class of commemorations which we propose as Minor Holy Days is not so great that it will not be possible to assign a Proper Epistle and Gospel to each of them, with no greater repetition than the use of the concordant but not identical passages of the same general import from different Gospels.

The use of the method of Commons will not be altogether discarded, however. Besides the Minor Holy Days, there will also be a more numerous listing of Black Letter Days as "Memorials," provided with a Collect only, where it does not seem advisable to allow the supersession of the service of the previous Sunday with a complete service of their own. Only when one of these is to be kept as a local Patronal will these require supplement; and this can be effected by bringing in the use of Commons, according to the designation of such days in the Calendar.

Martyrs

The first class of saints to be honored by an annual commemoration was the Martyrs of the early Church. The first institution of such an observance of which we have record was the Martyrdom of Polycarp about the year 155, attested in the circular letter of the Church of Smyrna. Such commemorations were so numerous in the age of the persecutions that Bishop Frere well observed that the early Roman Calendar was essentially "the *sanctorale* of the cemeteries."[9]

We therefore find that the Roman Missal provides no less than twelve Common Masses for Martyrs, quite elaborately arranged. There are two for Bishops who were Martyrs, named (as are all masses) from the first words of their Introits, *Statuit* and *Sacerdotes*; two, *In virtute* and *Laetabitur*, for Martyrs other than Bishops; *Protexisti* for one Martyr, and *Sancti tui* for more than one Martyr, in Eastertide; three for Martyrs outside Eastertide, *Intret*, *Sapientiam*, and *Salus autem*; two for Virgin Martyrs, *Loquebar* and *Me exspectaverunt*, with a further version of the latter under the same title for a female Martyr who was not a virgin. These dozen Commons are then skillfully assigned in the Missal to secure an approximately equal use of each of them in the course of the year, and to prevent any one of them recurring a wearisome number of times. But that is really all the arrangement there is. Any Epistle or Gospel of any one of them would be equally in place in any other, with the possible exception of the Parable of the Ten Virgins in the mass *Loquebar*.

Most of the Epistles and Gospels here assigned are very fine, with telling use of such themes as following the example of Christ's Passion, the fortitude of the Christian under persecution, and the heavenly reward. Some,

---

9. *Studies in Early Roman Liturgy*, 1. 29.

however, fall short of being satisfactory. The mass *Statuit*, for example, has as its Epistle James 1:12-18 — exactly the selection which the Committee on the Liturgical Lectionary proposed to assign to Easter IV, in a readjustment of the poorly divided material on this Sunday and the following.[10] Nothing could be finer than the verse "when he is tried, he shall receive the crown of life, which the Lord hath promised to them that love him." But unfortunately, the thought of this selection depends on the Greek use of one word for what English has discriminated into two rather divergent terms, namely "temptation" and "trial."

Most of the passage is taken up with "temptations" in quite the modern sense, and seems an irrelevant digression for the day of a Martyr.

Several of the assignments concern themselves with fortitude under persecutions, without observing that the passages speak of persecutions short of death, and in some cases explicitly promise a physical protection and preservation against that extremity. Wisdom 10:10-14 in the mass *In virtute* reviews the protection of Jacob in exile and Joseph in bondage — utterly inadequate for a Martyr, besides being a somewhat unconscionable accommodation of a text designed for a quite different purpose. The selections from the "Prayer of Jesus the Son of Sirach" in Ecclesiasticus 51 in the masses *Loquebar* and *Me exspectaverunt* are thanksgivings for deliverance actually effected. Matthew 24:3-13, the persecutions of the Last Days, in the mass *Salus autem*, is entirely in place; and so is Matthew 10:26b-32, "Fear not them which kill the body, but are not able to kill the soul," in the mass *Laetabitur*. But the combination of the thought of the two in Luke 21:9-10 in the mass *Intret* is distinctly not happy, since it is given an entirely wrong twist for this purpose in verse 18: "But there shall not an hair of your head perish," while the Matthaean version says "But the very hairs of your head are all numbered."

Also, the selections from the allegory of the Vine and the Branches in John 15 in the masses *Protexisti* and *Sancti tui*, however fitting for any saint whatever, have not the slightest allusion to martyrdom. And Luke 6:17-23a in the mass *Sapientiam* is the Lucan parallel of St. Matthew's Beatitudes which is the Gospel for All Saints. Persecutions, and the heavenly reward, are mentioned; but verses 17-19 are completely irrelevant mere filling for 'liturgical length' — and the passage as a whole is distinctly weak.

The manner in which we suggest that the remaining material be utilized, and in some cases supplemented, is as follows:

For the feast of Polycarp, Bishop and Martyr of Smyrna, on January 26, Rome provides a special Epistle, 1 John 3:10b-16, "We ought to lay down our lives for the brethren." This, which includes part of the Prayer Book Epistle for Trinity II, contains nothing particularly applicable to St. Polycarp:

---

10. See *Prayer Book Studies*, II, p. 83.

whereas the use of that passage for Alban (June 22) would be most significant for the circumstances of the latter's martyrdom. We think we can do better for Polycarp with Revelation 2:8-11: "Unto the angel of the Church Smyrna write: . . . Fear none of the things which thou shalt suffer: . . . be thou faithful unto death, and I will give thee a crown of life." The Roman Gospel is Matthew 10:34-42, from the Common *In virtute* for a Martyr *not* a Bishop, "He that loseth his life for my sake shall find it." That is all very well; but as it goes admirably with the above Epistle from 1 John, this Gospel also may advantageously be transferred to Alban; and in this place we suggest instead Matthew 20:20-23, which speaks of drinking our Lord's cup and being baptized with His baptism, a selection which Rome provides for the feast of St. John at the Latin Gate.

Ignatius of Antioch on February 1 also has true Propers in the Missal: Romans 8:35-39, "Who shall separate us from the love of Christ?" and John 12:24-26, "Except a grain of wheat fall into the ground and die," etc. It would seem difficult to improve upon either of these fine passages, and we would adopt them as they stand.

Perpetua and Felicitas on March 7 afford one of the noblest and most authentic of the early Acts of the Martyrs. Rome has reduced this primitive feast to a mere commemoration to make room for Thomas Aquinas on this day. We propose to commemorate Thomas on March 8, and to restore Perpetua to her ancient rights. Rome assigns to her, if her service is to be kept, the Common *Me exspectaverunt*. We have seen that the Epistle of this mass is beside the point; its Gospel is Matthew 13:44-52, the Parables of the Hid Treasure, the Pearl, and the Net — obviously a (rather perfunctory) assignment to a female saint (it is used also for one neither a Virgin nor a Martyr), rather than to a Martyr as such. We think much greater justice will be done by apportioning Hebrews 10:32-39, "a great fight of afflictions, . . . a great recompense of reward . . . the just shall live by faith," which is the Epistle for the mass *Salus autem*, lengthened by one verse; and Matthew 24:9-14a, a modification of the verses 3-13 from the same mass, "Then shall they deliver you to be afflicted, and shall kill you . . . but he that shall endure unto the end, the same shall be saved."

On June 2, Blandina and the Martyrs of Lyons furnish another of the really great stories of the heroisms of the early Church, fully recounted from contemporary documents in the *Ecclesiastical History* of Eusebius. Rome does not list her at all. We propose 1 Peter 1:3-9, a slight lengthening of the verses 3-7 of the Epistle of the Common *Sancti tui*: "A lively hope by the resurrection of Jesus Christ from the dead, to an inheritance incorruptible . . . in heaven . . . that the trial of your faith . . . might be found unto . . . glory at the appearing of Jesus Christ; . . . receiving the end of your faith, even the salvation of your souls." For the Gospel, we offer Matthew 16:24-27, from the mass *Sacerdotes*: "If any man will come after me, let him . . . take up his cross, and follow me . . . For what is a man profited, if he shall gain the whole world, and lose his own soul? . . . For the Son of man shall come in the glory of his Father with his angels: and then he shall reward every man according to his works." The common elements of this Epistle and Gospel reenforce each other admirably; it might seem that a more careful selection would have conjoined them, as we have done, rather than to have distributed them to separate masses.

We have mentioned that we consider the Epistle and Gospel which Rome assigned to Polycarp to be more applicable to Alban on June 22 ; though we recommend reducing the Epistle from 1 John 3:10b-16 to verses 13-16. This Epistle is particularly applicable to Alban, who was martyred for protecting a hunted Christian priest, mentioning as it does that "We ought to lay down our lives for the brethren." We might be tempted to collate with this John 15:12-16, "Greater love hath no man than this, that a man lay down his life for his friends." But in the first place this is the Prayer Book Gospel for St. Barnabas on June 11, which is much too close in the Calendar; in the second, Alban did not give his life for a friend, but a stranger; and finally, the remaining content of this Gospel is with special reference to the Apostles: "I have chosen you, and ordained you, that ye should go and bring forth fruit, and that your fruit should remain" — a saying without relevance to a man who seems not previously to have confessed Christ, and whose life was brought to an end at this point. The Supplement for England in the Roman Missal gives for Alban Matthew 10:34-42, which is identical with the Gospel for Polycarp, and is in fact the provision for the Common *In virtute*: "He that loseth his life for my sake shall find it. He that receiveth you receiveth me . . . And whosoever shall give to drink unto one of these little ones a cup of cold water only in the name of a disciple, verily I say unto thee, he shall in no wise lose his reward." Nothing could be more appropriate to the noble end of this Roman soldier, who forfeited his life for an act of common humanity to a disciple of the Lord.

For Cyprian of Carthage, which we have assigned to September 13, Rome uses the Common *Intret*, whose Gospel is the rather inapplicable Luke 21:9-19 already noted. Its Epistle, Wisdom 3:1-8, the beautiful poem on "the souls of the righteous," we consider will be more useful elsewhere. As Cyprian was an outstanding champion of Episcopacy, we propose the above Gospel of John 10:11-16, "The good shepherd giveth his life for the sheep," as the ideal Gospel for a Bishop and Martyr. The best Epistle to go with this seems to be 1 Peter 5:1-4, 10-11, "When the chief Shepherd shall appear, ye shall receive a crown of glory that fadeth not away," and the concluding mention of sufferings and their ultimate rewards.

Cyprian of Carthage was originally commemorated on September 14, and his day was actually a Cardinal Feast, determining the whole block of the Summer Sundays, and also the autumnal Ember Days. The great popularity of the feast of the Exaltation of the Holy Cross on this date caused Rome to shift him to the date of a namesake on the 16th of this month, to clear the Octave of the Nativity of the Blessed Virgin on the 8th to the 15th. As we do not have to concern ourselves with that, and have only the Ember Days to consider, the logical expedient is to put Cyprian on the 13th, as near as possible to his actual *natale*, which has been permanently usurped by Holy Cross Day.

For Justin Martyr and Boniface, see below pages 75 and 69, respectively.

Confessors

Originally, a Confessor was a saint who valiantly confessed his faith at the peril of his life in the face of persecution, without actually paying the ultimate penalty by his death. After the period of the persecutions, the term was relaxed and broadened to take in any saint not a Martyr, who had been outstanding in his services to the Church.

The Roman provisions under this general heading include two Commons for Confessors who were Bishops, called, like the corresponding masses for Martyrs, *Statuit* and *Sacerdotes*; one, *In medio ecclesiae*, for Doctors of the Church, with an extra, alternative Epistle; two, *Os justi*, and *Justus ut palma*, for Confessors who were neither high ecclesiastics nor theologians; and another *Os justi* for Abbots.

The first mass, *Statuit*, for a Bishop, is used in whole or in part for more than twenty feasts in the Roman Missal, including Patrick on our list, with the Epistle only for Martin of Tours and the scriptural Titus, and the Gospel only for Nicholas. The supplement for England has it also for Aidan and David.

The matter assigned for the Epistle is perhaps the most factitious and least authentic in the book. A passage from Ecclesiasticus which commemorates by name the contributions of Abraham, Enoch, Noah, Moses, and Jacob, has been shredded into its constituent phrases, and passed through a colander to remove the original attributions, and all elements of Jewish setting. This comminuted hash has then been flavored to taste by outright alterations of the text; and then allowed to consolidate in a new mold. The source of this kind of ecclesiastical veal-loaf seems to be the following fragments of our "King James" text: Ecclesiasticus 44:20a, 16a, 17, 20b, 22a, 23a, 26a, 27 and 45:3ac, 8, 10 and 20b. Such is the celebrated "Ecce sacerdos magnus" passage, which has even been set to music for the pomp of pontifical processions! It is impressive enough in a way; but it definitely is not Scripture, not even apocryphal Scripture; and we certainly cannot use it.

The Gospel is Matthew 25:14-23, which presents the incidents of the Five and the Two Talents out of the parable. While the figure of the servant who had been faithful over a few things made ruler over many things has an obvious applicability to any eminent figure of the hierarchy, the real application of the parable as our Lord intended it to be used certainly lies in the concluding, contrasting treatment of the timorous soul who hid the one talent that he had. The radical surgery which deprives the story of its necessary conclusion (since the One Talent is mentioned in the first part of the passage) therefore cannot be approved. We do not recommend that the mutilated parable be used for anyone.

The other mass for a Confessor-Bishop, *Sacerdotes*, has Hebrews 7:23-27, which emphasizes the sacrificing priesthood of the Episcopate; and Matthew 24:42-47, "the faithful and wise servant, whom his lord hath made ruler over his household, to give them their meat in due season," which in turn underscores the ruling and the teaching functions of the pastoral office. All this is by no means a bad combination; it certainly is immeasurably superior to the Common *Statuit*. Yet the body of the Roman Missal uses it for only four days, none of them of any interest to us, though the Supplement for England indicates its Epistle for Augustine of Canterbury.

There does not seem to be any commemoration on our list which calls for the particular "sacerdotal" emphasis of that Epistle. But the Gospel will do very well for Theodore of Tarsus (September 19) — that Archbishop of Canterbury to whom the unification and definitive organization of the Church of England was due. (No provision is made for Theodore anywhere in the Roman Missal.) An appropriate Epistle to go with this Gospel would be 2 Timothy 2:1-5, 10: "The things that thou hast heard among many witnesses, the same commit thou to faithful men, who shall be able to teach others also:" a form of which (verses 1-7) Rome uses for Alfonso Liguori on August 2.

Martin of Tours on November 11, besides the abominable Epistle "Ecce sacerdos," has, in the Missal, the special Gospel of Luke 11:35-36, the Candle on the Candlestick. There would be no special objection to having that for Martin, who was certainly a "bright and shining light" of the early Church in France. However, passages in the Gospels applicable to the outstanding teachers of the Church are few in relation to the number of such entries to be supplied; we would prefer to transfer this particular attribution to Irenæus. Martin was, however, notable for his charity in word and deed; and we would like to appoint for him one of the most touching passages in the Gospels, Matthew 25:34-40: "Inasmuch as ye have done it unto one of the least of these my brethren, ye have done it unto me." A proper Epistle to go with this would be Isaiah 58:10-12 — sharing one's bread with the hungry, satisfying the afflicted soul, etc. — a variant of the Epistle (verses 7-11) which Rome uses on July 20 for Jerome Emiliani.

Of the two Commons for Confessors who were not Bishops, the prevailing mass is the *Os justi*, also used on more than twenty occasions. In fact it is a sort of general catch-all. A considerable majority of those occasions are indeed the commemorations of monastic clergy — chiefly, perhaps, because most of the medieval canonizations were in that class — but of Regulars more distinguished for their organizing ability than their asceticism; and this mass is also used for a handful of Seculars, four Kings, and a professor!

The Epistle for this Common is Ecclesiasticus 31:8-11, and again cannot be said to be honestly used. The original text is concerned with the praise of the rich man — not, as the liturgical version disingenuously cites it, any man — without blemish, who has not gone after gold, who might have offended, and has not offended, or done evil, and has not done it. We may sympathize with the maker of this assignment in his apparent regret as to the infrequency of a rich man's actually entering the kingdom of heaven, and in his wish to preserve such direct and profitable phrases for more general application: yet it hardly seems candid to convert this passage to be used mainly for those who on the contrary were committed to the profession of a holy poverty. The Gospel to go with this is Luke 12:35-40, "Let your loins be girded about, and your lights burning; and ye yourselves like unto men that wait for their Lord," etc.

We can use that Gospel, but not in this classification. The only Confessor not otherwise determined, for whom we would like proper lections, is King Alfred, as the founder of the unity of the English nation, and an outstanding example of a really religious King, on October 26. Rome has not made much for its royal Confessors. Edward the Confessor of England and Henry II of Germany are simply assigned to the above rather monkish Common *Os justi* — quite appropriately; they were both monks more than kings at heart. Louis of France and Stephen of Hungary are provided with the same framework, but with the Lucan Parable of the Pounds for a Gospel. For King Alfred we propose a rather notable passage on the Reward of Wise Kings, derived from Wisdom 6 by the excision of some irrelevancies, taking verse 1-3, 9-12, and 24-25; and for the Gospel, Luke 6:43-45: "Every tree is known by its own fruit ... A good man out of the good treasure of his heart bringeth forth that which is good," etc. This parallels some of the matter of the Gospel lection for Trinity VIII, but with sufficient independence to make it worth including in an appropriate place: which we consider this to be.

Ascetics

Examples of the ascetic life are not separately categorized in the Roman Missal, save as they are intimated by the variant *Os justi* mass for Abbots. Nevertheless the second Common for a Confessor not a Bishop, *Justus ut palma*, was apparently intended for such, as it is assigned for nine commemorations, all of them monastic. The Epistle is 1 Corinthians 4:10-14, the famous "Fools for Christ's sake" passage, which has given its name to a class of saints in the Eastern Orthodox Church. It was really written of the perils of the Apostolic office, and avoids that definite designation limiting it to Apostles only by amputating verse 9a. The Gospel is Luke 12:32-34, "Sell that ye have, and give alms."

The *Os justi* for Abbots has for its Epistle Ecclesiasticus 45:113-2, 3b-5, another evasive rewriting and accommodation of the work of Moses: and for its Gospel, Matthew 19:27-29, "We have left all, and followed thee," and the same 'isapostolic' Twelve Thrones, as that now appointed for the Conversion of St. Paul.

The Ascetics for whom we wish to make provision are Anthony, Benedict, and Francis of Assisi. Rome uses the Abbots' *Os justi* for Benedict: and indeed this mass may originally have been appointed for this first Western head of a monastic order. The factitious Epistle, of course, cannot be considered. Nor are we much interested in giving a kind of "mitred Abbot" Gospel, which by implication would promote that sort of functionary to apostolic rank. To do honor, however, to the considerable services of Benedict, we can offer the substantial assignment of Luke 14:26-33, which is the Gospel for the mass *Statuit* for a Bishop and Martyr, but which Rome also assigns to Benedict's 'opposite number' in Eastern monasticism, Basil the Great; "Whosoever doth not bear his cross, and come after me, cannot be my disciple. . . So likewise, whosoever he be of you that forsaketh not all that he hath, he cannot be my disciple." A suitable Epistle with this might be Acts 2:44-47a, describing the religious communism, and the constant worship, of the primitive Church. The proposed date of July 11 for Benedict, by the way, is Sarum from the time of Lanfranc to the Reformation. Lanfranc apparently chose this day of the translation of the Saint's relics to Fleury in preference to the obit date on March 21, which Rome still observes, in order to clear the Lenten month of March as far as possible. This is still good reasoning.

For Anthony on January 17, Rome has the same impossible Epistle from the Abbots' *Os justi*, but for the Gospel takes that for the Common of the same name for Confessors, Luke 12:35-40, which has no particular applicability to Anthony, or any other ascetic. The Gospel for the second Common, *Justus*, Luke 12:32-34, "Sell that ye have, and give alms," would be perfectly in keeping. For an Epistle, we offer Philippians 3:7-14 (R.V., for a question of taste), with the theme of counting all things but loss of Christ, and pressing toward the mark for the prize of the high calling of God, which Rome uses two days earlier, on the feast of Paul the First Hermit.

Francis of Assisi on October 4 is much too individual a figure to be dismissed with a Common of any sort. Rome has for his Gospel Matthew 11:25-30 — Revealed to babes; Take my yoke upon you, etc. This of course is the same as that appointed (with much less cogency, be it said) for St. Matthias on February 24 — a date sufficiently removed in the year to cause no inconvenience if it is repeated here; and its content is virtually ideal for a saint with the complete loving simplicity of St. Francis. The Roman Epistle is Galatians 6:14-18, "I bear in my body the marks of the Lord Jesus." This is certainly specific enough — none more so in the entire Calendar of saints outside the New Testament — and its allusion to the *Stigmata* presents an indubitable historical and scientific fact.

Missionaries

There is another class of Confessors to which we desire to give a new emphasis. These are the founding fathers of national Churches, who accomplished a kind of Apostolate to new regions of the faith; in modern terms, Missionaries.

Augustine of Canterbury on May 26, who converted the South of England, has in the English supplement to the Missal the Epistle from the second Common for a Confessor-Bishop, *Sacerdotes*, as we have observed, and the Roman Gospel for St. Mark's Day, Luke 10:1-9, which is approximately our assignment for St. Luke (verses 1-7) — the Sending of the Seventy; chosen apparently for the verse about sending forth labourers into the harvest. We consider that Augustine's contributions as a Missionary were of far greater significance than his routine liturgical functions, as implied in that 'sacerdotal' Epistle. We propose instead 2 Corinthians 5:17-20, which stresses "the ministry of reconciliation," and the note of "ambassadors for Christ"; and Matthew 13:31-33, the brief parables of the Mustard Seed and the Leaven, with their intimations of the great growth from small beginnings which has made the Anglican Church into an ecumenical communion.

The same English supplement appoints the other Common for Confessor-Bishops, the mass *Statuit*, on August 31 for Aidan, the Celtic Apostle to the North of England. We have seen that the Epistle for this mass is intolerable, and its mutilated Gospel inadvisable. Again we prefer to emphasize the missionary contribution of St. Aidan with 1 Corinthians 9:16-23, "Woe is me, if I preach not the Gospel;" and to recognize his ascetic devotion, and its great fruits, by appointing the Gospel which we recommend removing from St. Paul's Day, Matthew 19:27-30: "We have forsaken all, and followed thee," with the hundred-fold reward.

The same Common *Statuit* is also appointed for David of Wales on March 1 in the Anglo-Roman supplement. It will be remembered that David is a partly factitious figure. The tale that he sought and received episcopal consecration in Jerusalem itself first appears at the end of the eleventh century, 500 years after his death, in a work of one Rhygyfarch (latinized as Richemarchus), himself a son of a Bishop of St. David's, and a super-patriotic Welshman who wanted to make out that the Welsh Church was rightfully independent of Canterbury. This Welshman was, of course, right in his contention that his was the elder Church, being indeed the survival of the original British Church before the invasion of the pagan Angles and Saxons, and hence long before either Augustine or Aidan: though he was a bit unconscionable in trying to bolster up fact with pious fiction. David was not the founder of the Welsh Church; but though not the Augustine of that Church, he may have been in some ways the Theodore. As its first historic figure, and the Patron Saint of Wales, he is perhaps the best choice to represent the native British source, which was the third of the tributary streams which coalesced to form the Church of England. Since, then, he was associated with the small beginnings of a great work, we suggest as a Gospel Mark 4:26-29, "First the blade, then the ear;" and for an Epistle a neutral but very fine passage not used elsewhere, Ephesians 2:4-10: "By grace ye are saved . . . Created unto good works."

Patrick, Apostle of Ireland, (March 17), is also provided with the Common *Statuit*. We conceive that this outstanding missionary may be much more worthily characterized with 1 Thessalonians 2:2b-12: "Bold to preach the Gospel of God; . . . affectionately desirous of you . . . that ye would walk worthy of God, who hath called us unto his kingdom and glory" (June 16, *aliquibus*) ; and Matthew 5:43-48, "Love your enemies" (Abbot John Gualbert, July 12) — the last in tribute to the man who deliberately devoted his life to the pagans among whom he had been a captive slave in his young days.

Finally, on June 5 we have the English monk Boniface who became the Apostle of Germany. He has in the Missal a proper mass, with Ecclesiasticus 44:1-15, the Praise of Famous Men, for the Epistle, and Matthew 5:1-12, the Beatitudes, from All Saints' Day, for the Gospel. It seems to us that Boniface's great services in the founding of the Church in Germany, and his indefatigable missionary career right up to his tragic end at the hands of pagan bandits, demand something rather more distinctive than these. Rome's use of Acts 20:17-21 for Pope Stephen on August 2 suggests the employment of the more inclusive Acts 20:18b-27, presenting the moving and instructive parallel of St. Paul's account of his own valiant missionary efforts in his farewell address to the Elders of Ephesus, concluding with the forecast of his coming afflictions. With such an Epistle, we need a very strong missionary Gospel: and our choice is the Great Commission in Matthew 28:18-20.

Doctors

But of all the saints whom Rome commemorates under the general category of Confessors, the most numerous and significant of those we desire to observe are those outstanding teachers of the faith who are known as Doctors of the Church.

The Common *In medio ecclesiæ* has as its Epistle 2 Timothy 4:1-8 — an extremely effective all-round passage, which makes the point that the Church's doctrine is no abstract theology or esoteric learning, but the proclamation of a dynamic Gospel. "Preach the word!" is its primary adjuration: that is the "sound doctrine" which some will resist. The Christian teacher must persevere in doing the work of an evangelist, and make full proof of his ministry. The peroration is the Apostle's farewell to such an active life himself: "I have fought a good fight, I have finished my course, I have kept the faith," to the final reward of the crown of righteousness. This Epistle serves in the Roman rite for SS. Hilary, Chrysostom, Gregory the Great, Ambrose, Anselm, Bede, Basil, Augustine of Hippo, and

Jerome, out of those for whom we desire to provide liturgical commemorations; as well as for Francis de Sales, Peter Damian, Isidore of Seville, Bonaventure, Peter Chrysologus, and Alfonso Liguori, with whom we are not concerned.

This mass also includes the alternative Epistle of Ecclesiasticus 39:5-10, whose general theme is wisdom through meditation. This is appointed for SS. Leo the Great, Gregory Nazianzen, and Bernard.

The Common Gospel is Matthew 5:13-19, the Salt and the Light of the world, and the saying that whosoever shall do and teach the Commandments shall be called great in the kingdom of heaven.

Nowhere is the desirability of assigning proper lections to each day, so far as possible, in order to secure an appropriate adaptation to each individual case, more evident than in the class we are now considering. The Doctors of the Church are all outstanding and distinctive personalities, who have made their own mark. They cannot adequately be treated by the blanket prescriptions of a Common, made to serve for any and all of the intellectual leaders of the Church.

A small start toward the selection of *propria* has been made in the Roman Missal itself. Wisdom 7:7-14, "Wisdom makes men friends of God," is assigned to Thomas Aquinas; variant Gospels, to be discussed later, are indicated for Basil and Leo the Great. And both a proper Epistle and Gospel are set forth for Athanasius on May 2, in a quite significant way. The Epistle is 2 Corinthians 4:5-14, mentioning "the knowledge of the glory of God in the face of Jesus Christ," which is certainly eminently suitable for this champion of an orthodox Christology, and "we believe, and therefore speak," which underscores the boldness of that figure which has become proverbial in the phrase "Athanasius contra mundum." The Gospel is Matthew 10:23-28, beginning "But when they persecute you in this city, flee ye into another," which bespeaks a quite living memory at Rome of Athanasius' fruitful exile there, which brought to the West a knowledge of the organization of Eastern monasticism. He actually spent a good part of his troubled episcopate practically commuting between his see city and various ports of exile: four times he had to flee his persecutors. And as for the rest of that Gospel, Athanasius was certainly persecuted as his Master was; he did proclaim from the housetops what he had heard in the ear from the Spirit. We should prefer to read Matthew 10:23-32, for the sake of a fuller treatment and a better ending; otherwise the Roman assignments for this Saint may be adopted just as they stand.

If we may take this Proper for Athanasius as a standard for the sort of choice of really apposite Scriptures which we consider desirable, the defects of the Roman provision of one Gospel and two Epistles for the great Doctors become somewhat striking. The normal Epistle, 2 Timothy 4:1-8 is, as we have remarked, most excellent in itself: but few indeed of the theological thinkers whom the Church has distinguished with the title of Doctor are accurately described by it, or come even close to realizing the clear moral valor intimated in it. Athanasius did, of course; but he is well taken care of by his Proper Epistle. Leo the

Great, dominating an ecumenical council from his distant see, and confronting the invading Huns, with the same resolution, might be considered to qualify; but curiously, and quite inappropriately, the Roman Church appoints for his feast the alternative Epistle, that 'wisdom through meditation' passage from Ecclesiasticus. Anselm no doubt was steadfast in difficulties; but other notes of the passage, intimating a firm governance of rebellious people through sound doctrine, seem none too applicable to this first scholar of Europe, who was only too thoroughly conscious of his own inadequacy to meet the administrative problems that confronted him. The only Doctor with whom we are concerned to whom this Epistle might apply without reservation seems to be Hilary of Poictiers, who in every respect measured up to the high standards there set forth.

As to the somewhat undistinguished Common Gospel, Matthew 5:13-19, it would really have a distinctly happy application to Leo the Great, with its allusion to the right of those who do and teach God's commandments to be called "great" in the kingdom of heaven. But again, Rome has unaccountably "missed the boat," and for Leo gives the Gospel for St. Peter's Day. No doubt this was intended to emphasize Leo's championship of "the Christ, the Son of the living God" at the great Council of Chalcedon, which accepted his famous *Tome*, and endorsed it with an ecumenical authority on a par with the Creeds. No doubt it was also intended to underscore the Roman claims that the successors of St. Peter possessed a universal *Magisterium*, infallible before and without a General Council, of which claims Leo's victory at Chalcedon is one chief ground of argument. Whether or not one is disposed to agree with Jalland that the Roman Church has *de facto* proved indefectible in preserving "the faith once delivered to the saints," all this is far too much weight to put upon Leo. Actually, he was not an original theological thinker at all — that passage from Ecclesiasticus is almost ludicrously misapplied in his case. He was a practical man, who supported vigorously the traditional faith of his see, where the real thinking had been done and the essential working conclusions established in the days of Hippolytus and Callistus, a century before Nicaea. He had the rare and valuable capacity to write in the very style of the Creeds; but he was not himself a creative theologian. The Common Gospel of Matthew 5:13-19 is quite exactly applicable to him; his greatness lay in the fact that he did teach and practice the "commandments" that had been handed down to him.

Therefore we propose to assign to Leo the Great on April this Gospel from the mass *In medio*. For an Epistle, 2 Timothy 1:12b-14, "Hold fast the form of sound words, which thou hast heard of me, in faith and love which is in Christ Jesus. That good thing which was committed unto thee keep by the Holy Ghost which dwelleth in us," is a quite accurate characterization.

We also find that we must make some similar qualifications in the case of the "Four Latin Doctors" of medieval tradition — Gregory the Great, Ambrose, Augustine, and Jerome. The Westerns felt they had to have such a list to balance the four Greek Doctors already acclaimed by the Eastern Church. Properly speaking, Augustine is the only one of them who actually deserves such a classification. Gregory and Ambrose were both liturgists and administrators, rather than theologians; and Jerome was a specialized Scriptural scholar.[11]

For Augustine on August 28, we suggest John 17:1-8, as perhaps the most adequate passage for the greatest of Western theologians: "This is life eternal, that they might know surely that I came from thee, and they have believed that thou didst send me." For the Epistle, it seems a justifiable 'accommodation' to allude to a majestic concept of Augustine's which is one of his greatest and most enduring contributions to the Church, by reading Hebrews 12:22-24, 28-29, with its explicit mention of "the city of the living God."

Ambrose the administrator is well characterized by Luke 12:42-44, the "faithful and wise steward, whom his lord shall make ruler over his household, to give them their portion of meat in due season." This is of course a 'concord' of Matthew 24:45-47, part of the Gospel of the mass Sacerdotes for a Bishop-Confessor, which we have proposed to apportion to Theodore on September 19; however, there would be no bar to having this for Ambrose on April 4, even if it were identical, which it is not. An appropriate Epistle to go with this would be Ecclesiasticus 2:7-11, 16-18, "Ye that fear the Lord, believe him, and your reward shall not fail."

For Gregory the Great on March 12, the obvious Gospel is Mark 10:42-45, "Whosoever will be great among you, shall be your minister, and whosoever of you will be the chiefest, shall be your servant," in allusion to the designation of *Servus servorum Dei*, which Gregory was the first to attach to his see, and which remains today the most basic title of the papacy. This again is a 'concord' with the Matthæan version for St. James on July 25, and permissible for the same reason as above.

As an Epistle, Ecclesiasticus 47:8-11 presents what may be held to be a justifiable 'accommodation' of some attributions to Nathan the prophet: "He set singers before the altar . . . He beautified their feasts, and set in order the solemn times," etc: which may or may not be an accurate description of the liturgical contributions of Nathan (the "Book of Nathan," mentioned in the Kings, has perished, and the canonical Old Testament says nothing about that), but it certainly is apropos of Gregory.

For Jerome on September 30, Nehemiah 8:1-3, 5-6, 8-9, the account of how Ezra the Scribe read the Book of the Law "distinctly, and gave the sense, and caused them to understand the reading;" and Luke 24:44-48, how our Lord taught the disciples of "all things . . . written in the law of Moses, and in the prophets, and in the Psalms," and "opened their understanding, that they might

---

11. Ed. Note: This is a revealing sentence that says more about the reception of these patristic thinkers in the mid-twentieth century than a clear-eyed appraisal of their respective works. Gregory's homilies on the Gospels, Ezekiel, and Job formed the preaching of the Western Church for the next 600 years, while Jerome decisively shaped the course of Western Monasticism for centuries in his lives, letters, and translations of Origen's spirituality.

understand the scriptures," might serve as background for the man who founded all biblical scholarship in the Western Church.

As to the four great "Greek Doctors," we have already considered Athanasius. For Basil on June 14, Rome uses the Epistle for the Common of Doctors, but for the Gospel takes Luke 14:26-35, which is a version lengthened by two verses of that from the mass *Statuit* for a martyred Bishop; apparently for the passages about hating father and mother, and counting the cost, which were perhaps thought suitable to Basil as the great regulator of Eastern monasticism — and, if the whole truth were better known, of Western also, since Benedict's reputation along that line rests in part upon his having promulgated much of Basil's rules and services. For our purposes, however, Basil's contributions to the cause of monasticism appear to be of little relevance. What is of enduring importance, namely his outstanding defense of the office and work of the Holy Spirit, and of Nicene theology generally, would be much better presented by 1 Corinthians 2:6-13a, "The Spirit searcheth all things, yea, the deep things of God," and Luke 10:22-24, "No man knoweth who the Son is, but the Father; and who the Father is, but the Son, and he to whom the Son will reveal him."

Chrysostom was less of a creative theologian than an indefatigable and nearly inexhaustible expositor of Scripture and preacher of the Word. For the day of John "of the Golden Mouth" on January 27, we suggest therefore Jeremiah 1:6-9, "I have put my words in thy mouth," (Rome has Jeremiah 1:5-10 for the Vigil of St. John Baptist); and Luke 21:12b-15, "I will give you a mouth and wisdom." This mild play upon words seems almost called for in the case of this man, whose own name has been all but wholly supplanted by the epithet universally applied by the admiring Church to his eloquence of speech; and it may readily be defended by pointing out that these passages convey a substantial and perfectly serious idea, which would be equally intelligible, and equally appropriate, if they contained no entertaining verbal echoes whatever.

The last of these four is Gregory of Nazianzus, assigned to May 9. With the other "great Cappadocians," Basil and Gregory of Nyssa, he was of the utmost service in consolidating the Athanasian position after Nicaea. His learning, and his triumphant labors, may be represented by Wisdom 7:7-14, "Wisdom makes men friends of God," which is the selection used in the Missal for Thomas Aquinas, and John 8:25-32, "The truth shall make you free."

In the rest of the list for which we desire Propers, we have already mentioned that Hilary of Poictiers on January 14 can best use the Epistle of the Common *In medio* (2 Timothy 4:1-8). For the Gospel we propose Luke 12:8-12: the reward of those who confess their Lord before men, and the inspiration of the Holy Ghost for their answers when they are brought before "magistrates and powers" — a reminder of Hilary's valiant defiance of Constantius.

As to the alternative Epistle for the mass *In medio*, Bernard on August 20 is the only Doctor to whom Rome assigns that Common for whom it is really in place, with its message of "wisdom through meditation:" though we think that Ecclesiasticus 39:1-10 will make a better lection than the Roman use of verses 5-10. Bernard is the principal mystic among those who have been named Doctors of the Church; and to express his warm devotion to the love of God, we suggest John 15:7-11 — a selection suggested by the use of verses 8-16 as a Gospel for St. Exsuperantius on January 24 in the appendix *pro aliquibus locis*.

Anselm of Canterbury can hardly be omitted from an Anglican list, though his two intellectual contributions which won him a European reputation and a place in the Roman Missal as a Doctor of the Church, namely his doctrine of the Atonement, and his ontological proof of the existence of God, are both now rather under an eclipse. The latter has been assailed as a mere logomachy, the former as the root-stock of that type of medieval Romanism which persists to this day in fundamentalist Protestantism. Yet it is to be said that he did not originate so much as clarify the doctrine of the Atonement prevalent in his time: it really represents a purification and crystallization out of much muddied thinking; it is an indispensable step in the history of thought on that subject, and became the starting point for further and higher consideration of what after all is doubtless an inexhaustible mystery of the faith.

Both of Anselm's chief contributions are well intimated in Romans 1:16-20a: "The gospel of Christ . . . is the power of salvation to every one that believeth . . . For the invisible things of him from the creation of the world are clearly seen, being understood by the things that are made, even his eternal power and Godhead." For a Gospel on his day of April 21, we suggest John 7:16-18 and 8:12. The saying, "If a man will do his will, he shall know of the doctrine" is a profoundly significant expression, which ought to have its place in any extended liturgical lectionary. Incidentally, it is all the safeguard that could be needed against the possibility of interpreting the Epistle along too rigidly Anselmian lines, since it makes the point that the basic reality is the witness of united Christian experience, not the theological formulations of those who profess to interpret it. The single added verse from the eighth chapter, on Christ the Light of the world, stands in Scripture in a kind of solitary splendor, between the *Pericope adulterae* and some Pharisaic wrangling, in such wise as to be absolutely unusable as part of any conceivable lection taken out of the chapter in which it occurs. To be made available at all, it must be combined with precisely these verses from the seventh chapter. Here, it affords a perfect ending to this Gospel for a Doctor of the Christian Church.

The Venerable Bede, whom Rome canonized late in the nineteenth century, with the honorary title of Doctor of the Church, was of course not a theologian, but an exegete and church historian. Rome uses for his day on May 27 the common *In medio*. But we would prefer Malachi 3:16-18, which mentions the "Book of Remembrance," and Matthew 13:47-52, the parable of the Net (which we consider eminently suitable to a historian like Bede, whose Calendar displayed such an interest in the history of the universal Church, and actually led the way to all modern Calendars which concern themselves with ecumenical rather than merely local commemorations), and the "scribe who is instructed, . . . bringing forth out of his treasure things new and old."

This completes the list of those we desire to commemorate, out of those whom the Church of Rome has designated as Doctors of the Church. But there are three more Confessors, two primitive apologists and one early theologian, to whom proper Scripture lessons may be assigned on the same general principles as the Doctors.

For Justin, Martyr and Apologist, on his day of April 13, we propose as an Epistle 1 Peter 3:14-22, "If ye suffer for righteousness' sake, happy are ye: . . . and be ready to give . . . a reason of the hope that is in you"; since this, and the further mention of "suffering for well-doing," are very germane to Justin's life. The remaining verses, 19-22, are a little less *ad rem*, and might be omitted; but the theme of Baptism bulked large in Justin's thought, so including them would be more useful than not. John 12:44-50, our Lord's intimation that belief on Him is the road to the knowledge of the Father, and that His "commandment is life everlasting," provides a Gospel quite in line with Justin's apologetic for the Christian faith.

Irenaeus' services to the early Church were very great, asserting the living continuity of Christian experience in the Church's tradition as a basic historic fact, and thereby defending its theology from being subverted into a theosophy. It is most unfortunate that the growing desuetude of the knowledge of the Greek language in those days when culture was decaying and the Church was forming in the West, allowed so much of his works to be lost. The fragments that have survived are among the most precious and vital of intimations for one of the most obscure periods in the Church's history. The Roman Missal commemorates him with 2 Timothy 3:14-4:5, and John 10:11-16. This Epistle is part of that in the Common of Doctors *In medio*, with the addition of "from a child thou hast known the holy scriptures," etc. This seems a rather roundabout and unsatisfactory way of making the point of Irenaeus' training in the Ephesian tradition. And the Gospel for Easter II, while perfectly suitable for Irenaeus as a martyred Bishop, we have already appropriated for Cyprian.

For Irenaeus' day on June 28, we are much inclined to one suggestion that has been made, to use Malachi 2:5-7 for the Epistle: chiefly for the very significant final verse, "For the priest's lips should keep knowledge, and they should seek the law at his mouth: for he is the messenger of the Lord of hosts;" though there is a certain permissible pleasure to be derived also from the subtle connotations of the phrases, "My covenant was with him of life and *peace*," and "he walked with me in *peace* and equity," as intimations, vocal to the intelligent, of the meaning of

Irenaeus' distinguished name.[12] And Luke 11:33-36, the Candle upon the Candlestick, seems quite in keeping with one of the most illustrious of "the lights of the world in their several generations."

Clement of Alexandria is not in the Roman Calendar; and in general his fame in the Western Church has been somewhat neglected till recent times. Writing before the period of the great heresies and the great councils, his figure was not illuminated by the lurid fires of controversy. His thought moves in the same spheres, with the same limitations, as the sub-apostolic Fathers; yet he is not to be blamed for expressing a Christology which, after later controversies, would have been condemned as a heretical Subordinationism. He was eminent among the founders of the first great Christian School for the cultivation of sacred studies for their own sake. He may be called the last of the early apologists, and the first of modern theologians. Indeed, in many ways he was very modern: much that he said about the application of the Christian faith to the tasks of Christian living is as vital and valid today as when he wrote it; he was the first to relate Christianity to the general picture of Comparative Religion, and to recognize its dominion over the spirits of all men through all religions. And as for his attempts to give Christian theology a place among the philosophical systems of thought in his day, it should be noted that of late years he has been viewed with increasing interest and respect by the historians of philosophy, and acclaimed as a neglected philosopher in his own right.

Besides, a Calendar which aims to represent the most eminent figures of Christian history ought to have at least one from the Church in Egypt, whose early contributions to the thought and life of the Christian society were so great, and which in many ways was the preceptor of Imperial Rome itself. Alexandrian Christianity has suffered in the eyes of orthodox theologians, first, by its defeat by the Antiochenes in the Christological controversies; second, by the schism which took it out of communion with the Orthodox East; and finally, by its submergence by the Mohammedan flood. Yet its inherent vitality may be gauged by the fact that the Copts to this day are far and away the most considerable of the separated Churches.

As an Epistle on Clement's day of December 4, we propose that uniquely assigned to St. Exsuperantius in the Supplement to the Missal, 2 Peter 1:2-8, mentioning "the knowledge of him that hath called us to glory and virtue; . . . Add to your faith virtue, and to virtue knowledge, . . . that ye shall neither be barren nor unfruitful in the knowledge of our Lord Jesus Christ." And for the Gospel, John 6:57-63, we suggest a passage much beloved by Clement, who favored the Fourth Gospel as one that was "spiritual."

---

12. Ed. Note: The point being made here is that the name "Irenaeus" comes from the Greek word for "peace" — *eirēnē*.

Scriptural Saints

Archbishop Cranmer, in his revision of the Calendar, reduced the Red Letter Days to saints mentioned in Scripture, under the apparent impression that because the persons mentioned belonged to the Primitive Church, the observance of their festivals must have done so too.[13] This last was anything but the case. Outside of Easter and Pentecost, it is doubtful if even any Scriptural event was regularly commemorated by the Church before the fourth century. Certainly the first persons to be so distinguished were contemporary martyrs; and the one class of festivals whose antiquity Cranmer simply took for granted, and incorporated entire, namely the Apostles, were all of later origin, in a piecemeal elaboration that lasted into the thirteenth century before the list was complete.

Hence we are considering last the possibility of supplementing the Prayer Book commemorations of figures in Holy Scripture by optional observances of some others.

There can be no doubt of the entire suitability for this purpose of such persons as Joseph, Mary Magdalene, Timothy, and Titus; or such events as the Conversion of Cornelius, and the Visitation of the Blessed Virgin. It is doubtful however whether anything would be gained by celebrating the Decollation of St. John Baptist. We celebrate his Nativity; his figure, as the precursor of our Lord, dominates two of the Sundays in Advent; his Baptism of our Lord is commemorated on Epiphany II. This about exhausts his significance for the Christian religion: he was not, strictly speaking, a Christian saint. His death was pure tragedy, and contributes nothing distinctive to Christian history or doctrine.

But there is another class of feasts featured by the Roman Church where the persons are found in Holy Scripture, but the events are not. Such are the Martyrdom of St. Paul; St. John at the Latin Gate, which celebrates his traditional escape from being boiled in oil; St. Peter "ad Vincula," in commemoration of the *Quo vadis?* story — an admirable fiction, perfect in its verisimilitude, but an absolute invention for all that; and also, the Conception and Nativity of the Blessed Virgin. The great difficulty in all these cases is the utter lack of any scriptural passages whatsoever, not only to recount such events, but even to be stretched by any ingenuity to be even congruous with them.

This is especially evident in the insuperable difficulties in which the Church of Rome has involved itself in attempting to find Scriptures appropriate to its very numerous festivals of the Blessed Virgin. The great difficulty, of course, is that St. Mary's significance, and nearly all that is said about her, is tied to the Incarnation. The festivals of the Annunciation and the Purification of the Blessed Virgin Mary are really just as much feasts of the Incarnation as Christmas Day itself, as is very properly indicated by the Proper Preface of the Nativity, taken from the

---

13. *Cf. Prayer Book Studies*, IX, Vol. 2, pp. 145-149, 159.

Roman rite for Christmas, and assigned them in our Church. Of course, this very fact gives rise to a desire to have some commemorations of the Blessed Virgin for her own sake. But when anyone tries to do that, he is not long in running into difficulties. There is no trouble in the Roman assignment of the Epistle and Gospel for the Annunciation for votive masses of the Virgin in Advent, or of the dawn Mass of Christmas for those between the Nativity and the Purification. The Visitation on July 2 takes Luke 1:39-47, the account of the incident through the first two verses of the *Magnificat*. That again is all very well, and naturally we are proposing something along that line also. This observance however concentrates attention on the event, and is a little too particular to serve for the sole commemoration of the first of all saints.

Relatively early ages of the Church, therefore, added commemorations of her Nativity and her Falling Asleep. But while both of these events obviously occurred, nothing whatever is said about them in Scripture. The best the Roman Church has been able to think of was to apportion to these occasions two utterly and completely irrelevant passages: to the Nativity, Matthew 1:1-16, the genealogy of our Lord from Adam down to "Joseph, the husband of Mary, of whom was born Jesus, who is called Christ;" and to the *Dormitio*, now unconscionably distorted into the purely mythological "Assumption," Luke 10:38-42, the incident of Mary and Martha of *Bethany*, for the sake of the verse "Mary hath chosen that good part, which shall not be taken away from her." This undoubtedly intentional confusing of identities is about on the same intellectual level as the story of the ignorant monk in the Middle Ages who crossed himself whenever he came to the word "maria" (seas) in the Psalms of the Breviary, taking it for "Maria!" Even if the Mary at Bethany had been the Blessed Virgin, it would require a brain-wrenching allegorization to connect it in any manner with the fact of her death.

When, not content with this, medieval devotion went further, and attempted to parallel the life of our Lord with such observances as the Conception and the Presentation of the Blessed Virgin, to celebrate her shrines and her attributes, and to provide variety for votives throughout the year (for to this day the ancient Sabbath is as much hers as Sunday is our Lord's; any Saturday without propers of its own is expected to be solemnized with a votive Mass of the Virgin,) still more remote expedients had to be resorted to. The Immaculate Conception on December 8 has Luke 1:26-28, the Angelic Salutation only: not bad at all in itself, but what has it to do with the purported subject of the feast? The "Seven Dolors," and votives between Easter and Whitsunday, take John 19:25-27: the *Stabat mater* passage, which again is all very well, though its actual content is exceedingly little, and its real point, "Behold thy mother," is either irrelevant in its actual contextual significance to a feast glorifying the Virgin, or very actively objectionable if forced into any accommodated sense. Finally, Luke 11:27-28, "Blessed is the womb that bare thee, and the paps which thou hast sucked," used for the universal Carmel feast, and a flock of others of more local currency, and for all the votives between the Purification and Advent, is to any modern mind in poor taste; we can only echo our Lord's answer, "Yea, rather, blessed are they that hear the word of God, and keep it."

One might have imagined that the paucity and aridity of the available passages from the New Testament might be in some degree relieved and enriched from the very wide variety of material in the Old. In fact, all Epistles for feasts of the Virgin, with the exception of the repetition of that Christmas mass, are from the Old Testament. But the results are even more futile. The Song of Solomon 2:8b-14, used for the Visitation is a very pretty spring love-lyric; but as applied to the Virgin, it is utterly sentimental. The same may be said of Ecclesiasticus 24:17-18a, 19-22, though it has some distinct overtones of goddess-worship: "I am the mother of fair love, and fear, and knowledge, and holy hope: . . . he that obeyeth me shall not be confounded, and they that work by me shall not do amiss." This is used for the Assumption, and the Carmel feast. But Ecclesiasticus 24:9-12, used for all votives from the Purification to Advent, and Proverbs 8:22-35, on the Nativity and the Immaculate Conception, are not short of blasphemy: "He created me from the beginning before the world;" and "I was set up from everlasting, from the beginning, or ever the world was. . . . Then was I by him, . . . and I was daily his delight. . . . Now, therefore, hearken unto me, 0O ye children: for blessed are they that keep my ways. . . . For whoso findeth me findeth life, and shall obtain favour of the Lord." How any living being, in this age or any other, can be content to repeat these words, intended to celebrate the Co-Eternal Wisdom of God, in such a setting of application to even the holiest of created beings, frankly surpasses even our attempt to conceive of a charitable interpretation. Scarcely less objectionable on these lines, and subject to grave criticism on others, is the peculiar rewriting of fragments from Judith 13:17-20, employed on the Seven Dolors: "Blessed art thou of the most high God above all the women upon the earth" is well enough; but it must be noted that the one who "hast this day brought to nought the enemies of thy people" has been transformed from God to Mary! — and this, with the concluding "hast avenged our ruin," was unquestionably included to inculcate the peculiar Roman distortion that it was in Mary, as the Second Eve, that the original sin of the race was wiped out.

In the light of all this, we have concluded to adopt the Visitation on July 2 as a Minor Holy Day, but not, as Bishop Frere suggested, to make it a Red Letter Day. Its Gospel should be Luke 1:39-45: and for an Epistle, perhaps the least objectionable and most adaptable selection would be Zechariah 2:10-13, "Sing and rejoice, O daughter of Zion," with its intimations of the coming of the Saviour to Jerusalem.

Of the two oldest feasts of the Blessed Virgin, we have, with some hesitation, recommended the Falling Asleep on August 15. Our hesitation, of course, is due to what the Roman Church has made of this day. But the Eastern Church has not fallen victim to the Roman exaggerations. There is no advantage in choosing arbitrarily some other *natale* of the chief of all saints than the traditional deathday. The feast of the Nativity of the Virgin is as purely apocryphal, if not more so. For a Gospel, the only completely unobjectionable selection is Luke 1:46-55, the *Magnificat*; and for an Epistle, apparently the very best that can be done would be Isaiah 61:7c-11: "Everlasting joy shall be unto them . . . They are the seed which the Lord hath blessed. I will greatly rejoice in the Lord, my soul shall be joyful in my God; for he hath clothed me with the garments of salvation . . . the Lord God will cause righteousness and praise to spring forth before all the nations."

The feast of St. Joseph on March 19 suffers in part from the difficulties of the commemorations of the Blessed Virgin. The Roman Gospel of Matthew 1:18b-21 is all right, though 18-25, as on the First Sunday after Christmas at present, would be much better. But Rome uses as an Epistle Ecclesiasticus 45:1b-2, 3b-5, which is precisely the same selection as in their Common for Abbots! — a cut and accommodated version of the work of Moses. We propose instead Isaiah 63:7-9,16, on the sheltering paternity of the Almighty as the Father of Israel: "I will mention the loving-kindnesses of the Lord, . . . in his love and in his pity he redeemed them; and he bare them, and carried them all the days of old . . . Doubtless thou art our father, though Abraham be ignorant of us, and Israel acknowledge us not: thou, O Lord, art our father, our redeemer; thy name is from everlasting." It would seem that such a divine pattern of foster fatherhood would give the best background for that "just man" who was the protector of the infancy of our Lord.

The proposed commemoration of the Martyrdom of St. Paul, with St. Peter, on June 29, demands some readjustment of the lections, as well as a new Collect. For both the present lessons are entirely devoted to St. Peter. We would keep the present Gospel, the great confession by Peter of our Lord's Messiahship and Sonship. For an Epistle, we propose Galatians 2:1-2, 7-10, which relates the common apostleship of Peter and Paul. The Roman Epistle for St. Paul's commemoration (on June 30), Galatians 1:11-20, is not appropriate to a festival commemorating the death of St. Paul, being in fact the Apostle's own comment on his conversion and his own inner preparation for his ministry.

Another Scriptural commemoration is the Conversion of Cornelius on February 4. This observance is only too bountifully provided with Scriptural authentication, since the story occupies all 48 verses of Acts 10, much of it told quite repetitiously. Verses 34 to the end, the climax of the narrative, are doubly bespoken for the Mondays after Easter and Whitsunday. Fortunately, the next chapter retells the whole in the words of St. Peter, and Acts 11:1-18 would cover the matter. As it happens that St. Peter does not mention the name of Cornelius in the course of his recital, a liturgical text might legitimately supply this by substituting "Cornelius'" for the words "the man's" in verse 12.

There is a little difficulty about a Gospel suitable for this significant commemoration of the firstfruits of the Gentiles. Rome gives us no hints, not having preserved this observance. Perhaps the best selection would be John 4:4-14, the first part of the incident of the Woman of Samaria, which is not otherwise used.

For Titus on February 6, Rome has not been able to do better than the unacceptable "Ecce sacerdos magnus" Epistle from the Common *Statuit* of Confessor-Bishops, and Luke 10:1-9, a slight lengthening of our Gospel for St. Luke's Day. We propose Titus 1:1-5 "To Titus, mine own son after the common faith; . . . For this cause left I thee in Crete, that thou shouldest set in order the things that are wanting, and ordain elders in every city, as I had appointed thee." With this we would bracket John 10:1-5 "He that entereth in by the door is the shepherd of the sheep . . . and he calleth his own sheep by name, . . . and the sheep follow him." We believe this combination will be a very useful witness to the Apostolic Succession, and the nature of the pastoral office.

For Timothy on January 24, Rome has 1 Timothy 6:11b-16, "Fight the good fight of faith, lay hold on eternal life, whereunto thou art also called, and hast professed a good profession before many witnesses," etc., an undoubtedly stirring and beautiful passage, which might well be adopted as it stands. We have however a certain preference for 2 Timothy 1:1-7, which mentions by name "Timothy, my dearly beloved son," (as the Roman selection does not,) which speaks most tenderly of the faith of his mother and grandmother before him, and which makes another point of value for the Apostolic Succession, "Wherefore I put thee in remembrance that thou stir up the gift of God, which is in thee by the putting on of my hands." (Of course, if anyone would prefer an undoubtedly historical notice of Timothy, in lieu of the possibly deutero-canonical attestation of the Pastoral Epistles, there are intrinsically fine passages of unquestioned Pauline authorship available in the form of 1 Corinthians 4:9-17, and Philippians 2:14-24.) For the Gospel, the Missal uses that of the Common *Statuit* for a martyred Bishop: "If any man come to me, and hate not his father, and mother, . . . yea, and his own life also, he cannot be my disciple," etc., with the reflections on "counting the cost." But the point about St. Timothy is not the tradition that he was martyred, but the fact that he stands in Scripture as a type of the pastoral office; and for this we prefer John 10:7-10, "I am the door of the sheep: . . . by me if any man enter in, he shall be saved, and shall go in and out, and find pasture . . . I am come that they might have life, and that they might have it more abundantly." Certainly this should be chosen, if Timothy 1:1-7 is to be the Epistle.

The Roman assignments for St. Mary Magdalene on July 22 must be rejected, with a certain justifiable indignation. It was Gregory the Great who made the unwarrantable and obviously erroneous identification of the "woman in the city, which was a sinner," who anointed Jesus' feet at the house of the Pharisee in Luke 7:36-50, the Roman Gospel for this feast, with the "Mary called Magdalene, out of whom went seven devils," in the second verse of the following chapter, who is there mentioned in the entirely honorable company of "certain women, which had been healed of evil spirits and infirmities," together with "Joanna the wife of Chuza, Herod's steward, and Susanna, and many others, which ministered to him of their substance." That the Mary of Magdala who stood by the Cross with the Mother of our Lord, and who herself was the first witness of the Resurrection, had ever been a public harlot, is quite out of the question; and this senseless identification of Gregory's has been decisively rejected by recent Roman Catholic scholars. (*Cf.* Hastings *Dictionary of the Bible* III.283.) Yet the Roman Epistle underscores this blunder with the Song of Solomon 3:2-5 and 8:6-7, which is neither more nor less than a literal and vivid description of the life of a street-walker; something which it would be inconceivable to read in English for the consideration of a modern congregation, on any hypothesis. Cranmer found this too much for him in the First Prayer Book, which retained the feast, and took instead the passage on the "Worthy woman" from Proverbs 31 from the mass *Cognovi*, the Common for a woman neither a virgin nor a martyr.

We can certainly dignify her by reciting the crowning act of her life in that first meeting with the Risen Lord in John 20:1, 11-18, since this is our chief motive for honoring her memory by including her in the liturgical list. For an Epistle, we may make a real enrichment of the liturgical lectionary with a passage not otherwise used, which, without calling her any names, does answer the latent question in people's minds which they have inherited from Gregory's malignings by reminding them that we are all redeemed sinners, in 2 Corinthians 5:14-18a: "For the love of Christ constraineth us: . . . therefore if any man be in Christ, he is a new creature: old things have passed away; behold, all things are become new. And all things are of God, who hath reconciled us to himself by Jesus Christ."

Events

Beside the above individual commemorations, we wish to make provisions for the two events of the First Book of Common Prayer, and the Consecration of Samuel Seabury; and for one theological festival, the Exaltation of the Holy Cross.

The Exaltation of the Holy Cross on September 14 can take the Roman selections unaltered: Philippians 2:5-11, "He became obedient unto death, even the death of the Cross. Wherefore God also hath highly exalted him," etc.; and John 12:31-36a, "And I, if I be lifted up from the earth, will draw all men unto me."

For the First Prayer Book on June 9, we have selected Acts 2:38-42, "Be baptized every one of you in the name of Jesus Christ for the remission of sins, and ye shall receive the Holy Ghost. . . . And they continued steadfastly in the apostles' doctrine and fellowship, and in the breaking of bread, and in prayers "; and Matthew 6:5-15, our Lord's instructions about sincerity in prayer, and the imparting of the Lord's Prayer.

Finally, for the Bestowal of the American Episcopate through Bishop Seabury's Consecration, on November 14, we propose Acts 20:28-32, part of the alternative Epistle for the Consecration of Bishops: "Take heed to yourselves, and to all the flock, over which the Holy Ghost hath made you overseers, to feed the church of God, which he hath purchased with his own blood . . . And now, brethren, I commend you to God, and to the word of his grace, which is able to build you up, and to give you an inheritance among all them which are sanctified." For the Gospel, Matthew 9:35-38: "But when he saw the multitudes, he was moved with compassion on them, because they fainted, and were scattered abroad, as sheep having no shepherd. Then saith he unto his disciples, The harvest truly is plenteous, but the labourers are few; pray ye therefore the Lord of the harvest, that he will send forth labourers into his harvest."

Commons

As we have intimated, we propose to supplement the foregoing specific assignments of Proper Epistles and Gospels for the Minor Holy Days with selections for Commons. These would be available for use when such day is the Patron or Title of a parish church: to be celebrated in such church as a Patronal Festival. This use however at the most would be only marginal, for one day a year. Moreover, no churches are dedicated to the modern worthies of our communion whom we have thought worthy of commemoration in the Calendar. And in America, very few bear the names of even the ancient saints of the Church Universal; though it may well be that the inclusion of them in the Calendar may in the future inspire greater variety and imagination in the naming of parishes than has been the case in time past.

The Commission offers three sets of Epistles and Gospels for these Commons. One, Hebrews 12:1-2 and Matthew 25:31-40, is the lections now provided in the Prayer Book for A Saint's Day. A second group emphasizes the qualities of Christian character that are exemplary: Philippians 4:4-9, and the Lucan form of the Beatitudes, Luke 6:17-23a. The third pair provides an Epistle, 2 Esdras 2:42-48, that relates the triumphal glory and immortality of the saints, and a Gospel, John 17:18-23, that underscores the basis of that glory by union with Christ through obedience to His commissioning. None of these sets, however, should be viewed as severally distinct. The celebrant should be permitted to select any one of the three Epistles and three Gospels, respectively, according to the character and teaching of the particular saint being commemorated.

Part Three: Movable Octaves and Seasons

The Easter and Whitsun Octaves

Within the Easter Octave, the Monday and Tuesday are already provided for, with Gospels comprising St. Luke's accounts of the Appearance at Emmaus, and the Appearance to the Disciples paralleling St. John's account which is used on Low Sunday. The Committee on the Prayer Book Epistles and Gospels found it inadvisable to disturb these ancient and very important assignments for two days which, at least in theory, have always enjoyed the same exalted rank as the Feast of Easter itself. But the retention of this pattern renders it quite impossible even to attempt an arrangement of the ample Gospel narratives available into anything like a day-to-day order of events as they occurred — even if there were any general agreement as to what that order actually was; which there certainly is not. The Evangelists were deeply concerned about recording the facts of those Appearances which made such an indelible impression upon the apostolic band; but nowhere in the Gospels is there a greater unconcern about fitting together any series of events into a time-pattern. It is doubtful if they knew; and they certainly did not care. Therefore, neither did the Roman Missal; and no more need we.

The Missal assigns St. Matthew's and St. Mark's narratives of the Empty Tomb to the Easter Vigil and Easter Day; St. Luke's Emmaus and the Upper Room as above to Monday; St. John's Appearance in Galilee to Wednesday; then on Thursday goes back to St. John's story of the first Appearance to Mary Magdalene; on Friday goes forward to St. Matthew's last Appearance on the Mount of the Ascension; and on Saturday reverts to St. John's Empty Tomb, in preparation for that Evangelist's narrative of the Appearance to the Disciples on the evening of the first Easter, and the second Appearance to the Disciples together with Thomas "after eight days" which is the inevitable assignment for the Easter Octave in all lectionaries Eastern and Western — which, although curtailed at the Reformation, is now proposed to be restored to its ancient form.

The Committee on the Liturgical Lectionary is advocating the appropriation of the primary narratives of St. Mark and St. Matthew to Easter Day, displacing the Johannine version which has appeared there only since the Reformation. This leaves St. John's Empty Tomb free for use within the Octave, as the Roman Missal has it. There is obviously, however, no point in reversing the order of the Johannine lections, with the Empty Tomb on Saturday, and the immediately following Appearance to Mary Magdalene on the previous Thursday. The fact is that all Thursdays in the Missal were eighth century afterthoughts, to fill up days previously deliberately left vacant, as "Jupiter's Day." The logical expedient is to assign John 20:1-10, the Empty Tomb, to Friday; John 20:11-18, the lovely 'Easter Idyl' of the first Appearance to Mary of Magdala, on Saturday: bringing us right up to John 20:19-29 on Low Sunday. We may however accept the Roman assignment of John 21:1-14, the "third" Appearance to the Disciples on the Lake of Galilee, on Wednesday, following the two Lucan narratives. The Committee on the Liturgical Lectionary is suggesting Matthew 28:18-20, the Mount of the Ascension and the Great Commission, for Ascension Day. But in view of the fact that after the later narratives which preoccupy the first half of Easter Week we must in any case make a new beginning with the Empty Tomb, leading up to Low Sunday, we may as well make that beginning on Thursday by assigning to that day the beginning of the Lucan narrative, in Luke 24:1-12. This passage makes its own entirely individual contributions to the whole picture (*e.g.* "Why seek ye the living among the dead?") and therefore certainly should be included; and this certainly seems the place for it in the existing pattern.

This arrangement brings into use all the important Gospel accounts, in what is virtually two consistent sequences of four days each, Easter Day through Wednesday, and Thursday through Low Sunday. Repetition there must be in any event, if we are to incorporate the contributions of all four Evangelists; and it would appear that this apportioning would make the best of that necessity, and the least of the difficulties of harmonizing the accounts.

As to Epistles for Easter Week, the Roman assignments are even less satisfactory than their arrangement of the Gospel narratives. On Wednesday, they have the instancing by Peter of the healing of the lame man at the Beautiful Gate as an example of the power of the Resurrection, in Acts 3:13-15, 17-19a, though with a neat excision of the reference to the lame man, and a not very good conclusion. Verses 13-15,17-19,26, would make a better lection. Friday has 1 Peter 3:18-22a, presenting Christian Baptism as the application and appropriation of the Easter Gospel, through the somewhat roundabout mentions of Christ's preaching "unto the spirits in prison," and of Noah's Ark — on the Easter analogy of Baptism in our Epistle for Trinity VI. But the Epistles for Thursday, Acts 8:26-40, the Conversion of the Ethiopian Eunuch, and for Saturday, 1 Peter 2:1-10, Christ the Chief Cornerstone, are selections bearing upon the Easter Baptisms which make no allusion whatever to the Resurrection.

As a matter of fact, apostolic preaching and writing overflows with eloquent attestations of the theme of the Resurrection, which, as the great fact of their own experience, they hailed as the prime warrant of the Christian faith. It is therefore quite possible, without trenching on the important passages of this sort which appear as Epistles on Trinity VI and XI,[14] to provide Epistles for the four days in Easter Week which will afford selections of much influence on Christian thought, but lacking hitherto in the liturgical lections. Our choice is Acts 3:3-15, 17-19, 26; Colossians 1:18-23a (ending ". . . to every creature which is under heaven"); Colossians 2:10-15; and 1 Peter 1:3-4, 15-21; all of them passages

---

14. Ed. Note: The Epistles alluded to are Romans 6:3-11 and 1 Corinthians 15:1-11 respectively.

which underscore the theme of the Easter Baptisms, as the Roman selections do, but all of them bearing strong witness to the power of the Resurrection.

The Octave of Pentecost again comprises only six days, since its Octave Day has been converted to the Feast of the Holy Trinity. Like Easter, it already has "Red Letter" provisions for Monday and Tuesday. The Whitsuntide Ember Days take care of Wednesday, Friday, and Saturday. This leaves only Thursday to be filled up. The Roman assignment of the apostolic commission to preach and heal, in Acts 8:5-8 and Luke 9:1-6, has no mention of the Holy Spirit; it is difficult to imagine why this carefully matched selection of an Epistle and Gospel was ever made. Our only difficulty has been to settle upon a single pair as representing the best available choice out of the numerous fine passages on the work of the Spirit not now in liturgical use.

The Ember Days

The Ember Days constitute a very interesting feature of the Christian Year, possessing one characteristic which is entirely unique. They are the only component of our annual observances in the Church whose ultimate origin lay only in the 'Natural' or Solar Year, which gave form to most primitive pagan religions. The fact that Christmas approximates the date of the Winter Solstice, and Easter the Vernal Equinox, does not relegate Christianity to the status of a Solar Myth, as some opponents have suggested: it happens that both festivals were assigned for quite independent reasons; so that the circumstance that they fit so beautifully into the rhythms of the Natural Year is reduced to the level of a happy coincidence. But "The Ember Days of the Four Seasons" began by being exactly what that name implies. They were in Latin the *Quattuor Tempora* — a term fused into the Teutonic *Quatember* and curtailed to the English *Ember*. They were derived from pagan agricultural observances which originally were three in number, devoted to the Winter Sowing in December, the Summer Reaping in June, and the Autumn Vintage in September. It was Leo the Great who added the Lenten days, to bring the number up to the four annual fasts of the Jews. The tie of these last with the season of Lent is therefore genuine; but the alliance of the December days with Advent is coincidental, and still more so is the attaching of the June week to Whitsunday it is actually unfortunate that the Octave of Pentecost has been invaded by fasting days, and that the Sunday which once belonged to them appears at Trinity IV!

The agricultural origin of these days is still discernible in some of the lections and proper antiphons prescribed for them in the Roman Missal. It also accounts for the fact that not one single lection therein has the slightest bearing upon the Holy Ministry. It merely happens to be the case that from early times the Roman Church adopted them as stated times for Ordinations, because they were already solemn fasting seasons at convenient quarterly intervals in the year — perhaps to supplement the two days at climaxes of the Great Fast, the Saturdays before Passion Sunday and Easter Day, which still remain as canonical times of Ordination, though now not often used as such.

The Roman assignments for the Ember Days in Advent are all pre-Christmas, with Gospels of the Annunciation, the Visitation, and the Voice crying in the wilderness (the same as the following day, Advent IV), and typological Epistles from the Old Testament to correspond.

The days in Lent again are strictly appropriate to that season — except when they are completely irrelevant to anything. The Wednesday cites Moses' Forty Days on Sinai, and Elijah's on his journey to the same place; and the Gospel is the Matthaean parallel to St. Luke's parable of the Empty House on Lent III, with the Sign of Jonah and the 'mother and brethren' passage added on for good measure. The Friday has Ezekiel's "The soul that sinneth, it shall die," in conjunction with the healing of the impotent man at the pool of Bethesda — perhaps to reflect the saying "Sin no more, lest a worse thing come unto thee." The Saturday, with its seven lections for a solemn Vigil service, is an unintelligible miscellany, with two lections on keeping the commandments; two prayers from the Apocrypha, that God will receive the sacrifice, and that he will show his power against the suppliant's enemies; the Song of the Three Children; the moralistic peroration of 1 Thessalonians; and in conclusion, with a certain sublime *non sequitur*, the Gospel of the Transfiguration of our Lord!

Whit-Wednesday presents the exordium of St. Peter's sermon on the Day of Pentecost, containing a quotation from the prophet Joel of the promise to pour out the Spirit upon all flesh as its chief content; then the healing of the sick by Peter's shadow; and finally, for some reason lost to history, St. John's discourse on the "Bread of Life." The Friday with equal artlessness conjoins Joel's mention of "the former and the latter rain" with St. Luke's account of the healing of the paralytic, paralleling St. Matthew's version which is the Gospel for Trinity XIX. The Saturday continues the reading of Joel with the passage already quoted in the Wednesday lection from Acts; goes on with three selections from Leviticus and Deuteronomy, all bearing on the Offering of the First-Fruits, and one of them mentioning the "seventh sabbath," and the "fifty days" after the celebration of the barley-harvest at Passover which determined the Jewish observance of the wheat-harvest at their "Pentecost;" then the inevitable "Three Children;" then a return to the theme initiated by the lection from Joel, with a short passage from Romans concluding with the mention of "the love of God shed abroad in our hearts by the Holy Ghost which is given unto us"; and finally the healing of Peter's wife's mother! It is probable that the papal Station at St. Peter's on this Saturday influenced the choice of this last, to bring in the Apostle's name. If so, one might surmise that the assignment is older than the effective establishment of the discipline of clerical celibacy, since it displays no self-consciousness about the fact that the Prince of the Apostles was a married man.

The primitive agricultural notes of these Whitsuntide selections are particularly marked. It may be reasonably surmised that the lections were all chosen for the Summer Harvest in June, and that it was the coincidence of the three passages mentioning the Spirit, and the First-fruits passage indicating the Jewish Pentecost, which finally, after a number of hesitations, determined the certainly very awkward intrusion of all this matter into Whit-Week. Though Leo the Great observed the Ember Days of this season immediately after Pentecost, apparently as a solemn resumption of the weekly Wednesday and Friday fasts which were then completely pretermitted between Easter and Whitsunday, as soon as the feast of Pentecost acquired an Octave the June dates resumed their sway in most places. It was not until 1078 that Gregory VII definitely attached them to Whit-Week in Rome, and not until the thirteenth century that this usage became universal.

Agricultural notes are also found in the autumnal days. The Wednesday begins with a lection from Amos specifically mentioning the vintage. Then Ezra's reading aloud of the Book of the Law is brought in for some reason which no longer appears. The Gospel relates the incident of the exorcism of the Dumb Spirit, with the final note "This kind can come forth by nothing, but by prayer and fasting." Beside the obvious application to a fast-day, it may be noted that some scholars have suggested that the mention of exorcism, which also occurs in the Gospel on the Whitsuntide Saturday, marks a definite Christianization of the previously existing pagan agricultural festivals, in a sort of formal abjuration of the demonic powers to which they had formerly been dedicated.

The September Friday combines Hosea 14, which is a promise of plenty to those who forsake their sins, with the Gospel on the anointing of Jesus' feet by the woman who was a sinner, with the comment "Her sins, which are many, are forgiven; for she loved much." The seven lections of the Saturday are all — for once, and with the exception of the conventional penultimate "Three Children" — intelligently put together around the closely affiliated themes of the Sabbath, the Fast of the Seventh Month, and the Day of Atonement, intimating a clear awareness of the analogies of the Jewish observances at this same period of the year.

All this is extremely interesting, and even diverting, for its own sake, bringing the enjoyment which anyone finds in exploring an attic containing the quaint, if dusty, inheritances of bygone generations. But when we turn our practical minds to asking what use we can make of these venerable antiquities, we are forced to the reluctant conclusion that there is none at all. The sole importance which the Ember Days carries for us is that they are traditionally the stated times of Ordination, and occasions which it is desirable to have observed throughout the Church, in a recurring reminder of the very basic and utterly indispensable task of ever sending new laborers into the ever growing harvest. Selections of Scripture whose significance is wholly along lines of liturgical archeology, however engaging, and which do not contribute one word to furthering this major concern of the Church, are utterly lacking in utility for our purposes. The only thing to do with them is to put them back respectfully in the archives.

The American Prayer Book of 1928 provides a single Epistle and Gospel as a sort of Common for all Ember Days. The theme of both these lections is the Preaching of the Word: which is all very well, as far as it goes, but by no manner of means exhausts the significance of the ministry of Christ's Church. Moreover, the repetition of this single assignment twelve times a year entails a cumulative monotony, calculated to deaden enthusiasm for this subject rather than to arouse it. Frankly, there is no excuse for allowing this situation to persist. The Holy Scriptures provide a great wealth of telling passages on what is after all one of their main interests and objectives, God's sending his ministers to be the shepherds of the people. There was not the slightest difficulty in finding enough substantial passages to provide lessons morning and evening for every one of the Ember Days; neither is there any in finding sufficient of the shorter and more pregnant selections suitable for Epistles and Gospels for each several day. Moreover, it does not demand much labor and ingenuity to arrange these Epistles and Gospels so that they are not only congruous with each other, but suitable to the tone and meaning of the particular ecclesiastical seasons to which they are now attached.

This does not seem to have been realized in the latest English and Scottish revisions, which took only a faltering step or two in that direction. Both incorporated some of the Roman provisions for the Lenten and Whitsuntide days, but merely as a part of the general pattern of Lent and Whit-Week, and with no apparent realization that these days were intended to be Ember Days — as we have seen, the Roman assignments are completely useless in that category for our objectives. In addition the English book suggests three Epistles and three Gospels for use in the other two seasons; and the Scottish book stipulates that in Advent the Ember Days shall use the Gospel of the previous Sunday (Advent III), and in September provides one Epistle and a choice of two Gospels. It seems to us that these half-measures miss a great tactical opportunity.

We propose to begin the Advent Ember Days by apportioning to the Wednesday John 4:31-38, where our Lord makes the very interesting point that at the moment he spoke "there are yet four months, and then cometh harvest," yet spiritually, "behold, I say unto you, Lift up your eyes, and look on the fields; for they are white already to harvest." This incident must have occurred at just about the time of the Palestinian Winter Sowing, four months before the barley-harvest in April. Thus chronologically it is ear-marked for this position in the year; and moreover, its use permits us to connect the agricultural origins of the Ember Seasons with the spiritual purpose into which they have evolved, in a manner which the Roman provisions never attain; it really seems remarkable that they do not, if only by sheer coincidence, since the relating of the ideas of physical and spiritual harvests is by no means uncommon in Scripture. Other constituents of this Gospel make it still more valuable for our purpose, e.g., "My meat is to do the will of him that sent me, and to finish his work," and "Other men laboured, and ye are entered into their labours," which has a most significant application to what might be called the cumulative continuity of parish life, handed on by one priest to his successor. And the verse "One soweth, and another reapeth" forms a tie with the suggested Epistle, 1 Corinthians 3:5-11, "I have planted, Apollos watered; but God gave the increase," with its weighty conclusion on the laying of sure foundations upon the One Foundation of Jesus Christ.

The Friday brings in certain apocalyptic notes which are in place in the season of Advent: 1 Peter 4:7-11, "The end of all things is at hand: be sober, and watch unto prayer;" and Luke 12:35-44, "Blessed are those servants, whom the Lord when he cometh shall find watching." This similar framework then encloses the corresponding expression of the same essential thought, in "As every man hath received the gift, even so minister the same one to another, as good stewards of the manifold grace of God" in the Epistle, and "Who then is that faithful and wise steward, whom his lord shall make ruler over his household, to give them their portion of meat in due season?" in the Gospel.

The Ember Saturday stresses what might be called the Ministry of Example, in 1 Timothy 1:12-17, in which the Apostle thanks our Lord for 'putting him into the ministry,' though he had been the 'chief of sinners,' saying, "Howbeit for this cause I obtained mercy, that in me first Jesus Christ might show forth all long-suffering, for a pattern to them which should here after believe on him to life everlasting." The Gospel, Matthew 16:24-27 expresses our Lord's challenge to follow his example, "If any man will come after me, let him deny himself, and take up his cross, and follow me;" with the promised reward in such eschatological terms as mark this lection for the season of Advent: "For the Son of man shall come in the glory of his Father with his angels; and then he shall reward every man according to his works."

In like manner the assignments to the Lenten days are such as to harmonize with a penitential season. Their full rationale will be discussed later, in the section on the Lenten week-days. The Epistles for Wednesday and Friday, and the Gospel for Saturday preserve the most ancient sequence of the week: the fasts of Moses and Elijah, and the Transfiguration, where Moses and Elijah stand beside Jesus on the mount. These scenes are certainly appropriate as models for the ministry in its demand of prayer, of hidden self-denial, and of complete obedience to God's will that His revelation may be made known to His people at whatever cost.

For the Gospels for Wednesday and Friday, we have assigned two Matthaean passages, 20:17-28 and 21:33-44, respectively. (In the old Roman sequence these lections are read in the second week of Lent.) The first one presents the request of the mother of James and John, and brings out the demands of suffering that the Lord expects of His ministers, if they are to obtain a place of honor in His kingdom. The second is the parable of the Wicked Husbandmen. It also stresses the theme of rejection and suffering. Thus both Gospels are linked, with the Transfiguration on Saturday, as they look forward to the Lord's Passion.

The Epistle for Saturday, 2 Corinthians 3:4-18, combines in a most remarkable way both the "ministry" and the "transfiguration" themes. It is the obvious lesson to go with the Transfiguration, even though it repeats part of the Ember Sunday Epistle of Trinity XII.

Naturally the Whitsuntide assignments comprise those passages bearing on the Ministry which explicitly mention the work of the Holy Spirit. We may begin on Wednesday with the Prayer Book Common Gospel, our Lord's words at the synagogue at Nazareth, quoting Isaiah's "The Spirit of the Lord is upon me, because he hath anointed me to preach the gospel to the poor," etc., and concluding, "And he began to say unto them, This day is this scripture fulfilled in your ears." But because the content of this Gospel is rather slight, and its meaning largely an implication, we propose to introduce it by a very powerful Epistle, 2 Corinthians 3:17-4:6 "Where the Spirit of the Lord is, there is liberty. But we all, . . . beholding . . . the glory of the Lord, are changed into the same image from glory to glory even as by the Spirit of the Lord. Therefore, seeing we have this ministry, . . . we faint not; . . . for God, who commanded the light to shine out of darkness, hath shined in our hearts, to give the light of the knowledge of the glory of God in the face of Jesus Christ."

On Friday, Titus 3:4-8 presents the work of the Spirit in Baptism and Confirmation: "According to his mercy he saved us, by the washing of regeneration, and renewing of the Holy Ghost;" with Matthew 28:16-20, the Great Commission to "go . . . and teach all nations, baptizing them in the name of the Father, and of the Son, and of the Holy Ghost." (This has been assigned as the Gospel for St. Boniface's Day on June 5; but the "closed Octave" of Whitsunday prevents an actual juxtaposition. But if the repetition is objected to, we would rather apportion say Luke 10:1-9 — sending laborers into the great harvest; the Gospel for St. Luke's Day, lengthened — to St. Boniface, rather than to adopt here other passages from the Gospels mentioning the Spirit, such as Luke 12:8-12 — "the Holy Ghost shall teach you what ye ought to say," — or John 16:12-15, borrowed from Easter III, "The Spirit of Truth": neither of which would go well with this Epistle, or indeed any other available for this place.)

We propose to conclude the Whitsuntide days on Saturday with Ephesians 2:13-22, a great passage, reciting the reconciliation through Christ, who "came and preached peace to you which were afar off, and to them that were nigh: for through him we both have access by one Spirit unto the Father . . . and are built upon the foundation of the apostles and prophets, Jesus Christ himself being the chief corner stone; . . . in whom ye also are builded together for an habitation of God through the Spirit." With this we would give John 20:19-23, the Apostolic Commission, "Receive ye the Holy Ghost." This is a repetition from Low Sunday; and, like the Gospel suggested for Whit-Friday, occurs in the service of the

Consecration of Bishops. But both are needed to round out the picture of the work of the Holy Spirit in the ministry.

Finally, the September Ember Days have, of course, no seasonal color whatever. Any lections could be assigned here. But there surely will be no harm in putting here, as in the December place, a passage which happily reflects the agricultural origins of the Ember Seasons. The September days having been derived from the Autumnal Vintage, nothing could be more in place than John 15:1-8, the Vine and the Branches, with its concluding "Herein is my Father glorified, that ye bear much fruit: so shall ye be my disciples." With this a harmonious Epistle would be Ephesians 4:11-18, mentioning the diversity of offices ("some apostles; and some, prophets;" etc.) "for the work of the ministry," unified by the fact that they "grow up into him in all things, which is the head, even Christ."

The Common Epistle now in the Prayer Book, Acts 13:44-49, can go here, with its fine missionary implications of "I have set thee to be a light of the Gentiles, that thou shouldest be for salvation unto the ends of the earth;" with perhaps Matthew 10:24-32, "What ye hear in the ear, that preach ye upon the housetops. . . Whosoever will confess me before men, him will I also confess before my Father which is in heaven."

We suggest concluding this season with two fine and evenly matched passages on the requirements and results of an effective pastoral ministry: Acts 20:28-32, "Take heed therefore unto yourselves, and to all the flock over which the Holy Ghost hath made you overseers. . . And now, brethren, I commend you to God, and to the word of his grace, which is able to build you up, and to give you an inheritance among all them that are sanctified "; and John 10:1-10, "The shepherd of the sheep . . . calleth his own sheep by name, . . . and the sheep follow him, for they know his voice . . . I am come that they might have life, and that they might have it more abundantly."

Rogation Days

The Rogation Days constitute the one feature of the Christian Year that not only was but is purely agricultural in significance. It is the other pole of the year from our characteristic American festival of Thanksgiving Day; it is a vernal supplication for the future harvests of the year.

The Rogation Days originated in the solemn Litany Days of Mamertus of Vienne in Gaul in the fifth century. Rome, which already had a corresponding occasion on April 25, adopted as a backfire to the pagan Robigalia, eventually but rather reluctantly made place for these Gallican Rogations, but called them the "Lesser Litanies," reserving the "Greater Litanies" for the April date; and assigned only a single mass, that already appropriated for the native Roman observance, to the three days. The later addition of a Vigil of the Ascension cut off the Wednesday entirely from being celebrated as a true Rogation.

As a sort of three-day pseudo-Lent before the Ascension, the Rogation Days are a liturgical blunder; the Three Hundred Eighteen Fathers at Nicaea would have excommunicated the Gauls for importing fasting-days into the great season of rejoicing between Easter and Pentecost. Our Prayer Book of 1928 tried to retrieve that by giving the Rogation Days a separate heading, "Days of Solemn Supplication," which seems to have been intended to be a coordinate and contrasting classification to the "Other Days of Fasting;" though since both still remain under the general title, "A Table of Fasts," it may be doubted if the point has been made sufficiently clear. They are not in fact penitential days at all, as Rome would seem to intimate by using the Gloria in Excelsis at their mass. Viewed however simply as "Days of Solemn Supplication," they are well enough in place here, as they would be in any other part of the Christian Year; and especially so, in that they carry out the implications of the Gospel for Easter V, which is very properly known as "Rogation Sunday," from its keynote of "Whatsoever ye shall ask the Father in my name, he will give it you."

The one Roman provision is James 5:16-20, "The effectual fervent prayer of a righteous man availeth much," which is certainly excellent, though the example which is given, Elijah's prowess as a weather-maker, seems calculated to arouse an inconvenient amount of skepticism now in the twentieth Christian century; and Luke 11:5-13, "Ask, . . . seek, . . . knock."

The American Prayer Book of 1928 retained the Roman Gospel in its single Common for the three days, but substituted Ezekiel 34:25-31 for that dubious Epistle. This last contains nothing about weather-prayers, but is an excellent selection about God's providence in caring for his people with peace and plenty.

The English and Scottish follow Rome for Rogation Tuesday, and on the Wednesday for the Ascension Vigil; and for Monday improvise James 5:7-11 for the sake of its mention of "the former and the latter rain" in v. 7 only, and the apparently irrelevant Gospel of the Mote and the Beam, borrowed from Trinity IV.

We propose to retain the assignments of the 1928 Prayer Book for Rogation Monday, that is, the new Epistle from Ezekiel, and the Roman Gospel. That Gospel is unexceptionable in this place.

No Vigils are recognized in the American Prayer Book, and we do not intend to begin here. So for Rogation Tuesday and Wednesday we suggest Joel 2:21-27, another admirable passage on the promises of plenty in God's good providence, and Mark 11:22-26, the Prayer of Faith; and Micah 6:6-8, the true Sacrifice, with Matthew 6:5-8, true prayer.

Weekdays of Lent

One of the most persistent problems brought again and again to the attention of the Commission has been the inadequacy of our present provisions in the Prayer Book for the Lenten season. These problems are basically twofold. On the one hand, there is much dissatisfaction with some of the Sunday lections, despite their time-honored place in our liturgy, deriving as they do from the Sarum appointments. And these, in turn, with the exception of the Epistle and Gospel for the Second Sunday, come to us ultimately from the Roman appointments of the seventh century. The common grievance against some of these propers relates either to their obscurity (e.g., the Gospel for the Second Sunday and the Epistle for the Fourth Sunday), or to their seeming lack of relevance to modern religious concerns (e.g., the Gospels for the Third and the Fifth Sundays). Such dissatisfactions become intensified when these lections are repeated several times, if not daily, during the week.

This latter circumstance brings to the fore the other facet of the problem of the Lenten propers. In most parishes, it is customary to schedule one, two, or more celebrations of the Holy Communion on weekdays of Lent; and in a considerable number of churches there is a daily celebration throughout the season. Accordingly, there is a strong groundswell of demand for a much larger amount of suitable material for these extra celebrations than the Sunday propers provide. In a season when so many church people practice a more intensive and extensive devotion, by a greater frequency of participation in the Eucharistic sacrament, it would seem a pity not to feed them with a more plenteous supply of the Scriptural Word.

The Commission made a preliminary study of the question, on the basis of providing a daily schedule of propers for Lent, somewhat along the lines suggested by the English Proposed Book of 1928, the Scottish and South African Prayer Books, and, more recently, by the Indian Prayer Book. Partial results of this work were included in *Prayer Book Studies*, No. II, on the Eucharistic lectionary, where certain alterations in the Sunday propers of Lent were proposed, in view of fitting them more nearly to the projected scheme of daily propers. However, no thorough presentation of the rationale of the plan was presented in the Study; and as a consequence, perhaps, there has been little interest shown in it, if we may judge from the correspondence received by the Commission to date.

Basically, this earlier project of the Commission was built around a course sequence of Gospel lections from the Sermon on the Mount (Matthew 5-7), distributed among the weekdays through the first four weeks of Lent. Other pericopes from Matthew 20-23 were appointed for the fifth week, which had themes more directly relevant to the Passion. Epistle lections from both the Old and the New Testament were then selected to harmonize in theme with the several Gospel lessons from the Sermon on the Mount. The scheme was admittedly novel. It had little relation to the ancient Roman-Sarum sequence of Lenten propers, except in so far as it agreed with it in the principle of thematic unity between Epistle and Gospel. At the same time, it was not in any agreement with the scheme of other Anglican Prayer Books. For in these Books the daily Lenten propers are based upon a course reading of Hebrews and

Colossians for the Epistle lections, with scattered Gospel pericopes to match the themes of the Epistles.

Further reflection and study of the problem have convinced us that the type of lesson arrangement, both in our first plan as also in the other Anglican Prayer Books, is unsound. For a daily course sequence, by which a book of the Bible is read through in order, is not practically feasible. It is an excellent plan for the lectionary of the Daily Offices of Morning and Evening Prayer, since these offices are in their essential purpose designed for daily use. But it is not likely that, except for a relatively small number of people or for those who belong to collegiate and monastic groups, attendance at the Eucharist will be a daily occurrence, even during the season of Lent. There is no great value in a daily course sequence of lessons when there is little expectation that the same congregation will attend daily upon them. Furthermore, there is no indication as yet that the majority of our parish and mission churches and chapels will be able to provide a daily celebration of the Holy Communion during Lent, even assuming the fact that they desire or hope to make such provision for their people.

A more realistic approach to the actual, present needs of our Church as a whole calls for some other plan. For we must always bear in mind that the Prayer Book is primarily designed to be a liturgy suitable to the needs of the entire membership of the Church. It is not a specialized Breviary and Missal for a small and élite "advance guard" of devotés, however important and needful such smaller groups are to the spiritual health of the whole Church. The standards and disciplines of corporate worship as set forth in the Prayer Book should be, ideally speaking, those that can make a reasonable claim upon the time, energy, and devotion of all the Church's members. The Prayer Book ought not to lay out a program of liturgical worship which, in the circumstances of daily life, is beyond the capacity of the vast majority of the laity, not to speak of busy parish clergy without benefit of assistants, to fulfill. For this reason, therefore, the Commission, after careful thought and consideration, has come to the conclusion that a plan of daily celebrations of the Eucharist over any extensive period, such as Lent, is not at the present time a realistic way of meeting the conditions that obtain in the great majority of our congregations. By this statement, it does not mean to imply in any way that the Commission considers daily celebrations either undesirable or unimportant. But it believes that there is adequate recourse to canonical and rubrical law for supplementing what the Prayer Book officially prescribes, in places and under circumstances where such additional provisions are deemed necessary and essential.

The Commission has therefore made a new study of the whole problem of Lenten observance, so far as celebrations of the Holy Communion with specific propers for the day is concerned. And it has come to a unanimous conclusion that the most feasible plan would be to offer two sets of weekday propers for each week in Lent in addition to the Sunday propers. These two sets would be normally appointed for Wednesdays and Fridays — the ancient "station" days, observed in the Church since the second century as occasions for optional participation in the Church's liturgy. But a specific rubrical direction should accompany these propers that allows them to be used, at the discretion of the priest, on any other day of the week, when a celebration of Holy Communion is scheduled; or, if the priest so desires, allows the Sunday propers to be used instead of the weekday sets.

For example, if a parish has only one mid-week celebration during Lent, whatever the day of the week on which it may fall, the celebrant would have a choice of three propers for use — the Sunday propers or either of the weekday ones. If the parish had two mid-week celebrations, the priest might, if he so desired, repeat the Sunday propers at one celebration and select either of the two weekday sets for the other. In the case of a parish with a daily celebration, the priest could alternate day after day between the Sunday and the weekday propers, or he could use one of the weekday propers for Monday through Wednesday, and the other for Thursday through Saturday; or he might simply use one set every day in the week.

Every week in Lent would thus be provided with three available propers. The obvious exceptions to this would be: 1) the week after the First Sunday, which would have four propers, because of the three Ember Days; and 2) Holy Week, which would continue to have, as at present, propers for each day. In the former case, the Ember propers would necessarily be used on the days specifically appointed; but for other days of this week — namely, Monday, Tuesday, and Thursday — the celebrant would have choice of using any set of propers for the week.

We believe that this proposal, in view of the wide variations of usage from parish to parish, provides not only a realistic solution to the pressing needs before the Church for additional propers for Lenten weekdays. We believe also that it is a plan that is sufficiently flexible to meet almost any situation. Furthermore, it has, for those who find such arguments significant, a rootage in ancient practices of the universal Church; namely, the recognition of the values of the old "station" days of Wednesday and Friday.

Having satisfied ourselves of the reasonableness of this plan, the Commission next faced the task of finding sure principles for the selection of Scriptural passages for these extra days. We gave up the principle of a course reading type of schedule, even though it would have been done on a more modest scale; and we did so for the same reason as noted above: there is no likelihood that the same congregation would be present at each successive celebration on weekdays during Lent. Hence the values of a course reading of any single Biblical book or part of a book would be largely missed.

The only other course that seemed to be open to us was to examine the ancient schedules for Lent in the Roman-Sarum tradition, and see if there were any fundamental rules that governed its development. We were not disappointed. For despite the apparently chaotic way in which the Epistles and Gospels seem to be selected in the ancient Missals, for the weekdays of Lent, there were recoverable certain underlying principles that could be identified behind the varied strata of addition and revision in the course of their development from the fifth to the seventh centuries. Thanks to the labors of liturgical scholars during the past generation, and the discovery and publication of a larger number of ancient liturgical manuscripts, it is now possible to give a fairly coherent account of how the Lenten lectionary of the Western Church, and more particularly that of the Church of Rome, came into being in the classic age of formulation of the great historic rites of Latin Christendom. It is from these rites, especially that of Rome, that our own Prayer Book tradition descends by way of the use of Sarum. It is impossible in a Study of this kind to attempt a detailed demonstration of this history. Nor is it necessary to do so. We shall content ourselves with marking out in broad strokes the major stages of development.

It has always been recognized that the Lenten season came into being as a preparation for Easter, and more particularly as a time for the instruction and discipline of converts to the faith who awaited the initiatory experience of Baptism, Confirmation, and first Communion at the Paschal mysteries. The specific themes of the liturgy during Lent were therefore originally aimed at the conformation of these initiants to a spiritual and sacramental experience of death to sin and resurrection to life in union with the Passion and victorious Resurrection of the Lord. One cannot understand the origin of Lent, much less its primary significance in the total life of the Church unless one always bears in mind that Lent leads up to Easter. The Lenten mysteries and disciplines are preparatory to the fullness of the Easter faith and experience.

As early as the time of Pope Leo the Great (440-461) we can outline the broad frame of the Lenten devotion and liturgy. The season began on what we call the First Sunday in Lent, and the same Epistle and Gospel were appointed as are read today. The account of our Lord's Temptation brought to the fore the three renunciations of the flesh, the world, and the devil, which the Lord having made immediately following His Baptism would require of the initiants before their Baptism on Easter Even. At the close of the season, in Holy Week, the Gospel Passions were read, thus bringing the catechumens to the decisive and final point of faith in Christ as the Redeemer and Saviour from sin.

We do not know whether the lections for the intervening weeks were fixed so early as Leo's time; but by the beginning of the sixth century, we can deduce, from a comparative study of the oldest surviving service books, a generally accepted group of Gospel lections for these Sundays in use among most of the Western Churches, including also the church in Rome. These lessons were selected also for the special instruction of catechumens. With slight variations both as to selection and to order of arrangement, these Gospels were all drawn from the Johannine pericopes of the great Messianic signs, whereby the Lord revealed Himself as the Saviour from sin, error, want, and death.

The group included such stories as the Samaritan woman, the Healing of the Man Born Blind, the Feeding of the Multitude, the Healing of the Paralytic, and the Raising of Lazarus. (It is interesting to note, incidentally, that to this day the Byzantine lectionary in use in the Orthodox Church draws from this group for Gospel lections during Eastertide. Their association is also confirmed by sixth-seventh century Christian ivories emanating from Egypt.)

By the turn of the sixth century, however, the Roman liturgy of Lent had already undergone a fair amount of elaboration. The season now began on Ash Wednesday, so as to allow an exact counting of forty days of fast (Sundays always being excluded from this discipline). Moreover, the "scrutiny" masses as they were called, those that were specially designed for catechetical instruction, were appointed not on the Sundays of Lent, but distributed over a number of masses assigned to Wednesdays, Fridays, and a few Saturdays. The Lenten Ember Days were also fully developed by the time of Pope Gelasius (492-496). It is now an established opinion among liturgical scholars that the oldest recoverable sequence of Lenten masses underlying the Roman rite are those for the Sundays, Wednesdays, Fridays, and a few Saturdays. In this early stage of development, it appears also that some of the lessons originally used at Rome on Sundays were transferred to the weekday scrutiny masses.

About the same time, the Roman rite added the Monday and Tuesday masses of Lent. Thus by the time of Pope Gregory the Great (590-604) a definitive settlement had been made at Rome for most of the Lenten observance. As the liturgy left this great Pope's reforming hand, there were masses provided for all Sundays, Mondays, Tuesdays, Wednesdays, and Fridays of Lent, and also for a few Saturdays. All of the ancient lessons of an earlier time were preserved, albeit not always on their original days. The pope visited on successive days for these masses each one of the major patriarchal basilicas and almost every one of the parish or "titular" churches. These "stations" of the pope, as they were called, are still preserved in the headings of these masses in the modern Roman Missal. This day-by-day perambulation of the pope in visiting and celebrating Mass in his churches was the occasion of suggesting new themes for the selection of proper lessons. Many of the Epistles and Gospels for the non-scrutiny masses were chosen, not so much for the special instruction of the catechumens, as for some illustration or theme in them that supposedly recalled a familiar association of the basilica where the pope said mass. Thus, for example, the famous allegory on Jerusalem, contained in our Epistle for the Fourth Sunday in Lent, was selected not solely because of its great theme of bondage versus freedom, but also because the papal mass of the day was held at the basilica of the "Holy Cross in Jerusalem."

It was not until the eighth century that the Roman church filled the remaining vacant days of Lent — i.e., the Thursdays and other Saturdays — with proper formularies, thus completing the full round of daily masses for the entire Lenten season. One of these Thursday masses had assigned the pericope of the Syrophoenician woman, which, by a strange accident of transmission, passed into the Sarum use as the Gospel for the Second Sunday of Lent. What is of particular interest about the scheme of Lenten propers, as they were finally determined, is that the Epistles are almost entirely drawn from the Old Testament, and are selected to undergird the themes of the several Gospels. With one or two exceptions, the Gospel lessons are all taken from Matthew and John. In fact, the lections from John utilize almost the entire contents of the Gospel except for those portions at the beginning and the end of the book that had already been employed in the Christmas-Epiphany and the Easter seasons respectively.

With this broad reconstruction of the development of the Lenten propers before us, the Commission felt that certain basic principles were at hand to guide our own task of re-forming a Lenten sequence of lessons for our more modest scheme of Wednesdays, Fridays, and Sundays. Without any concern to follow slavishly the exact appointments of the ancient schedules or to avoid, where it seemed appropriate, the introduction of some new lessons into the sequence, we felt nonetheless that there were fundamental values in the old tradition that ought not to be lost; particularly, the emphasis in these ancient lessons upon the great Old Testament types and New Testament signs of salvation as they are consummated in the Paschal mystery. In sum, the principles that we have sought to recover for the Lenten propers are as follows:

1. The Gospel lections should serve as the primary basis of the sequence, with Epistles chosen to match them.
2. These Gospel lessons should in the main be drawn from Matthew and John, especially the latter, with emphasis upon the chief Messianic signs of our Lord's redemption of us in death and resurrection.
3. Certain of these great Messianic signs of the Johannine Gospel should replace some of the present Sunday Gospels — namely, those of the Second, Third, and Fifth Sundays. But the present Sunday Gospels so replaced should not be lost altogether, but rather shifted to weekday appointments.
4. The New Testament selections for the Epistles now used in the Lenten season should also be retained; but all new lessons employed for Epistles should be drawn from the Old Testament. In this way, a great enrichment from the Old Testament can be provided for our Prayer Book lectionary for the Eucharist — a matter that has been strongly urged from many quarters in the Church.

In detail, we propose to the consideration of the Church the following application of these principles:

After Ash Wednesday

	Epistle	**Gospel**
Ash Wednesday	Joel 2:12-17	Matthew 6:16-21
Friday after Ash Wednesday	Isaiah 58:1-12	Matthew 5:43-6:8

No change is contemplated in the Ash Wednesday lections. For the Friday following, we suggest the Roman-Sarum lections, with a slight lengthening of both the Epistle and the Gospel. The whole group of lessons for these two days treats of the three major disciplines of Lent: almsgiving, fasting, and prayer. The prophetic teaching of the Epistles is summed up in the applications of our Lord. This group of lessons is the one thing we have salvaged from our original plan of utilizing the Sermon on the Mount for a Gospel sequence throughout Lent. The teaching seems an admirable introduction to Lent, and specifically a preparation for the lections of the First Sunday. (It may be noted also that the theme of prayer on the Friday fits in very well with a custom now observed by women of all the Churches on this first Friday of Lent — the day is set apart by them as a "World Day of Prayer.")

Lent I

	Epistle	**Gospel**
Sunday	2 Corinthians 6:1-10	Matthew 4:1-11
Wednesday (Ember)	Exodus 24:12-18	Matthew 20:17-28
Friday (Ember)	1 Kings 19:1-8	Matthew 21:33-44
Saturday (Ember)	2 Corinthians 3:4-18	Luke 9:28-36

The Sunday lections — the most ancient introduction to Lent — remain unchanged. For the Ember Days, we suggest using from the Roman material the two lections of Moses' and Elijah's fasts as Epistles on Wednesday and Friday, respectively. These find a suitable summation in the Gospel lesson of the Transfiguration on Saturday, where Moses and Elijah appear on either side of the Christ. The Lucan version of the Transfiguration is preferable to the Matthean or Marcan, for St. Luke links the Transfiguration experience of the Lord with His coming "exodus" in Jerusalem (vs. 31). In a future revision of the Prayer Book, we believe that it would be desirable to shift the Lucan version of the Transfiguration to this place, and assign the Matthean version to the feast on August 6. The Epistle we have assigned to Saturday, 2 Corinthians 3:4-18, has a "transfiguration" theme. It also links the experience of Moses and of our Lord, by contrasting the veil that Moses had to place over his face when it shone with God's glory, with the "open face" by which we behold God's glory in the face of Jesus Christ. (Verses 4-9 of this Epistle are at present read on the Twelfth Sunday after Trinity.)

The two Gospel selections from St. Matthew, assigned to Wednesday and Friday, occur in the Roman-Sarum Lenten sequence on these weekdays within the second week of Lent. We propose using them here for they are good Embertide lessons that bring out the demands of suffering expected from Christ's ministers. They also fit the opening of Lent, as does the Transfiguration lesson, by the way they look forward to the Lord's Passion.

Lent II

	Epistle	**Gospel**
Sunday	Jeremiah 2:4-13	John 4:5-26
Wednesday	1 Thessalonians 4:1-7	Matthew 15:10-28
Friday	Numbers 20:1-13	Luke 11:14-28

The many dissatisfactions expressed in the Church about the selection of lessons for the Second and Third Sundays of Lent have been discussed in the Commission's Prayer Book Studies II. The Epistle and Gospel for the Second Sunday do not belong to the more ancient Lenten selections of the Western Church. The Roman liturgy originally had no propers for this Sunday, because of the lengthy ordination rites that carried over from the Saturday Ember Day. In the eighth century, the propers which we now use on the Sunday were assigned in the Roman rite to Thursday. It was the Sarum Missal that adopted them for the "vacant" Sunday. The Commission recommends that these propers, which are by no means unsuited to the Lenten season, be transformed to Wednesday, with a lengthening of the Gospel lection so as to give it a better and more extensive context.

For the Sunday, we would return to the most ancient Western sequence and begin the great Johannine signs for the Gospels, starting with the *Samaritana*. This lection picks up from the Johannine Gospels appointed in the post-Epiphany Sundays. The Roman-Sarum sequence provides it on the Friday after the Third Sunday of Lent; but there is sufficient evidence that at one time most of the Western Churches read this Gospel on a Sunday of Lent, either the second or the third. To go with this Gospel, the Commission has chosen as Epistle, Jeremiah 2:4-13, though this selection does not occur in the ancient Lenten propers. Its theme fits the Gospel as background ("they have forsaken me, the fountain of living waters," etc.), and is also an excellent Lenten lesson.

On Friday, the Commission proposes using one of the most ancient and favored Lenten Epistles, Numbers 20:1-13, the story of Moses smiting the rock at Meribah to bring forth water. It has from New Testament times been one of the chief Old Testament "types" of the Easter Baptism (*cf.* 1 Cor. 10:4). The Gospel assigned to the day is transferred from the Third Sunday, in order to make way for a Johannine Gospel on the Sunday.

Lent III

	Epistle	Gospel
Sunday	Ephesians 5:1-9	John 5:1-16
Wednesday	2 Samuel 12:1-14	John 8:12, 28-36
Friday	1 Kings 21:1-20	John 8:46-59

The Sunday Gospel continues the great Johannine signs of the Messiah, with the story of the Healing of the Paralytic. The present Gospel has been shifted to the preceding Friday. The Gospels of Wednesday and Friday form a sequence, from the controversy of Jesus with the Jews, culminating in what is now our Gospel for the Fifth Sunday. These lections were favorites in the ancient lectionary of the season. For they not only provide the baptismal theme of Christ as "the light of the world," but they prepare the way for the story of the Passion.

The Epistle for the Sunday is recommended to be kept unchanged. For Wednesday and Friday, the Commission proposes two Old Testament lessons that are not part of the ancient sequence, but which it believes are among the most significant passages of the Old Testament background of Christian ethical teaching. The first is the parable told by Nathan to David, to bring him to repentance for the death of Uriah; the second is the account of Ahab's robbery of Naboth's vineyard, and his subsequent rebuke by Elijah. These stories are too tremendous to be neglected in the Church's lectionary of the Eucharist.

Lent IV

	Epistle	Gospel
Sunday	Isaiah 55:1-11	John 6:1-14
Wednesday	Jeremiah 31:31-34	John 9:1-38
Friday	Ezekiel 34:11-16	John 10:17-31

The Johannine account of the Feeding of the Multitude is now seen to fit into the ancient sequence of Johannine signs. Hence it is left unaltered. For the Sunday Epistle, the Commission returns to its suggestion of providing Isaiah 55:1-11, as a fitting companion piece to the Gospel (see *Prayer Book Studies* II, Vol 1, pp. 58f.), in place of the difficult allegory of the present Epistle from Galatians.

The weekday Gospels, all drawn from the ancient ones of the season, continue the Johannine accounts: on Wednesday, the Healing of the Man Born

Blind; on Friday, the discourse and controversy with the Jews following upon the pronouncement of the Good Shepherd theme. The Jeremiah Epistle is a new one, but contains the important prophecy of the New Covenant. The Ezekiel lection goes with the "Good Shepherd" theme of the Gospel material. In the Roman-Sarum sequence it is assigned to the Monday of the first week of Lent.

Lent V

	Epistle	Gospel
Sunday	Hebrews 9:11-15	John 11:1-46
Wednesday	Isaiah 49:1-6	John 11:47-54
Friday	Isaiah 50:5-10	John 12:23-32

These lessons are virtually self-explanatory. The Gospel provides the last of the great signs in St. John, the Raising of Lazarus — an account read in almost all Western Churches in ancient times on this Sunday. The present Gospel that is displaced by it has been assigned to the Friday of the third week of Lent. The Gospels proposed for the Wednesday and Friday of the week carry the Johannine narrative sequentially up to the very eve of Palm Sunday.

The Epistle for "Passion Sunday" is left unchanged. On the weekdays, the Epistles begin the reading of the Servant Songs of Isaiah. Isaiah 49:1-6 is new, 50:5-10 has been transferred here from its place on Tuesday of Holy Week. This transfer makes possible some changes in the Holy Week sequence, without losing this important song of the Suffering Servant from the lectionary.

Holy Week

Working from its suggestions in *Prayer Book Studies* II, the Commission recommends certain alterations in the lectionary of Holy Week to bring it more nearly in line with ancient custom. In the Epistles, a better grouping of material is offered for Monday, namely, Isaiah 63:7-64:12. And the greatest of the Servant Songs, Isaiah 52:13-53:12, is proposed for Tuesday its present Epistle having been shifted to Friday of the preceding week. Otherwise the Epistles remain the same.

In the matter of the Gospels, it has been felt that the splitting of the Marcan and Lucan Passions into two was not altogether felicitous. Hence the Commission recommends that on Monday the Gospel be John 12:1-11, the account of the Anointing at Bethany, which certainly belongs to the cycle of Passion narratives. Then, the Marcan Passion would be read on Tuesday, the first half of it being assigned to the second lesson at Morning Prayer. A similar arrangement of the Lucan Passion is suggested for Wednesday. This leaves Maundy Thursday free for the sole use of the properly "Maundy" Gospel, John 13:1-17, which is now provided as an alternative to the second portion of the Lucan Passion. Good Friday remains with its lections as now appointed.

Part Four: The Proposed Propers

The Proposed Calendar

		JANUARY
1	A	THE HOLY NAME OF OUR LORD JESUS CHRIST
2	b	
3	c	
4	d	
5	e	
6	f	THE EPIPHANY OF OUR LORD JESUS CHRIST
7	g	
8	A	
9	b	
10	c	William Laud, Archbishop of Canterbury, 1645
11	d	
12	e	
13	f	
14	g	*Hilary*, Bishop of Poitiers, 367,
15	A	
16	b	
17	c	*Antony*, Abbot in Egypt, 356
18	d	
19	e	
20	f	
21	g	Agnes, Martyr at Rome, 304
22	A	Vincent, Deacon of Saragossa, and Martyr, 304
23	b	Phillips Brooks, Bishop of Massachusetts, 1893
24	c	*Saint Timothy*
25	d	THE CONVERSION OF SAINT PAUL THE APOSTLE
26	e	*Polycarp*, Bishop of Smyrna, and Martyr, 156
27	f	*John Chrysostom*, Bishop of Constantinople, 407

		JANUARY (continued)
28	g	
29	A	
30	b	
31	c	

		FEBRUARY
1	d	*Ignatius*, Bishop of Antioch, and Martyr, c. 115
2	e	THE PRESENTATION OF OUR LORD JESUS CHRIST IN THE TEMPLE
3	f	Ansgarius, Archbishop of Hamburg, Missionary to Denmark and Sweden, 865
4	g	*Cornelius*, the Centurion
5	A	
6	b	*Saint Titus*
7	c	
8	d	
9	e	
10	f	
11	g	
12	A	
13	b	
14	c	
15	d	Thomas Bray, Priest and Missionary, 1730
16	e	
17	f	
18	g	
19	A	
20	b	
21	c	
22	d	
23	e	
24	f	SAINT MATTHIAS THE APOSTLE
25	g	

PRAYER BOOK STUDIES XII

			FEBRUARY (continued)
	26	A	
	27	b	George Herbert, Priest, 1633
	28	c	
	29		

			MARCH
	1	d	*David*, Bishop of Menevia, Wales, c. 544
	2	e	
	3	f	
	4	g	
	5	A	
	6	b	
	7	c	*Perpetua and her Companions*, Martyrs of Carthage,
	8	d	Thomas Aquinas, Friar, 1274
	9	e	
	10	f	
	11	g	
	12	A	*Gregory the Great*, Bishop of Rome, 604
	13	b	
	14	c	
	15	d	
	16	e	
	17	f	*Patrick*, Bishop and Missionary of Ireland, 461
	18	g	
	19	A	*Saint Joseph*
	20	b	Thomas Ken, Bishop of Bath and Wells, 1711
	21	c	
14	22	d	
3	23	e	Gregory the Illuminator, Bishop and Missionary of Armenia, c. 332
	24	f	
11	25	g	THE ANNUNCIATION OF THE BLESSED VIRGIN MARY

			MARCH (continued)
	26	A	
19	27	b	
8	28	c	
	29	d	John Keble, Priest, 1866
16	30	e	
5	31	f	

			APRIL
	1	g	John Frederick Denison Maurice, Priest, 1872
13	2	A	
2	3	b	
	4	c	*Ambrose*, Bishop of Milan, 397
10	5	d	
	6	e	William Law, Priest, 1761
18	7	f	
7	8	g	William Augustus Muhlenberg, Priest, 1877
	9	A	
15	10	b	
4	11	c	*Leo the Great*, Bishop of Rome, 461
	12	d	George Augustus Selwyn, Bishop of New Zealand, 1878
12	13	e	
1	14	f	*Justin*, Martyr at Rome, c. 167
	15	g	
9	16	A	
17	17	b	
6	18	c	
	19	d	
	20	e	
	21	f	*Anselm*, Archbishop of Canterbury, 1109
	22	g	
	23	A	
	24	b	
	25	c	**SAINT MARK THE EVANGELIST**

			APRIL (continued)
	26	d	
	27	e	
	28	f	
	29	g	
	30	A	

			MAY
1	b	SAINT PHILIP AND SAINT JAMES, APOSTLES
2	c	*Athanasius*, Bishop of Alexandria, 373
3	d	
4	e	Monnica, Mother of Augustine of Hippo, 387
5	f	
6	g	John of Damascus, Priest, c. 760
7	A	
8	b	
9	c	*Gregory of Nazianzus*, Bishop of Constantinople, 389
10	d	
11	e	Cyril and Methodius, Missionary Bishops to the Slavs, 869, 885
12	f	
13	g	
14	A	
15	b	
16	c	
17	d	
18	e	
19	f	Dunstan, Archbishop of Canterbury, 988
20	g	Alcuin, Deacon, and Abbot of Tours, 804
21	A	
22	b	
23	c	
24	d	Jackson Kemper, First Missionary Bishop in the United States, 1870
25	e	

		MAY (continued)
26	f	*Augustine*, First Archbishop of Canterbury, 605
27	g	*Bede*, the Venerable, Priest, and Monk of Jarrow, 735
28	A	
29	b	
30	c	
31	d	

		JUNE
1	e	
2	f	*The Martyrs of Lyons*, 177
3	g	
4	A	
5	b	*Boniface*, Archbishop of Mainz, Missionary to Germany, Martyr, 754
6	c	
7	d	
8	e	
9	f	*The First Book of Common Prayer*, 1549
10	g	Columba, Abbot of Iona, 597
11	A	SAINT BARNABAS THE APOSTLE
12	b	
13	c	
14	d	*Basil the Great*, Bishop of Caesarea, 379
15	e	
16	f	Joseph Butler, Bishop of Durham, 1752
17	g	
18	A	Ephrem of Edessa, Syria, Deacon, 373
19	b	
20	c	
21	d	
22	e	*Alban*, First Martyr of Britain, c. 304
23	f	
24	g	THE NATIVITY OF SAINT JOHN BAPTIST

		JUNE (continued)
25	A	
26	b	
27	c	
28	d	*Irenaeus*, Bishop of Lyons, c. 202
29	e	SAINT PETER AND SAINT PAUL, APOSTLES
30	f	

		JULY
1	g	
2	A	*The Visitation of the Blessed Virgin Mary*
3	b	
4	c	INDEPENDENCE DAY
5	d	
6	e	
7	f	
8	g	
9	A	
10	b	
11	c	*Benedict of Nursia*, Abbot of Monte Cassino, c. 540
12	d	
13	e	
14	f	
15	g	
16	A	
17	b	William White, Bishop of Pennsylvania, 1836
18	c	
19	d	
20	e	
21	f	
22	g	*Saint Mary Magdalene*
23	A	
24	b	
25	c	SAINT JAMES THE APOSTLE

		JULY (continued)
26	d	Thomas a Kempis, Priest, 1471
27	e	William Reed Huntington, Priest, 1909
28	f	
29	g	William Wilberforce, 1833
30	A	
31	b	

		AUGUST
1	c	
2	d	
3	e	
4	f	Dominic, Friar, 1221
5	g	
6	A	THE TRANSFIGURATION OF OUR LORD JESUS CHRIST
7	b	
8	c	
9	d	
10	e	Laurence, Deacon, and Martyr at Rome, 258
11	f	
12	g	
13	A	Hippolytus, Bishop, and Martyr, c. 235
14	b	Jeremy Taylor, Bishop of Down, Connor and Dromore, 1667
15	c	*Saint Mary the Virgin*, Mother of Our Lord Jesus Christ
16	d	
17	e	
18	f	
19	g	
20	A	*Bernard*, Abbot of Clairvaux, 1153
21	b	
22	c	
23	d	
24	e	SAINT BARTHOLOMEW THE APOSTLE

		AUGUST (continued)
25	f	Louis, King of France, 1270
26	g	
27	A	
28	b	*Augustine*, Bishop of Hippo, 430
29	c	
30	d	
31	e	*Aidan*, Bishop of Lindisfarne, 651

		SEPTEMBER
1	f	
2	g	
3	A	
4	b	
5	c	
6	d	
7	e	
8	f	
9	g	
10	A	
11	b	
12	c	John Henry Hobart, Bishop of New York, 1830
13	d	*Cyprian*, Bishop of Carthage, and Martyr, 258
14	e	*The Exaltation of the Holy Cross*
15	f	
16	g	
17	A	
18	b	
19	c	*Theodore of Tarsus*, Archbishop of Canterbury, 690
20	d	John Coleridge Patteson, Bishop of Melanesia, and Martyr, 1871
21	e	SAINT MATTHEW, APOSTLE AND EVANGELIST
22	f	
23	g	
24	A	

The Propers for the Minor Holy Days 113

		SEPTEMBER (continued)
25	b	Sergius, Abbot of Holy Trinity, Moscow, 1392
26	c	Lancelot Andrewes, Bishop of Winchester, 1626
27	d	
28	e	
29	f	SAINT MICHAEL AND ALL ANGELS
30	g	*Jerome*, Priest, and Monk of Bethlehem, 420

		OCTOBER
1	A	
2	b	
3	c	
4	d	*Francis of Assisi*, Friar, 1226
5	e	
6	f	William Tyndale, Priest, and Martyr, 1536
7	g	
8	A	
9	b	
10	c	
11	d	
12	e	
13	f	
14	g	
15	A	Samuel Isaac Joseph Schereschewsky, Bishop of Shanghai, 1906
16	b	Hugh Latimer and Nicholas Ridley, Bishops and Martyrs, 1555
17	c	
18	d	SAINT LUKE THE EVANGELIST
19	e	
20	f	
21	g	
22	A	
23	b	
24	c	
25	d	

		OCTOBER (continued)
26	e	*King Alfred the Great*, 899
27	f	
28	g	SAINT SIMON AND SAINT JUDE, APOSTLES
29	A	James Hannington and his Companions, Bishop and Martyrs of Uganda, 1885
30	b	
31	c	

		NOVEMBER
1	d	ALL SAINTS
2	e	
3	f	
4	g	
5	A	
6	b	
7	c	Willibrord, Archbishop of Utrecht, Missionary to Frisia, 738
8	d	
9	e	
10	f	
11	g	*Martin*, Bishop of Tours, 397
12	A	Charles Simeon, Priest, 1836
13	b	
14	c	*Consecration of Samuel Seabury*, First American Bishop, 1784
15	d	
16	e	Margaret, Queen of Scotland, 1093
17	f	Hilda, Abbess of Whitby, 680
18	g	
19	A	Elizabeth, Princess of Hungary, 1231
20	b	
21	c	
22	d	
23	e	Clement, Bishop of Rome, c. 100
24	f	

The Propers for the Minor Holy Days 115

		NOVEMBER (continued)
25	g	
26	A	
27	b	
28	c	
29	d	
30	e	SAINT ANDREW THE APOSTLE

		DECEMBER
1	f	
2	g	Channing Moore Williams, Missionary Bishop in China and Japan, 1910
3	A	
4	b	*Clement of Alexandria*, Priest, c. 210
5	c	
6	d	Nicholas, Bishop of Myra in Lycia, c. 342
7	e	
8	f	
9	g	
10	A	
11	b	
12	c	
13	d	
14	e	
15	f	
16	g	
17	A	
18	b	
19	c	
20	d	
21	e	SAINT THOMAS THE APOSTLE
22	f	
23	g	
24	A	

DECEMBER (continued)		
25	b	THE NATIVITY OF OUR LORD JESUS CHRIST
26	c	SAINT STEPHEN, DEACON AND MARTYR
27	d	SAINT JOHN, APOSTLE AND EVANGELIST
28	e	THE HOLY INNOCENTS
29	f	
30	g	
31	A	

Proposed Collects, Epistles, and Gospels for the Lesser Feasts and Fasts

ADVENT

WEDNESDAY IN THE THIRD WEEK OF ADVENT
EMBER DAY

The Collect.[15]

ALMIGHTY God, the giver of all good gifts, who of thy divine providence hast appointed divers Orders in thy Church: Give thy grace, we humbly beseech thee, to all those who are called to any office and administration in the same; and so replenish them with the truth of thy doctrine, and endue them with innocency of life, that they may faithfully serve before thee, to the glory of thy great Name, and the benefit of thy holy Church; through Jesus Christ our Lord. Amen.

The Epistle. 1 Corinthians 3:5-11.
The Gospel. St. John 4:31-38.

FRIDAY IN THE THIRD WEEK OF ADVENT

The Collect. (Same as on Wednesday)
The Epistle. 1 Peter 4:7-11.
The Gospel. St. Luke 12:25-44.

---

15. Prayer Book, page 39.

SATURDAY IN THE THIRD WEEK OF ADVENT

The Collect. (Same as on Wednesday)
The Epistle. 1 Timothy 1:12-17.
The Gospel. St. Matthew 16:24-27.

LENTEN SEASON

THE FIRST DAY OF LENT, COMMONLY CALLED ASH WEDNESDAY

The Collect. (Same as at present)
The Epistle. (Same as at present)
The Gospel. (Same as at present)

FRIDAY AFTER ASH WEDNESDAY

The Epistle. Isaiah 58:1-12.
The Gospel. St. Matthew 5:43-6:8.

THE FIRST SUNDAY IN LENT

The Collects. (Same as at present)
The Epistle. (Same as at present) [2 Cor. 6:1-10]
The Gospel. (Same as at present) [Matt. 4:1-11]

WEDNESDAY IN THE FIRST WEEK OF LENT EMBER DAY

The Collect.

ALMIGHTY God, who hast committed to the hands of men the ministry of reconciliation: We humbly beseech thee, by the inspiration of thy Holy Spirit, to put it into the hearts of many to offer themselves for this ministry; that thereby mankind may be drawn to thy blessed kingdom; through Jesus Christ our Lord. *Amen.*

The Epistle. Exodus 24:12-18.
The Gospel. St. Matthew 20:17-28.

FRIDAY IN THE FIRST WEEK OF LENT EMBER DAY

The Collects. (Same as on Wednesday)
The Epistle. 1 Kings 19:1-8.
The Gospel. St. Matthew 21:33-44.

SATURDAY IN THE FIRST WEEK OF LENT EMBER DAY

The Collects. (Same as on Wednesday)
The Epistle. 2 Corinthians 3:4-18.
The Gospel. St. Luke 9:28-26.[16]

THE SECOND SUNDAY IN LENT

The Collects. (Same as at present)
The Epistle. Jeremiah 2:4-13.
The Gospel. St. John 4:5-26.

WEDNESDAY IN THE SECOND WEEK OF LENT

The Epistle. 1 Thessalonians 4:1-7.
The Gospel. St. Matthew 15:10-28.

FRIDAY IN THE SECOND WEEK OF LENT

The Epistle. Numbers 20:1-13.
The Gospel. St. Luke 11:14-28.

THE THIRD SUNDAY IN LENT

The Collects. (Same as at present)
The Epistle. (Same as at present) [Eph. 5:1-14]
The Gospel. St. John 5:1-16.

---

16. When the next revision of the Prayer Book is undertaken, the Commission suggests that the Matthean version of the Transfiguration (St. Matthew 17: 1-9) be adopted for the Feast Day of August 6th, and the Lucan version be used on this Ember Day of Lent.

WEDNESDAY IN THE THIRD WEEK OF LENT

The Epistle. 2 Samuel 12:1-14.
The Gospel. St. John 8:12, 28-36.

FRIDAY IN THE THIRD WEEK OF LENT

The Epistle. 1 Kings 21:1-20.
The Gospel. St. John 8:46-59.

THE FOURTH SUNDAY IN LENT

The Collects. (Same as at present)
The Epistle. Isaiah 55:1-11.
The Gospel. (Same as at present)

WEDNESDAY IN THE FOURTH WEEK OF LENT

The Epistle. Jeremiah 31:31-34.
The Gospel. St. John 9:1-38.

FRIDAY IN THE FOURTH WEEK OF LENT

The Epistle. Ezekiel 34:11-16.
The Gospel. St. John 10:17-31.

PASSIONTIDE

THE FIFTH SUNDAY IN LENT, COMMONLY CALLED PASSION SUNDAY

The Collects. (Same as at present)
The Epistle. (Same as at present) [Heb. 9:11-15]
The Gospel. St. John 11:1-46.

WEDNESDAY IN THE FIFTH WEEK OF LENT

The Epistle. Isaiah 49:1-6.
The Gospel. St. John 11:47-54.

FRIDAY IN THE FIFTH WEEK OF LENT

The Epistle. Isaiah 50:5-10.
The Gospel. St. John 12:23-32.

THE SUNDAY NEXT BEFORE EASTER, COMMONLY CALLED PALM SUNDAY

The Collect. (Same as at present)
The Epistle. (Same as at present) [Phil. 2:5-11]
The Gospel. (Same as at present) [Matt. 27:1-54]

MONDAY BEFORE EASTER

The Collects. (Same as at present)
The Epistle. Isaiah 63:7-64:12.
The Gospel. St. John 12:1-11.

TUESDAY BEFORE EASTER

The Collects. (Same as at present)
The Epistle. Isaiah 52:13-53:12.
The Gospel. (Same as at present) [Mark 15:1-39][17]

WEDNESDAY BEFORE EASTER

The Collects. (Same as at present)
The Epistle. (Same as at present) [Heb. 9:16-28]
The Gospel. St. Luke 23:1-49.[18]

---

17. St. Mark 14, now read as the Gospel on Monday, would be assigned to the Second Lesson of Morning Prayer on this day.

18. St. Luke 22, now read as the Gospel on this day, would be assigned to the Second Lesson of Morning Prayer on this day.

THURSDAY BEFORE EASTER, COMMONLY CALLED MAUNDY THURSDAY

The Collects. (Same as at present)
The Epistle. (Same as at present) [1 Cor. 11:17-34]
The Gospel. St. John 13: 1-17.

GOOD FRIDAY

The Collects. (Same as at present)
The Epistle. (Same as at present) [Heb 10:1-25]
The Gospel. (Same as at present) [1 Pet. 3:17-22]

EASTER EVEN

The Collect. (Same as at present)
The Epistle. (Same as at present) [1 Pet. 3:17-22]
The Gospel. (Same as at present)[Matt. 27:57-66]

EASTERTIDE

EASTER DAY[19]
(First celebration of the Holy Communion)

The Collect. (Same as at present)
The Epistle. Colossians 3:1-4.
The Gospel. (Same as at present) [John 20:1-10]

(Second celebration of the Holy Communion)

The Collect. (Same as at present)
The Epistle. Philippians 3:7-14 RV.
The Gospel. St. Matthew 28:1-10.

---

19. See the proposals for Easter Day and week in *Prayer Book Studies* II, reprinted in Prayer Book Studies Volume 1, pp. 62-65.

MONDAY IN EASTER WEEK

The Collects. (Same as at present)
The Epistle. (Same as at present) [Acts 10:34-43]
The Gospel. (Same as at present) [Luke 24:13-35]

TUESDAY IN EASTER WEEK

The Collects. (Same as at present)
The Epistle. (Same as at present) [Acts 13:26-41]
The Gospel. (Same as at present) [Luke 24:36-48]

WEDNESDAY IN EASTER WEEK

The Epistle. Acts 3:13-15, 17-19, 26.
The Gospel. St. John 21:1-14.

THURSDAY IN EASTER WEEK

The Epistle. Colossians 1:18-23a.
The Gospel. St. Luke 24:1-12.

FRIDAY IN EASTER WEEK

The Epistle. Colossians 2:10-15.
The Gospel. St. John 20:1-10.

SATURDAY IN EASTER WEEK

The Epistle. 1 Peter 1:3-4, 15-21.
The Gospel. St. John 20:11-18.

THE FIRST SUNDAY AFTER EASTER

The Collects. (Same as at present)
The Epistle. (Same as at present) [1 John 5:4-12]
The Gospel. St. John 20:19-29.[20]

---

20. A lengthening of the present Gospel lesson, in order to include the appearance to Thomas. See *Prayer Book Studies*, II, Vol. 1, p. 65.

THE ROGATION DAYS MONDAY

(Same Collect, Epistle, and Gospel, as at present; Prayer Book, pages 261-263)
[Eze. 34:25-31] [Luke 11:5-13]

TUESDAY

The Collects. (Same as at present)
The Epistle. Joel 2:21-27.
The Gospel. St. Mark 11:22-26.

WEDNESDAY

The Collects. (Same as at present)
The Epistle. Micah 6:6-8.
The Gospel. St. Matthew 6:5-8.

WHITSUNTIDE

(Whitsunday, and Monday and Tuesday in Whitsun Week, as proposed in *Prayer Book Studies*, II, Vol. 1, pp. 67-69)

WEDNESDAY IN WHITSUN WEEKEMBER DAY

The Collect.[21]

ALMIGHTY God, our heavenly Father, who hast purchased to thyself an universal Church by the precious blood of thy dear Son: Mercifully look upon the same, and at this time so guide and govern the minds of thy servants the Bishops and Pastors of thy flock, that they may lay hands suddenly on no man, but faithfully and wisely make choice of fit persons, to serve in the sacred Ministry of thy Church. And to those who shall be ordained to any holy function, give thy grace and heavenly benediction; that both by their life and doctrine they may show forth thy glory, and set forward the salvation of all men; through Jesus Christ our Lord. *Amen.*

The Epistle. 2 Corinthians 3:17-4:6.
The Gospel. St. Luke 4:16-21.

---

21. Prayer Book page 38.

THURSDAY IN WHITSUN WEEK

The Epistle. Romans 8:1-11.
The Gospel. St. John 16:12-15.

FRIDAY IN WHITSUN WEEKEMBER DAY

The Collects. (Same as on Wednesday)
The Epistle. Titus 3:4-8.
The Gospel. St. Matthew 28:16-20.

SATURDAY IN WHITSUN WEEK EMBER DAY

The Collects. (Same as on Wednesday)
The Epistle. Ephesians 2: I 3-23.
The Gospel. St. John 20:19-23.

THE AUTUMN EMBER DAYS WEDNESDAY

The Collect.[22]

ALMIGHTY God, look mercifully upon the world which thou hast redeemed by the blood of thy dear Son, and incline the hearts of many to dedicate themselves to the sacred Ministry of thy Church; through the same thy Son Jesus Christ our Lord. *Amen.*

The Epistle. Ephesians 4:11-16.
The Gospel. St. John 15:1-8.

FRIDAY

The Collects. (Same as on Wednesday)
The Epistle. Acts 13:44-49.
The Gospel. St. Matthew 10:24-32.

---

22. Prayer Book, page 39.

SATURDAY

The Collects. (Same as on Wednesday)
The Epistle. Acts 20:28-32.
The Gospel. St. John 10:1-10.

THE GREATER HOLY DAYS

THE HOLY NAME OF OUR LORD JESUS CHRIST
[January 1.]

The Collect.

ETERNAL Father, who didst give thine incarnate Son a Name, betokening not his majesty but our salvation: We pray thee to set the Name of Jesus high above every name, and to plant in every heart the love of our only Saviour; who liveth and reigneth with thee and the Holy Ghost, one God, world without end. *Amen.*

The Epistle. (Same as at present) [Philippians 2:9-13].
The Gospel. (Same as at present) [St. Luke 2:15-21].

SAINT PETER AND SAINT PAUL, APOSTLES [June 29.]

The Collect.

ALMIGHTY God, whose blessed Apostles Peter and Paul hallowed this day by their martyrdom: Grant that thy household the Church, being instructed by their doctrine and example, and knit together in unity by thy Spirit, may ever stand firm upon the one Foundation, which is Jesus Christ our Lord, who liveth and reigneth with thee and the same Spirit, one God, world without end. *Amen.*

The Epistle. Galatians 2:1-2, 7-10.
The Gospel. (Same as at present) [St. Matthew 16:13-19].

THE LESSER HOLY DAYS

CHANNING MOORE WILLIAMS
Missionary Bishop in China and Japan
[December 2.]

The Collect.

ALMIGHTY and everlasting God, we thank thee for thy servant Channing Moore Williams, whom thou didst call to preach the Gospel to the people of China and Japan; Raise up, we pray thee, in this and every land, heralds and evangelists of thy kingdom, that thy Church may make known the unsearchable riches of Christ, and may increase with the increase of God; through the same thy Son, Jesus Christ our Lord. *Amen.*

CLEMENT OF ALEXANDRIA
Priest
[December 4.]

The Collect.

O GOD, who hast enlightened thy Church by the teaching of thy servant Clement: Enrich us evermore, we beseech thee, with thy heavenly grace, and raise up faithful witnesses who by their life and doctrine will set forth the truth of thy salvation; through Jesus Christ our Lord. *Amen.*

The Epistle. 2 Peter 1:2-8.
The Gospel. St. John 6:57-63.

NICHOLAS
Bishop of Myra
[December 6.]

The Collect.

ALMIGHTY and everlasting God, who didst enkindle the flame of thy love in the heart of thy servant Nicholas: Grant to us, thy humble servants, the same faith and power of love; that, as we rejoice in his triumph, we may profit by his example; through Jesus Christ our Lord. *Amen.*

WILLIAM LAUD
Archbishop of Canterbury
[January 10.]

The Collect.

ACCEPT, O Lord, our thanksgiving this day for thy servant William Laud, and grant unto us in like manner such constancy and zeal in thy service, that we may obtain with him and thy servants everywhere a good confession and the crown of everlasting life; through Jesus Christ our Lord. *Amen.*

HILARY
Bishop of Poitiers
[January 14.]

The Collect.

ALMIGHTY, everlasting God, whose servant Hilary steadfastly confessed the true faith of thy Son our Saviour Jesus Christ to be Very God and Very Man: Grant that we may hold fast to this faith, and evermore magnify his holy Name; through the same thy Son Jesus Christ our Lord, who liveth and reigneth with thee and the Holy Spirit ever, one God, world without end. *Amen.*

The Epistle. 2 Timothy 4:1-8.
The Gospel. St. Luke 12:8-12.

ANTONY
Abbot in Egypt
[January 17.]

The Collect.

ALMIGHTY God, who by thy Holy Spirit didst enable thy servant to withstand the temptations of the world, the flesh, and the devil: Grant that we, in the same Spirit, may with pure hearts and minds follow thee, the only God; through Jesus Christ our Lord. *Amen.*

The Epistle. Philippians 3:7-14 (RV).
The Gospel. St. Luke 12:32-34.

AGNES
Martyr at Rome
[January 21.]

The Collect.

ALMIGHTY and everlasting God, with whom thy meek ones go forth as the mighty: Grant us so to cherish the memory of thy blessed martyr Agnes, that we may share her pure and steadfast faith in thee; through Jesus Christ our Lord. *Amen.*

VINCENT
Deacon of Saragossa, and Martyr
[January 22.]

The Collect.

ALMIGHTY God, by whose grace and power thy holy Deacon and martyr Vincent triumphed over suffering and despised death: Grant, we beseech thee, that enduring hardness and waxing valiant in fight, we may with the noble army of martyrs receive the crown of everlasting life; through Jesus Christ our Lord. *Amen.*

PHILLIPS BROOKS
Bishop of Massachusetts
[January 23.]

The Collect.

ALMIGHTY and everlasting God, the source and perfection of all virtues, who didst inspire thy servant Phillips Brooks both to do what is right and to preach what is true: Grant that all ministers and stewards of thy mysteries may afford to thy faithful people, by word and example, the instruction which is of thy grace; through Jesus Christ our Lord. *Amen.*

SAINT TIMOTHY
[January 24.]

The Collect.

ALMIGHTY and merciful God, who didst call Saint Timothy to endure hardship for the sake of thy dear Son: Strengthen us in like manner to stand firm in adversity, through the grace of Christ Jesus, that we may obtain salvation with eternal glory, who livest and reignest with the same thy Son Jesus Christ and the Holy Ghost ever, one God, world without end. *Amen.*

The Epistle. 2 Timothy 1:1-7.
The Gospel. St. John 10:7-10.

POLYCARP
Bishop of Smyrna, and Martyr
[January 26.]

The Collect.

ALMIGHTY God, who didst give thy servant Polycarp boldness to confess the Name of our Saviour Jesus Christ before the rulers of this world, and courage to die for this faith: Grant that we likewise may ever be ready to give a reason for the hope that is in us, and to suffer gladly for his sake; through the same Jesus Christ our Lord. *Amen.*

The Epistle. Revelation 2:8-11.
The Gospel. St. Matthew 20:20-23.

JOHN CHRYSOSTOM
Bishop of Constantinople
[January 27.]

The Collect.

O GOD, who didst give grace to thy servant John, eloquently to declare thy righteousness in the great congregation, and fearlessly to bear reproach for the honour of thy Name: Mercifully grant unto all bishops and pastors such excellency in preaching, and fidelity in ministering thy Word, that thy people may be partakers with them of the glory that shall be revealed; through Jesus Christ our Lord. *Amen.*

The Epistle. Jeremiah 1:6-9.
The Gospel. St. Luke 21:12b-15.

IGNATIUS
Bishop of Antioch, and Martyr
[February 1.]

The Collect.

ALMIGHTY God, by whose grace and power thy holy Bishop and martyr Ignatius triumphed over suffering and despised death: Grant, we beseech thee, that enduring hardness, and waxing valiant in fight, we may with the noble army of martyrs receive the crown of everlasting life; through Jesus Christ our Lord. *Amen.*

The Epistle. Romans 8:35-39.
The Gospel. St. John 12:24-26.

ANSGARIUS
Archbishop of Hamburg, Missionary to Denmark and Sweden
[February 3.]

The Collect.

ALMIGHTY and everlasting God, we thank thee for thy servant Ansgarius, whom thou didst call to preach the Gospel to the people of Scandinavia: Raise up, we pray thee, in this and every land, heralds and evangelists of thy kingdom, that thy Church may make known the unsearchable riches of Christ, and may increase with the increase of God; through the same thy Son Jesus Christ our Lord. *Amen.*

CORNELIUS, THE CENTURION
[February 4.]

The Collect.

GOD, who by thy Spirit didst call Cornelius the Centurion to be the first Christian among the Gentiles: Grant to thy Church in every nation a ready mind and will to proclaim thy love to all who turn to thee with unfeigned hope and faith; for the sake of Jesus Christ our Lord, who liveth and reigneth with thee and the same Spirit ever, one God, world without end. *Amen.*

> *The Epistle.* Acts 11:1-18.
> *The Gospel.* St. John 4:4-14.

SAINT TITUS
[February 6.]

The Collect.

BLESSED Lord, who didst charge Saint Titus to speak the things that accord with sound doctrine and to offer himself a pattern of good works: Grant to all thy people to live soberly, righteously, and godly in this present age, that they may with sure confidence look for the blessed hope and glorious appearing of our great God and Saviour Jesus Christ, who liveth and reigneth with thee and the Holy Spirit ever, one God, world without end. *Amen.*

> *The Epistle.* Titus 1:1-5.
> *The Gospel.* St. John 10:1-5.

THOMAS BRAY
Priest and Missionary
[February 15.]

The Collect.

O GOD, who dost ever hallow and protect thy Church: Raise up therein through thy Spirit good and faithful stewards of the mysteries of Christ, as thou didst in thy servant Thomas Bray; that by their ministry and example thy people may abide in thy favour and walk in the way of truth; through Jesus Christ our Lord, who liveth and reigneth with thee in the unity of the same Spirit ever, one God, world without end. *Amen.*

GEORGE HERBERT
Priest
[February 27.]

The Collect.

ETERNAL Lord God, who holdest all souls in life: We beseech thee to shed forth upon thy whole Church in paradise and on earth the bright beams of thy light and thy peace; and grant that we, following the good examples of thy servant George Herbert, and of all those who loved and served thee here, may at the last enter with them into thine unending joy; through Jesus Christ our Lord. Amen.

DAVID
Bishop of Menevia
[March 1.]

The Collect.

ALMIGHTY God, who in thy providence didst choose thy servant David to be an apostle to the people of Wales, to bring those who were wandering in darkness and error to the true light and knowledge of thee: Grant us so to walk in that light, that we may come at last to the light of everlasting life; through the merits of Jesus Christ thy Son our Lord. Amen.

The Epistle. Ephesians 2:4-10.
The Gospel. St. Mark 4:26-29.

PERPETUA AND HER COMPANIONS
Martyrs of Carthage
[March 7.]

The Collect.

ALMIGHTY and everlasting God, with whom thy meek ones go forth as the mighty: Grant us so to cherish the memory of thy blessed martyrs Perpetua and her companions, that we may share their pure and steadfast faith in thee; through Jesus Christ our Lord. *Amen.*

> *The Epistle.* Hebrews 10:32-39.
> *The Gospel.* St. Matthew 24: 9-14a.

THOMAS AQUINAS
Friar
[March 8.]

The Collect.

ALMIGHTY God, who hast enriched thy Church with the singular learning and holiness of thy servant Thomas: Grant us to hold fast the true doctrine of thy Son our Saviour Jesus Christ, and to fashion our lives according to the same, to the glory of thy great Name and the benefit of thy holy Church; through the same Jesus Christ our Lord. *Amen.*

GREGORY THE GREAT
Bishop of Rome
[March 12.]

The Collect.

ALMIGHTY and merciful God, who didst raise up in Gregory the Great a servant of the servants of God, by whose labour the people of England were brought into the knowledge of the Catholic and Apostolic faith: Preserve in thy Church evermore a thankful remembrance of his devotion, that thy people, being zealous in every good work, may receive with him and thy servants everywhere the crown of glory that fadeth not away; through Jesus Christ our Lord. *Amen.*

> *The Epistle.* Ecclesiasticus 47:8-11.
> *The Gospel.* St. Mark 10:42-45.

PATRICK
Bishop and Missionary of Ireland
[March 17.]

The Collect.

ALMIGHTY God, who in thy providence didst choose thy servant Patrick to be an apostle to the people of Ireland, to bring those who were wandering in darkness and error to the true light and knowledge of thee: Grant us so to walk in that light, that we may come at last to the light of everlasting life; through the merits of Jesus Christ thy Son our Lord. *Amen.*

The Epistle. 1 Thessalonians 2:2b-12.
The Gospel. St. Matthew 5:43-48.

SAINT JOSEPH
[March 19.]

The Collect.

O GOD, who didst call blessed Joseph to be the faithful guardian of thine only-begotten Son, and the spouse of his virgin Mother: Give us grace to follow his example in constant worship of thee and obedience to thy commands, that our homes may be sanctified by thy presence, and our children nurtured in thy fear and love; through the same Jesus Christ our Lord. *Amen.*

The Epistle. Isaiah 63:7-9, 16.
The Gospel. St. Matthew 1:18-25.

THOMAS KEN
Bishop of Bath and Wells
[March 20.]

The Collect.

ALMIGHTY and everlasting God, we give thee thanks for the purity and strength with which thou didst endow thy servant Thomas Ken; and we pray that by thy grace we may have a like power to hallow and conform our souls and bodies, to the purpose of thy most holy will; through Jesus Christ our Lord. *Amen.*

GREGORY THE ILLUMINATOR
Bishop and Missionary of Armenia
[March 23.]

The Collect.

ALMIGHTY and everlasting God, we thank thee for thy servant Gregory, whom thou didst call to preach the Gospel to the people of Armenia: Raise up, we pray thee, in this and every land, heralds and evangelists of thy kingdom, that thy Church may make known the unsearchable riches of Christ, and may increase with the increase of God; through the same thy Son Jesus Christ our Lord. *Amen.*

JOHN KEBLE
Priest
[March 29.]

The Collect.

O ETERNAL Lord God, who holdest all souls in life: We beseech thee to shed forth upon thy whole Church in paradise and on earth the bright beams of thy light and thy peace; and grant that we, following the good examples of thy servant John Keble, and of all those who loved and served thee here, may at the last enter with them into thine unending joy; through Jesus Christ our Lord. *Amen.*

JOHN FREDERICK DENISON MAURICE
Priest
[April 1.]

The Collect.

LET thy continual mercy, O Lord, enkindle in thy Church the never-failing gift of charity, that, following the example of thy servant John Frederick Denison Maurice, we may have grace to defend the children of the poor, and maintain the cause of them that have no helper; for the sake of him who gave his life for us, thy Son our Saviour Jesus Christ. *Amen.*

AMBROSE
Bishop of Milan
[April 4.]

The Collect.

O GOD, who didst give grace to thy servant Ambrose, eloquently to declare thy righteousness in the great congregation, and fearlessly to bear reproach for the honour of thy Name: Mercifully grant unto all bishops and pastors such excellency in preaching, and fidelity in ministering thy Word, that thy people may be partakers with them of the glory that shall be revealed; through Jesus Christ our Lord. *Amen.*

> *The Epistle.* Ecclesiasticus 2:7-11, 16-18.
> *The Gospel.* St. Luke 12:42-44.

WILLIAM LAW
Priest
[April 6.]

The Collect.

ALMIGHTY and everlasting God, we give thee thanks for the purity and strength with which thou didst endow thy servant William Law; and we pray that by thy grace we may have a like power to hallow and conform our souls and bodies, to the purpose of thy most holy will; through Jesus Christ our Lord. *Amen.*

WILLIAM AUGUSTUS MUHLENBERG
Priest
[April 8.]

The Collect.

ALMIGHTY and everlasting God, who didst enkindle the flame of thy love in the heart of thy servant William Augustus Muhlenberg: Grant to us, thy humble servants, the same faith and power of love; that, as we rejoice in his triumph, we may profit by his example; through Jesus Christ our Lord. *Amen.*

LEO THE GREAT
Bishop of Rome
[April 11.]

The Collect.

ALMIGHTY, everlasting God, whose servant Leo steadfastly confessed the true faith of thy Son our Saviour Jesus Christ to be Very God and Very Man: Grant that we may hold fast to this faith, and evermore magnify his holy Name; through the same thy Son Jesus Christ our Lord, who liveth and reigneth with thee and the Holy Spirit ever, one God, world without end. *Amen.*

The Epistle. 2 Timothy 1:12b-14.
The Gospel. St. Matthew 5:13-19.

GEORGE AUGUSTUS SELWYN
Bishop of New Zealand
[April 12.]

The Collect.

ALMIGHTY and everlasting God, we thank thee for thy servant George Augustus Selwyn, whom thou didst call to preach the Gospel to the people of New Zealand: Raise up, we pray thee, in this and every land, heralds and evangelists of thy kingdom, that thy Church may make known the unsearchable riches of Christ, and may increase with the increase of God; through the same thy Son Jesus Christ our Lord. *Amen.*

JUSTIN
Martyr at Rome
[April 14.]

The Collect.

ALMIGHTY God, who didst give thy servant Justin boldness to confess the Name of our Saviour Jesus Christ before the rulers of this world, and courage to die for this faith: Grant that we likewise may ever be ready to give a reason for the hope that is in us, and to suffer gladly for his sake; through the same Jesus Christ our Lord. *Amen.*

The Epistle. 1 Peter 3:14-18, 22.
The Gospel. St. John 12:44-50.

ANSELM
Archbishop of Canterbury
[April 21.]

The Collect.

GOD, who hast enlightened thy Church by the teaching of thy servant Anselm: Enrich us evermore, we beseech thee, with thy heavenly grace, and raise up faithful witnesses who by their life and doctrine will set forth the truth of thy salvation; through Jesus Christ our Lord. *Amen.*

> *The Epistle.* Romans 1:16-20a.
> *The Gospel.* St. John 7:16-18; 8:1-2.

ATHANASIUS
Bishop of Alexandria
[May 2.]

The Collect.

ALMIGHTY, everlasting God, whose servant Athanasius steadfastly confessed the true faith of thy Son our Saviour Jesus Christ to be Very God and Very Man: Grant that we may hold fast to this faith, and evermore magnify his holy Name; through the same thy Son Jesus Christ our Lord, who liveth and reigneth with thee and the Holy Spirit ever, one God, world without end. *Amen.*

> *The Epistle.* 2 Corinthians 4:5-14.
> *The Gospel.* St. Matthew 10:23-32.

MONNICA
Mother of Augustine of Hippo
[May 4.]

The Collect.

ALMIGHTY and everlasting God, who didst enkindle the flame of thy love in the heart of thy servant Monnica: Grant to us, thy humble servants, the same faith and power of love; that, as we rejoice in her triumph, we may profit by her example; through Jesus Christ our Lord. *Amen.*

JOHN OF DAMASCUS
Priest
[May 6.]

The Collect.

ALMIGHTY God, who hast enriched thy Church with the singular learning and holiness of thy servant John: Grant us to hold fast the true doctrine of thy Son our Saviour Jesus Christ, and to fashion our lives according to the same, to the glory of thy great Name and the benefit of thy holy Church; through the same Jesus Christ our Lord. *Amen.*

GREGORY OF NAZIANZUS
Bishop of Constantinople
[May 9.]

The Collect.

ALMIGHTY, everlasting God, whose servant Gregory steadfastly confessed the true faith of thy Son our Saviour Jesus Christ to be Very God and Very Man: Grant that we may hold fast to this faith, and evermore magnify his holy Name; through the same thy Son Jesus Christ our Lord, who liveth and reigneth with thee and the Holy Spirit ever, one God, world without end. *Amen.*

The Epistle. Wisdom 7:7b-14.
The Gospel. St. John 8:25-32.

CYRIL AND METHODIUS
Missionary Bishops to the Slavs
[May 11.]

The Collect.

ALMIGHTY and everlasting God, we thank thee for thy servants Cyril and Methodius, whom thou didst call to preach the Gospel to the Slavic people: Raise up, we pray thee, in this and every land, heralds and evangelists of thy kingdom, that thy Church may make known the unsearchable riches of Christ, and may increase with the increase of God; through the same thy Son Jesus Christ our Lord. *Amen.*

DUNSTAN
Archbishop of Canterbury
[May 19.]

The Collect.

O GOD, who dost ever hallow and protect thy Church: Raise up therein through thy Spirit good and faithful stewards of the mysteries of Christ, as thou didst in thy servant Dunstan; that by their ministry and example thy people may abide in thy favour and walk in the way of truth; through Jesus Christ our Lord, who liveth and reigneth with thee in the unity of the same Spirit ever, one God, world without end. *Amen.*

ALCUIN
Deacon, and Abbot of Tours
[May 20.]

The Collect.

O ETERNAL Lord God, who holdest all souls in life: We beseech thee to shed forth upon thy whole Church in paradise and on earth the bright beams of thy light and thy peace; and grant that we, following the good examples of thy servant Alcuin, and of all those who loved and served thee here, may at the last enter with them into thine unending joy; through Jesus Christ our Lord. *Amen.*

JACKSON KEMPER
First Missionary Bishop in the United States
[May 24.]

The Collect.

ALMIGHTY and everlasting God, we thank thee for thy servant Jackson Kemper, whom thou didst call to preach the Gospel in this our land: Raise up, we pray thee, in every land, heralds and evangelists of thy kingdom, that thy Church may make known the unsearchable riches of Christ, and may increase with the increase of God; through the same thy Son Jesus Christ our Lord. *Amen.*

AUGUSTINE
First Archbishop of Canterbury
[May 26.]

The Collect.

ALMIGHTY God, who in thy providence didst choose thy servant Augustine to be an apostle to the people of England, to bring those who were wandering in darkness and error to the true light and knowledge of thee: Grant us so to walk in that light, that we may come at last to the light of everlasting life; through the merits of Jesus Christ thy Son our Lord. *Amen.*

The Epistle. 2 Corinthians 5:17-20.
The Gospel. St. Matthew 13:31-33.

BEDE THE VENERABLE
Priest and Monk of Jarrow
[May 27.]

The Collect.

ALMIGHTY God, who hast enriched thy Church with the singular learning and holiness of thy servant Bede: Grant us to hold fast the true doctrine of thy Son our Saviour Jesus Christ, and to fashion our lives according to the same, to the glory of thy great Name and the benefit of thy holy Church; through the same Jesus Christ our Lord. *Amen.*

The Epistle. Malachi 3:16-18.
The Gospel. St. Matthew 13:47-52.

THE MARTYRS OF LYONS
[June 2.]

The Collect.

ALMIGHTY and everlasting God, with whom thy meek ones go forth as the mighty: Grant us so to cherish the memory of thy blessed martyrs Blandina and her companions, that we may share their pure and steadfast faith in thee; through Jesus Christ our Lord. *Amen.*

The Epistle. 1 Peter 1:3-9.
The Gospel. St. Matthew 16:24-27.

BONIFACE
Archbishop of Mainz, Missionary to Germany and Martyr
[June 5.]

The Collect.

ALMIGHTY God, who didst call thy faithful servant Boniface to be a witness and martyr in the land of Germany, and by his labours and suffering didst raise up a people for thine own possession: Shed forth, we beseech thee, thy Holy Spirit upon thy Church in all lands, that by the sacrifice and service of many, thy holy Name may be glorified and thy blessed kingdom enlarged; through Jesus Christ our Lord, who liveth and reigneth with thee in the unity of the same Spirit ever, one God, world without end. *Amen.*

>*The Epistle.* Acts 20:18b-27.
>*The Gospel.* St. Matthew 28:18-20.

THE FIRST BOOK OF COMMON PRAYER
[June 9]

The Collect.

ALMIGHTY and everliving God, who didst guide thy servant Thomas Cranmer, with others, to render the worship of thy Church in a language understanded of the people: Make us ever thankful for this our heritage, and help us so to pray in the Spirit and with the understanding also, that we may worthily magnify thy holy Name; through Jesus Christ our Lord, who liveth and reigneth with thee and the same Holy Spirit ever, one God, world without end. *Amen.*

>*The Epistle.* Acts 2:38-42.
>*The Gospel.* St. Matthew 6:5-15.

COLUMBA
Abbot of Iona
[June 10.]

The Collect.

ALMIGHTY God, who in thy providence didst choose thy servant Columba to be an apostle to the people of Scotland, to bring those who were wandering in darkness and error to the true light and knowledge of thee: Grant us so to walk in that light, that we may come at last to the light of everlasting life; through the merits of Jesus Christ thy Son our Lord. *Amen.*

BASIL THE GREAT
Bishop of Caesarea
[June 14.]

The Collect.

ALMIGHTY, everlasting God, whose servant Basil steadfastly confessed the true faith of thy Son our Saviour Jesus Christ to be Very God and Very Man: Grant that we may hold fast to this faith, and evermore magnify his holy Name; through the same thy Son Jesus Christ our Lord, who liveth and reigneth with thee and the Holy Spirit ever, one God, world without end. *Amen.*

The Epistle. 1 Corinthians 6:2-15a.
The Gospel. St. Luke 10:22-24.

JOSEPH BUTLER
Bishop of Durham
[June 16.]

The Collect.

O GOD, who hast enlightened thy Church by the teaching of thy servant Joseph Butler: Enrich us evermore, we beseech thee, with thy heavenly grace, and raise up faithful witnesses who by their life and doctrine will set forth the truth of thy salvation; through Jesus Christ our Lord. *Amen.*

EPHREM OF EDESSA
Deacon
[June 18.]

The Collect.

ALMIGHTY God, who hast enriched thy Church with the singular learning and holiness of thy Deacon Ephrem: Grant us to hold fast the true doctrine of thy Son our Saviour Jesus Christ, and to fashion our lives according to the same, to the glory of thy great Name and the benefit of thy holy Church; through the same Jesus Christ our Lord. *Amen.*

ALBAN First Martyr of Britain
[June 22.]

The Collect.

ALMIGHTY God, by whose grace and power thy holy martyr Alban triumphed over suffering, and despised death: Grant, we beseech thee, that enduring hardness, and waxing valiant in fight, we may with the noble army of martyrs receive the crown of everlasting life; through Jesus Christ our Lord. *Amen.*

The Epistle. 1 John 3:13-16.
The Gospel. St. Matthew 10:34-42.

IRENAEUS Bishop of Lyons
[June 28.]

The Collect.

ALMIGHTY God, who didst uphold thy servant Irenaeus with strength to maintain the truth against every wind of vain doctrine: We beseech thee to keep us steadfast in thy true religion, that we may walk in constancy and in peace the way that leadeth to eternal life; through Jesus Christ our Lord. *Amen.*

The Epistle. Malachi 2:5-7.
The Gospel. St. Luke 11:33-36.

THE VISITATION OF THE BLESSED VIRGIN MARY
[July 2.]

The Collect.

O CHRIST, our God Incarnate, whose virgin Mother was blessed in bearing thee, but still more blessed in keeping thy word: Grant us, who honour the exaltation of her lowliness, to follow the example of her devotion to thy will; who livest and reignest with the Father and the Holy Ghost ever, one God, world without end. *Amen.*

The Epistle. Zechariah 2:10-13.
The Gospel. St. Luke 1:39-56.

BENEDICT OF NURSIA
Abbot of Monte Cassino
[July 11.]

The Collect.

ALMIGHTY and everlasting God, we give thee thanks for the purity and strength with which thou didst endow thy servant Benedict; and we pray that by thy grace we may have a like power to hallow and conform our souls and bodies to the purpose of thy most holy will; through Jesus Christ our Lord. *Amen.*

The Epistle. Acts 2:44-47a.
The Gospel. St. Luke 14:26-33.

WILLIAM WHITE
Bishop of Pennsylvania
[July 17.]

The Collect.

O GOD, who dost ever hallow and protect thy Church: Raise up therein through thy Spirit good and faithful stewards of the mysteries of Christ, as thou didst in thy servant William White; that by their ministry and example thy people may abide in thy favour and walk in the way of truth; through Jesus Christ our Lord, who liveth and reigneth with thee in the unity of the same Spirit ever, one God, world without end. *Amen.*

SAINT MARY MAGDALENE
[July 22.]

The Collect.

ALMIGHTY God, whose blessed Son did sanctify Mary Magdalene, and called her to be a witness to his Resurrection: Mercifully grant that by thy grace we may be healed of all our infirmities, and alway serve thee in the power of his endless life; who with thee and the Holy Ghost liveth and reigneth, one God, world without end. *Amen.*

The Epistle. 2 Corinthians 5:14-18a.
The Gospel. St. John 20:1, 11-18.

THOMAS A KEMPIS
Priest
[July 26.]

The Collect.

O ETERNAL Lord God, who holdest all souls in life: We beseech thee to shed forth upon thy whole Church in paradise and on earth the bright beams of thy light and thy peace; and grant that we, following the good examples of thy servant Thomas, and of all those who loved and served thee here, may at the last enter with them into thine unending joy; through Jesus Christ our Lord. *Amen.*

WILLIAM REED HUNTINGTON
Priest
[July 27.]

The Collect.

ALMIGHTY and everlasting God, the source and perfection of all virtues, who didst inspire thy servant William Reed Huntington both to do what is right and to preach what is true: Grant that all ministers and stewards of thy mysteries may afford to thy faithful people, by word and example, the instruction which is of thy grace; through Jesus Christ our Lord. *Amen.*

WILLIAM WILBERFORCE
[July 29.]

The Collect.

LET thy continual mercy, O Lord, enkindle in thy Church the never-failing gift of charity, that following the example of thy servant William Wilberforce, we may have grace to defend the children of the poor, and maintain the cause of them that have no helper; for the sake of him who gave his life for us, thy Son our Saviour Jesus Christ. *Amen.*

DOMINIC Friar
[August 4.]

The Collect.

ALMIGHTY and everlasting God, we give thee thanks for the purity and strength with which thou didst endow thy servant Dominic; and we pray that by thy grace we may have a like power to hallow and conform our souls and bodies to the purpose of thy most holy will; through Jesus Christ our Lord. *Amen.*

LAURENCE
Deacon, and Martyr at Rome
[August 10.]

The Collect.

ALMIGHTY God, by whose grace and power thy holy Deacon and martyr Laurence triumphed over suffering, and despised death: Grant, we beseech thee, that enduring hardness, and waxing valiant in fight, we may with the noble army of martyrs receive the crown of everlasting life; through Jesus Christ our Lord. *Amen.*

HIPPOLYTUS
Bishop and Martyr
[August 13.]

The Collect.

O GOD, who hast enlightened thy Church by the teaching of thy servant Hippolytus: Enrich us evermore, we beseech thee, with thy heavenly grace, and raise up faithful witnesses who by their life and doctrine will set forth the truth of thy salvation; through Jesus Christ our Lord. *Amen.*

JEREMY TAYLOR
Bishop of Down, Connor and Dromore
[August 14.]

The Collect.

ALMIGHTY God, who hast enriched thy Church with the singular learning and holiness of thy servant Jeremy Taylor: Grant us to hold fast the true doctrine of thy Son our Saviour Jesus Christ, and to fashion our lives according to the same, to the glory of thy great Name and the benefit of thy holy Church; through the same Jesus Christ our Lord. *Amen.*

SAINT MARY THE VIRGIN
[August 15.]

The Collect.

O GOD, who on this day didst take to thyself the blessed Virgin Mary, mother of thine only Son: Grant that we who have been redeemed by his blood may share her glory in thine eternal kingdom; through the same Jesus Christ our Lord, who liveth and reigneth with thee and the Holy Ghost ever, one God, world without end. *Amen.*

> *The Epistle.* Isaiah 61:7c-11.
> *The Gospel.* St. Luke 1:46-55.

BERNARD
Abbot of Clairvaux
[August 20.]

The Collect.

ALMIGHTY and everlasting God, who didst enkindle the flame of thy love in the heart of thy servant Bernard: Grant to us, thy humble servants, the same faith and power of love; that, as we rejoice in his triumph, we may profit by his example; through Jesus Christ our Lord. *Amen.*

> *The Epistle.* Ecclesiasticus 39:1-10.
> *The Gospel.* St. John 15:7-11.

LOUIS
King of France
[August 25.]

The Collect.

O GOD, who didst call thy servant Louis to an earthly throne that he might advance thy heavenly kingdom, and didst endue him with zeal for thy Church and charity towards thy people: Mercifully grant that we who commemorate his example may be fruitful in good works, and attain to the glorious fellowship of thy saints; through Jesus Christ our Lord. *Amen.*

AUGUSTINE
Bishop of Hippo
[August 28.]

The Collect.

O LORD God, who art the light of the minds that know thee, the life of the souls that love thee, and the strength of the hearts that serve thee: Help us, after the example of thy servant Saint Augustine, so to know thee that we may truly love thee, so to love thee that we may fully serve thee, whom to serve is perfect freedom; through Jesus Christ our Lord. *Amen.*

The Epistle. Hebrews 12:22-24, 28-29.
The Gospel. St. John 17:1-8.

AIDAN
Bishop of Lindisfarne
[August 31.]

The Collect.

ALMIGHTY God, who in thy providence didst choose thy servant Aidan to be an apostle to the people of England, to bring those who were wandering in darkness and error to the true light and knowledge of thee: Grant us so to walk in that light, that we may come at last to the light of everlasting life; through the merits of Jesus Christ thy Son our Lord. *Amen.*

The Epistle. 1 Corinthians 9:16-23.
The Gospel. St. Matthew 19:27-30.

JOHN HENRY HOBART
Bishop of New York
[September 12.]

The Collect.

O GOD, who dost ever hallow and protect thy Church: Raise up therein through thy Spirit good and faithful stewards of the mysteries of Christ, as thou didst in thy servant John Henry Hobart; that by their ministry and example thy people may abide in thy favour and walk in the way of truth; through Jesus Christ our Lord who liveth and reigneth with thee in the unity of the same Spirit ever, one God, world without end. *Amen.*

CYPRIAN
Bishop of Carthage and Martyr
[September 13.]

The Collect.

ALMIGHTY God, who didst give thy servant Cyprian boldness to confess the Name of our Saviour Jesus Christ before the rulers of this world, and courage to die for this faith: Grant that we likewise may ever be ready to give a reason for the hope that is in us, and to suffer gladly for his sake; through the same Jesus Christ our Lord. *Amen.*

The Epistle. 1 Peter 5:1-4, 10-11.
The Gospel. St. John 10:11-16.

THE EXALTATION OF THE HOLY CROSS
[September 14.]

The Collect.

ALMIGHTY God, whose beloved Son for our sake willingly offered himself to endure the agony and shame of the Cross: Remove from us all cowardice of heart, and give us courage to take up our cross and bear it patiently in his service; through the same thy Son Jesus Christ our Lord, who liveth and reigneth with thee and the Holy Ghost ever, one God, world without end. *Amen.*

The Epistle. Philippians 2:5-11.
The Gospel. St. John 1 2:31-36a.

THEODORE OF TARSUS
Archbishop of Canterbury
[September 19.]

The Collect.

O GOD, who dost ever hallow and protect thy Church: Raise up therein through thy Spirit, good and faithful stewards of the mysteries of Christ, as thou didst in thy servant Theodore; that by their ministry and example thy people may abide in thy favour and walk in the way of truth; through Jesus Christ our Lord, who liveth and reigneth with thee in the unity of the same Spirit, one God, world without end. *Amen.*

The Epistle. 2 Timothy 2:1-5, 10.
The Gospel. St. Matthew 24:42-47.

JOHN COLERIDGE PATTESON

Bishop of Melanesia and Martyr,
[September 20.]

The Collect.

ALMIGHTY God, who didst call thy faithful servant John Coleridge Patteson to be a witness and martyr in the isles of Melanesia, and by his labours and suffering didst raise up a people for thine own possession: Shed forth, we beseech thee, thy Holy Spirit upon thy Church in all lands, that by the sacrifice and service of many, thy holy Name may be glorified and thy blessed kingdom enlarged; through Jesus Christ our Lord, who liveth and reigneth with thee and the same Holy Spirit ever, one God, world without end. *Amen.*

SERGIUS

Abbot [September 25.]

The Collect.

ALMIGHTY and everlasting God, we give thee thanks for the purity and strength with which thou didst endow thy servant Sergius; and we pray that by thy grace we may have a like power to hallow and conform our souls and bodies, to the purpose of thy most holy will: through Jesus Christ our Lord. *Amen.*

LANCELOT ANDREWES

Bishop of Winchester
[September 26.]

The Collect.

ETERNAL Lord God, who holdest all souls in life: We beseech thee to shed forth upon thy whole Church in paradise and on earth the bright beams of thy light and thy peace; and grant that we, following the good examples of thy servant Lancelot Andrewes, and of all those who loved and served thee here, may at the last enter with them into thine unending joy; through Jesus Christ our Lord. *Amen.*

JEROME

Priest, and Monk of Bethlehem
[September 30.]

The Collect.

O GOD, who hast given us the holy Scriptures for a light to shine upon our path: Grant us, after the example of thy servant Jerome, so to learn of thee and of thy truth according to that Word, that we may find in it the light that shineth more and more unto the perfect day; through Jesus Christ our Lord. *Amen.*

> *The Epistle.* Nehemiah 8:1-3, 5-6, 8-9.
> *The Gospel.* St. Luke 24:44-48.

FRANCIS OF ASSISI

Friar
[October 4.]

The Collect.

MOST high, almighty, and good Lord: Grant thy people grace to renounce gladly the vanities of this world, that, after the example of blessed Francis, we may for love of thee delight in all thy creatures, with perfectness of joy; through Jesus Christ our Lord. *Amen.*

> *The Epistle.* Galatians 6:14-18.
> *The Gospel.* St. Matthew 11:25-30.

WILLIAM TYNDALE

Priest and Martyr
[October 6.]

The Collect.

ACCEPT, O Lord, our thanksgiving this day for thy servant William Tyndale; and grant unto us in like manner such constancy and zeal in thy service, that we may obtain with him and thy servants everywhere a good confession and the crown of everlasting life; through Jesus Christ our Lord. *Amen.*

SAMUEL ISAAC JOSEPH SCHERESCHEWSKY

Bishop of Shanghai
[October 15.]

The Collect.

ALMIGHTY God, who hast enriched thy Church with the singular learning and holiness of thy servant Samuel Isaac Joseph Schereschewsky: Grant us to hold fast the true doctrine of thy Son our Saviour Jesus Christ, and to fashion our lives according to the same, to the glory of thy great Name, and the benefit of thy holy Church; through the same Jesus Christ our Lord. *Amen.*

HUGH LATIMER AND NICHOLAS RIDLEY

Bishops and Martyrs
[October 16.]

The Collect.

ACCEPT, O Lord, our thanksgiving this day for thy servants Hugh Latimer and Nicholas Ridley; and grant unto us in like manner such constancy and zeal in thy service, that we may obtain with them and thy servants everywhere a good confession and the crown of everlasting life; through Jesus Christ our Lord. *Amen.*

ALFRED THE GREAT

King of England
[October 26.]

The Collect.

O GOD, who didst call thy servant Alfred to an earthly throne that he might advance thy heavenly kingdoms and didst endue him with zeal for thy Church and charity towards thy people: Mercifully grant that we who commemorate his example may be fruitful in good works, and attain to the glorious fellowship of thy saints; through Jesus Christ our Lord. *Amen.*

The Epistle. Wisdom 6:1-3, 9-12, 24-25.
The Gospel. St. Luke 6:43-45.

JAMES HANNINGTON AND HIS COMPANIONS

Bishop and Martyrs of Uganda
[October 29.]

The Collect.

ALMIGHTY God, who didst call thy faithful servants James Hannington and his companions to be witnesses and martyrs in the land of Africa, and by their labours and suffering didst raise up a people for thine own possession: Shed forth, we beseech thee, thy Holy Spirit upon thy Church in all lands, that by the sacrifice and service of many, thy holy Name may be glorified and thy blessed kingdom enlarged; through Jesus Christ our Lord, who liveth and reigneth with thee and the Holy Spirit ever, one God, world without end. *Amen.*

WILLIBRORD

Archbishop of Utrecht, Missionary to Frisia
[November 7.]

The Collect.

ALMIGHTY God, who in thy providence didst choose thy servant Willibrord to be an apostle to the Frisian people, to bring those who were wandering in darkness and error to the true light and knowledge of thee: Grant us so to walk in that light, that we may come at last to the light of everlasting life; through the merits of Jesus Christ thy Son our Lord. *Amen.*

MARTIN

Bishop of Tours
[November 11.]

The Collect.

O GOD, who by thy Holy Spirit didst enable thy servant Martin to withstand the temptations of the world, the flesh, and the devil: Grant that we, in the same Spirit, may with pure hearts and minds follow thee, the only God; through Jesus Christ our Lord. *Amen.*

The Epistle. Isaiah 58:10-12.
The Gospel. St. Matthew 25:34-40.

CHARLES SIMEON

Priest
[November 12.]

The Collect.

ETERNAL Lord God, who holdest all souls in life: We beseech thee to shed forth upon thy whole Church in paradise and on earth the bright beams of thy light and thy peace; and grant that we, following the good examples of thy servant Charles Simeon, and of all those who loved and served thee here, may at the last enter with them into thine unending joy; through Jesus Christ our Lord. *Amen.*

THE CONSECRATION OF SAMUEL SEABURY

First American Bishop
[November 14.]

The Collect.

ALMIGHTY GOD, who by thy divine providence hast appointed divers Orders of Ministers in thy Church, and by thy Son Jesus Christ didst give to thy holy Apostles many excellent gifts: Give grace, we beseech thee, to all Bishops of thy Church, and more especially to those who serve in that branch of the same planted by thee in this land; that, following the example of thy servant Samuel Seabury, they may diligently preach thy Word, and duly administer the godly Discipline thereof, to the glory of thy Name, and the edification of thy Church; through the same Jesus Christ our Lord. *Amen.*

The Epistle. Acts 20:28-32.
The Gospel. St. Matthew 9:35-38.

MARGARET

Queen of Scotland
[November 16.]

The Collect.

O GOD, who didst call thy servant Margaret to an earthly throne that she might advance thy heavenly kingdom, and didst endue her with zeal for thy Church and charity towards thy people: Mercifully grant that we who commemorate her example may be fruitful in good works, and attain to the glorious fellowship of thy saints; through Jesus Christ our Lord. *Amen.*

HILDA

Abbess of Whitby
[November 17.]

The Collect.

ALMIGHTY and everlasting God, we give thee thanks for the purity and strength with which thou didst endow thy servant Hilda; and we pray that by thy grace we may have a like power to hallow and conform our souls and bodies, to the purpose of thy most holy will; through Jesus Christ our Lord. *Amen.*

ELIZABETH

Princess of Hungary
[November 19.]

The Collect.

ALMIGHTY and everlasting God, who didst enkindle the flame of thy love in the heart of thy servant Elizabeth: Grant to us, thy humble servants, the same faith and power of love; that as we rejoice in her triumph, we may profit by her example; through Jesus Christ our Lord. *Amen.*

CLEMENT

Bishop of Rome
[November 23.]

The Collect.

O GOD, who hast enlightened thy Church by the teaching of thy servant Clement: Enrich us evermore, we beseech thee, with thy heavenly grace, and raise up faithful witnesses who by their life and doctrine will set forth the truth of thy salvation; through Jesus Christ our Lord. *Amen.*

A Saint's Day

> ¶ *The following Collects, Epistles, and Gospels may be used for the Patronal festival of a saint not listed in the Calendar, or for the commemoration of a Saint*

other than those for which provision is made in this Book, PROVIDED, that such commemoration is duly authorized by the Ordinary.

¶ *And NOTE, That no festival of a Saint shall be observed on a Sunday or Greater Holy Day, contrary to the Tables of Precedence as established in the Book of Common Prayer.*

The Collect.

ALMIGHTY God, who hast called us to faith in thee, and hast compassed us about with so great a cloud of witnesses: Grant that we, encouraged by the good examples of thy Saints, and especially of thy servant _____, may persevere in running the race that is set before us, until at length, through thy mercy, we with them attain to thine eternal joy; through him who is the author and finisher of our faith, thy Son Jesus Christ our Lord. *Amen.*

Or this,

ALMIGHTY and everlasting God, who didst strengthen thy servant (and blessed martyr) _____ with the virtue of constancy in faith and truth: Grant us in like manner for love of thee to despise the prosperity of this world, and to fear none of its adversities; through Jesus Christ our Lord. *Amen.*

Or this,

ALMIGHTY God, who willest to be glorified in thy Saints, and didst raise up thy servant _____ to shine as a light in the world: Shine, we pray thee, in our hearts, that we also in our generation may show forth thy praises, who hast called us out of darkness into thy marvellous light; through Jesus Christ our Lord. *Amen.*

Or this,

O God, who hast brought us near to an innumerable company of Angels, and to the spirits of just men made perfect: Grant us during our pilgrimage to abide in their fellowship, and in our Country to become partakers of their joy; through Jesus Christ our Lord. *Amen.*

The Epistle. Hebrews 12:1-2.

or

Philippians 4:4-9.

or

2 Esdras 2:42-48.

The Gospel. St. Matthew 25:31-40.

or

St. Luke 6:17-23a.

or

St. John 17:18-23.

Indices

Movable Days: Epistles and Gospels

Editor's Note: In this table, brackets indicate no change from the 1928 Prayer Book.

Day	Epistle	Gospel
ADVENT III		
Ember Wednesday	1 Cor. 3:5-11	John 4:31-38
Ember Friday	1 Pet. 4:7-11	Luke 12:25-44
Ember Saturday	1 Tim. 1:12-17	Matt. 16:24-27
LENT		
Friday after Ash Wednesday	Isa. 58:1-12	Matt. 5:43-6:8
LENT I	[2 Cor. 6:1-10]	[Matt. 4:1-11]
Ember Wednesday	Exod. 24:12-18	Matt. 20:17-28
Ember Friday	1 Kings 19:1-8	Matt. 21:33-44
Ember Saturday	2 Cor. 3:4-18	Luke 9:28-36
LENT II	Jer. 2:4-13	John 4:5-26
Wednesday	1 Thess. 4 : 1-7	Matt. 15:10-28
Friday	Num. 20:1-13	Luke 11:14-28
LENT III	[Eph. 5:1-14]	John 5:1-16
Wednesday	2 Sam. 12:1-14	John 8:12, 28-36
Friday	1 Kings 21:1-20	John 8:46-59
LENT IV	Isa. 55:1-11	[John 6:1-14]
Wednesday	Jer. 31:31-34	John 9:1-38

Day	Epistle	Gospel
Friday	Ezek. 34:11-16	John 10:17-31
LENT V	[Heb. 9:11-15]	John 11:1-46
Wednesday	Isa. 49:1-6	John 11:47-54
Friday	Isa. 50:5-10	John 12:23-32
PALM SUNDAY	[Phil. 2:5-11]	[Matt. 27:1-54]
Monday	Isa. 63:7-64:12	John 12:1-11
Tuesday	Isa. 52:13-53:12	[Mark 15:1-39]
Wednesday	[Heb. 9:16-28]	Luke 23:1-49
Maundy Thursday	[1 Cor. 11:17-34]	John 13:1-17
Good Friday	[Heb 10:1-25]	[John 19:1-37]
Easter Even	[1 Pet. 3:17-22]	[Matt. 27:57-66]
EASTER DAY		
First celebration	Col. 3:1-4	[John 20:1-10]
Second celebration	Phil. 3:7-14	Matt. 28:1-10
EASTER WEEK		
Monday	[Acts 10:34-43]	[Luke 24:13-35]
Tuesday	[Acts 13:26-41]	[Luke 24:36-48]
Wednesday	Acts 3:13-15,17-19,26	John 21:1-14
Thursday	Col. 1:18-23a	Luke 24:1-12
Friday	Col. 2:10-15	John 20:1-10
Saturday	1 Pet. 1:3-4,15-21	John 20:11-18
EASTER I	[1 John 5:4-12]	John 20:19-29
ROGATION DAYS		
Monday	[Eze. 34:25-31]	[Luke 11:5-13]
Tuesday	Joel 2:21-27	Mark 11:22-26
Wednesday	Micah 6:6-8	Matt. 6:5-8
WHITSUN WEEK		
Ember Wednesday	2 Cor. 3:17-4:6	Luke 4:16-21
Thursday	Rom. 8:1-11	John 16:12-15
Ember Friday	Tit. 3:4-8	Matt. 28:16-20
Ember Saturday	Eph. 2:13-23	John 20:19-23
AUTUMN EMBER DAYS		
Wednesday	Eph. 4:11-16	John 15:1-8

Day	Epistle	Gospel
Friday	Acts 13:44-49	Matt. 10:24-32
Saturday	Acts 20:28-32	John 10:1-11

Immovable Days: Epistles and Gospels

(In Chronological Order)

Dec. 4	Clement of Alexandria	2 Pet. 1:2-8	John 6:57-63
Jan. 1	Holy Name	[Phil. 2:9-13]	[Luke 2:15-21]
Jan. 14	Hilary	2 Tim. 4:1-8	Luke 12:8-12
Jan. 17	Antony	Phil. 3:7-14	Luke 12:32-34
Jan. 24	Timothy	2 Tim. 1:1-7	John 10:7-10
Jan. 26	Polycarp	Rev. 2:8-11	Matt. 20:20-23
Jan. 27	John Chrysostom	Jer. 1:6-9	Luke 21:12b-15
Feb. 1	Ignatius	Rom. 8:35-39	John 12:24-26
Feb. 4	Cornelius	Acts 11:1-18	John 4:4-14
Feb. 6	Titus	Tit. 1:1-5	John 10:1-5
Mar. 1	David	Eph. 2:4-10	Mark 4:26-29
Mar. 7	Perpetua and her Companions	Heb. 10:32-39	Matt. 24:9-14a
Mar. 12	Gregory the Great	Ecclus. 47:8-11	Mark 10:42-45
Mar. 17	Patrick	1 Thess. 2:2b-12	Matt. 5:43-48
Mar. 19	Joseph	Isa. 63:7-9,16	Matt. 1:18-25
Apr. 4	Ambrose	Ecclus. 2:7-11,16-18	Luke 12:42-44
Apr. 11	Leo the Great	2 Tim. 1:12b-14	Matt. 5:13-19
Apr. 14	Justin Martyr	1 Pet. 3:14-18, 22	John 12:44-50
Apr. 21	Anselm	Rom. 1:16-20a	John 7:16-18, 8:12
May 2	Athanasius	2 Cor. 4:5-14	Matt. 10:23-32
May 9	Gregory Nazianzen	Wis. 7:7b-14	John 8:25-32
May 26	Augustine of Canterbury	2 Cor. 5:17-20	Matt. 13:31-33
May 27	Bede the Venerable	Mal. 3:16-18	Matt. 13:47-52
June 2	Martyrs of Lyons	1 Pet. 1:3-9	Matt. 16:24-27
June 5	Boniface	Acts 20:18b-27	Matt. 28:18-20

June 9	First Prayer Book	Acts 2:38-42	Matt. 6:5-15
June 14	Basil the Great	1 Cor. 6:2-15a	Luke 11:22-24
June 22	Alban	1 John 3:13-16	Matt. 10:34-42
June 28	Irenaeus	Mal. 2:5-7	Luke 11:33-36
June 29	Peter and Paul	Gal. 2:1-2, 7-10	[Matt. 16:13-19]
July 2	Visitation B.V.M.	Zech. 2:10-13	Luke 1:39-56
July 11	Benedict	Acts 2:44-47a	Luke 14:26-33
July 22	Mary Magdalene	2 Cor. 5:14-18a	John 20:1, 11-18
Aug. 15	St. Mary the Virgin	Isa. 61:7c-11	Luke 1:46-55
Aug. 20	Bernard	Ecclus. 39:1-10	John 15:7-11
Aug. 28	Augustine of Hippo	Heb. 12:22-24, 28-29	John 17:1-8
Aug. 31	Aidan	1 Cor. 9:16-23	Matt. 19:27-30
Sept. 13	Cyprian	1 Pet. 5:1-4, 10-11	John 10:11-16
Sept. 14	Holy Cross	Phil. 2:5-11	John 12:31-36a
Sept. 19	Theodore of Tarsus	2 Tim. 2:1-5, 10	Matt. 24:42-47
Sept. 30	Jerome	Neh. 8:1-3, 5-6, 8-9	Luke 24:44-48
Oct. 4	Francis of Assisi	Gal. 6:14-18	Matt. 55:25-30
Oct. 26	Alfred the Great	Wis. 6:5-3, 9-12, 24-25	Luke 6:43-45
Nov. 11	Martin	Isa. 58:10-12	Matt. 25:34-40
Nov. 14	Consecration of Samuel Seabury	Acts 20:28-32	Matt. 9:35-38

Interim Epistles and Gospels Proposed for the Week Days of Lent

(Subject to due canonical legislation by the General Convention, and authorization of the Ordinary, the following schedule is offered for optional use, as a supplement to the present lections provided by the Prayer Book.)

Day	Epistle	Gospel
Friday after Ash Wednesday	Isa. 58:1-12	Matt. 5:43-6:8
Lent I		
Wednesday (Ember Day)	Ex. 24:12-18	Matt. 20:17-28
Friday (Ember Day)	1 Kgs. 19:1-8	Matt. 21:33-44
Saturday (Ember Day)	2 Cor. 3:4-18	Luke 9:28-36
Lent II		

Day	Epistle	Gospel
Wednesday	Jer. 2:4-13	John 4:5-26
Friday	Num. 20:1-13	John 5:1-16
Lent III		
Wednesday	2 Sam. 12:1-14	John 8:12, 28-36
Friday	1 Kgs. 21:1-20	John 7:14-18, 25-30
Lent IV		
Wednesday	Jer. 35:35-34	John 9:1-38
Friday	Ezek. 34:11-16	John 10:17-31
Lent V		
Wednesday	Isa. 50:5-10	John 11:1-46
Friday	Isa. 52:13-53:12	John 12:23-32

Immovable Days

(In Alphabetical Order)

Feast	Date	Pages
Agnes	(Jan. 21)	48, 127
Aidan	(Aug. 31)	148, 161
Alban	(June 22)	49, 143
Alcuin	(May 20)	54, 161
Alfred the Great	(Oct. 26)	51, 152
Ambrose	(Apr. 4)	52, 135
Lancelot Andrewes	(Sept. 26)	54, 150
Anselm	(Apr. 21)	53, 137
Ansgarius	(Feb. 3)	50, 130
Antony	(Jan. 17)	53, 127
Athanasius	(May 2)	52, 137
Augustine of Canterbury	(May 26)	51, 139
Augustine of Hippo	(Aug. 28)	46, 148
Basil the Great	(June 14)	52, 142
Bede the Venerable	(May 27)	52, 140
Benedict	(July 11)	55, 144

Feast	Date	Pages
Bernard	(Aug. 20)	55, 147
Boniface	(June 5)	49, 141
Book of Common Prayer, First	(June 9)	44, 141
Thomas Bray	(Feb. 15)	54, 131
Phillips Brooks	(Jan. 23)	54, 128
Joseph Butler	(June 16)	53, 142
Clement of Alexandria	(Dec. 4)	53, 126
Clement of Rome	(Nov. 23)	53, 155
Columba	(June 10)	51, 141
Cornelius the Centurion	(Feb. 4)	43, 130
Cyprian	(Sept. 13)	49, 149
Cyril and Methodius	(May 11)	50, 138
David	(Mar. 1)	51, 131
Dominic	(Aug. 4)	55, 145
Dunstan	(May 19)	54, 139
Elizabeth of Hungary	(Nov. 19)	55, 155
Ephrem	(June 18)	52, 142
Francis of Assisi	(Oct. 4)	47, 151
Gregory of Nazianzus	(May 9)	52, 138
Gregory the Great	(Mar. 12)	43, 132
Gregory the Illuminator	(Mar. 23)	50, 134
James Hannington and Companions	(Oct. 29)	49, 153
George Herbert	(Feb. 27)	54, 131
Hilary	(Jan. 14)	51, 127
Hilda	(Nov. 17)	55, 155
Hippolytus	(Aug. 13)	53, 146
John Henry Hobart	(Sept. 12)	54, 148
Exaltation of Holy Cross	(Sept. 14)	46, 149
Holy Name	(Jan. 1)	41, 125
William Reed Huntington	(July 27)	54, 145

The Propers for the Minor Holy Days 163

Feast	Date	Pages
Ignatius	(Feb. 1)	49, 129
Irenaeus	(June 28)	45, 143
Jerome	(Sept. 30)	47, 151
John Chrysostom	(Jan. 27)	52, 129
John of Damascus	(May 6)	52, 138
Joseph	(Mar. 19)	44, 133
Justin Martyr	(Apr. 13)	49, 136
John Keble	(Mar. 29)	54, 134
Jackson Kemper	(May 24)	50, 139
Thomas Ken	(Mar. 20)	55, 133
Hugh Latimer	(Oct. 16)	50, 152
William Laud	(Jan. 10)	50, 126
Laurence	(Aug. 10)	49, 146
William Law	(Apr. 6)	55, 135
Leo the Great	(Apr. 11)	52, 136
Louis	(Aug. 25)	51, 147
Margaret	(Nov. 16)	51, 154
Martin	(Nov. 11)	53, 153
Martyrs of Lyons	(June 2)	48, 140
Saint Mary The Virgin	(Aug. 15)	46, 147
Mary Magdalene	(July 22)	45, 144
John Frederick Denison Maurice	(Apr. 1)	55, 134
Monnica	(May 4)	55, 137
William Augustus Muhlenberg	(Apr. 8)	55, 135
Nicholas	(Dec. 6)	55, 126
Patrick	(Mar. 17)	51, 133
John Coleridge Patteson	(Sept. 20)	49, 150
Perpetua and Companions	(Mar. 7)	48, 132
Peter and Paul	(June 29)	41, 125
Polycarp	(Jan. 26)	49, 129

Feast	Date	Pages
Nicholas Ridley	(Oct. 16)	50, 152
Samuel Isaac Joseph Schereschewsky	(Oct. 15)	52, 152
Consecration of Samuel Seabury	(Nov. 14)	48, 154
George Augustus Selwyn	(Apr. 12)	50, 136
Sergius	(Sept. 25)	55, 150
Charles Simeon	(Nov. 12)	54, 154
Jeremy Taylor	(Aug. 14)	52, 146
Theodore of Tarsus	(Sept. 19)	54, 149
Thomas a Kempis	(July 26)	54, 145
Thomas Aquinas	(Mar. 8)	52, 132
Timothy	(Jan. 24)	42, 128
Titus	(Feb. 6)	43, 130
William Tyndale	(Oct. 6)	50, 151
Vincent	(Jan. 22)	49, 128
Visitation of the Blessed Virgin Mary	(July 2)	45, 143
William White	(July 17)	54, 144
William Wilberforce	(July 29)	55, 145
Channing Moore Williams	(Dec. 2)	50, 126
Willibrord	(Nov. 7)	51, 153

PRAYER BOOK STUDIES XIII: THE ORDER FOR THE BURIAL OF THE DEAD

The Standing Liturgical Commission
of the Protestant Episcopal Church in the
United States of America

1959

PREFACE

The last revision of our Prayer Book was brought to a rather abrupt conclusion in 1928. Consideration of it had preoccupied the time of General Convention ever since 1913. Everyone was weary of the long and ponderous legislative process, and desired to make the new Prayer Book available as soon as possible for the use of the Church.

But the work of revision, which sometimes has seemed difficult to start, in this case proved hard to stop. The years of debate had aroused widespread interest in the whole subject: and the mind of the Church was more receptive of suggestions for revision when the work was brought to an end than when it began. Moreover, the revision was actually closed to new action in 1925, in order that it might receive final adoption in 1928: so that it was not possible to give due consideration to a number of very desirable features in the English and Scottish revisions, which appeared simultaneously with our own. It was further realized that there were some rough edges in what had been done, as well as an unsatisfied demand for still further alterations.

The problem of defects in detail was met by continuing the Revision Commission, and giving it rather large 'editorial' powers (subject only to review by General Convention) to correct obvious errors in the text as adopted, in the publication of the new Prayer Book. Then, to deal with the constructive proposals for other changes which continued to be brought up in every General Convention, the Revision Commission was reconstituted as a Standing Liturgical Commission. To this body all matters concerning the Prayer Book were to be referred, for preservation in permanent files, and for continuing consideration, until such time as the accumulated matter was sufficient in amount and importance to justify proposing another Revision.

The number of such referrals by General Convention, of Memorials from Dioceses, and of suggestions made directly to the Commission from all regions and schools and parties in the Church, has now reached such a total that it is evident that there is a widespread and insistent demand for a general revision of the Prayer Book.

The Standing Liturgical Commission is not, however, proposing any immediate revision. On the contrary, we believe that there ought to be a period of study and discussion, to acquaint the Church at large with the principles and issues involved, in order that the eventual action may be taken intelligently, and if possible without consuming so much of the time of our supreme legislative synod.

Accordingly, the General Convention of 1949 signalized the Fourth Centennial Year of the First Book of Common Prayer in English by authorizing the Liturgical Commission to publish its findings, in the form of a series of *Prayer Book Studies*.

It must be emphasized that the liturgical forms presented in these *Studies* are not — and under our Constitution, cannot be — sanctioned for public use. They are submitted for free discussion. The Commission will be grateful for copies or articles, resolutions, and direct comment, for its consideration, that the mind of the Church may be fully known to the body charged with reporting it.

In this undertaking, we have endeavored to be objective and impartial. It is not possible to avoid every matter which may be thought by some to be controversial. Ideas which seem to be constructively valuable will be brought to the attention of the Church, without too much regard as to whether they may ultimately be judged to be expedient. We cannot undertake to eliminate every proposal to which anyone might conceivably object: to do so would be to admit that any constructive progress is impossible. What we can do is to be alert not to alter the present *balance* of expressed or implied doctrine of the Church. We can seek to counterbalance every proposal which might seem to favor some one party of opinion by some other change in the opposite direction. The goal we have constantly had in mind — however imperfectly we may have succeeded in attaining it — is the shaping of a future Prayer Book which *every* party might embrace with the well-founded conviction that therein its own position had been strengthened, its witness enhanced, and its devotions enriched.

The objective we have pursued is the same as that expressed by the Commission for the Revision of 1892: "*Resolved*, That this Committee, in all its suggestions and acts, be guided by those principles of liturgical construction and ritual use which have guided the compilation and amendments of the Book of Common Prayer, and have made it what it is."

THE STANDING LITURGICAL COMMISSION:

GOODRICH R. FENNER, *Chairman*
ALBERT R. STUART
JOHN W. SUTER, *Custodian*
MASSEY H. SHEPHERD, JR., *Vice Chairman*
CHARLES W. F. SMITH
FRANCIS B. SAYRE, JR.
BERTRAM L. SMITH
SPENCER ERVIN, *Secretary*
JOHN W. ASHTON
FRANK STEPHEN CELLIER

The sub-committee for drafting the Study on the Burial Office has been in charge of Dr. Ashton. The Commission gratefully records the assistance, in preparing the first materials of this Study, of the late Reverend Dr. Bayard H. Jones.

MASSEY H. SHEPHERD, JR.
Editor, for the Commission.

General Comments

From very early times the Church has provided a service for the dead. Over the course of the centuries, however, the nature and intent of the service have changed in accord with changing concepts of the nature of death to the Christian. In the early days the dominant note was joy at the release of the soul from the vicissitude of the earth and its attaining to full happiness in heaven. With the development of the doctrine of Purgatory in the Middle Ages the emphasis changed to prayers for the release of the soul from punishment. In turn, in the Prayer Book of 1549 — since the doctrine of Purgatory was rejected — there was a return to the early sense of rejoicing, and at the same time a considerable shortening of the service, which had become crowded with prayers, processions, selections from Scripture, etc., over the course of centuries.

It was further shortened in the 1552 Book by combining the services in the church and at the grave, and by omitting the Psalms and the Requiem. Indicative of the state of the theological discussion was the exclusion of any passages in the prayers that might be construed as intercession for the departed, and hence suggestive of a belief in Purgatory. It was not until the revisions of the 1920's that this last was restored. The 1662 Book had already restored the Psalms, and the distinction of services in the church and at the grave.

The present study for revision presents no radical changes in the text of the Office, but attempts to clarify and make more effective certain parts by some rearrangement and by a few additions and small deletions. In its totality it attempts to provide appropriately for the departed, for the bereaved, and for the total congregation. We have tried to follow the principle that the Office should be designed for the comfort of the living rather than for the benefit of the dead. The revisions proposed also take into account the needs recognized from pastoral experience. Since often many of those attending burial services are not Christians, it is important that a proper concept of the nature of life and death be inculcated. We have also attempted to revise such passages as have been misinterpreted by the laity, such as references to the angels in the Office for a Child, where experience has shown that this has sometimes been understood as meaning that the children become angels.

The Revisions

The initial rubrics reflect the concern of the Commission with the tendency sometimes found to secularize the Burial service and to focus attention on the body of the departed. It is hoped that frequent admonitions from the Minister may counteract the suggestions of undertakers that the service be held in funeral parlors or elsewhere than in the church. The closing of the coffin and the use of only a pall (which is preferred) or "some other proper covering" is designed to diminish a curious or morbid or sentimental concern with the body. The use of a pall is also designed to prevent the use of flowers or other inappropriate covering.

Of the Sentences, the present third one (from Job 1:21) has been omitted as being essentially negative in its statement and is replaced by two: one from Romans 14:7-8, the second a revision of the committal anthem (Rev. 14:13) on page 333 of the Prayer Book.

The Psalms have been rearranged in numerical order as a matter of simple logic, and Psalm 23 has been added to the group as one obviously appropriate to such a service and occasion.

In the Lessons, the only significant change is the deletion of the last three sentences in the first paragraph of the selection from 1 Corinthians, on the grounds that it is likely to be confusing to the laity and it is not pertinent to the occasion. The verse numbers have been omitted from the selections, since they are misleading. A minor alteration in the King James translation of the lesson from Romans has been made to improve the sense.

To make clear the limits of choice of the Minister, the rubric immediately following the Lessons has been broken into two: one providing for a hymn or anthem and the discretionary saying of the Creed; the second requiring the Sentences, Lord's Prayer, and the prayers following. The Thanksgiving is moved from the service at the grave, and a choice of forms is offered. This seems to the Commission a more appropriate place for a thanksgiving than is the grave-side. It serves also to shorten the service at the grave, often necessary in inclement weather.

At the Grave

In addition to the verses which serve as an introduction here, we suggest the inclusion of verses 13-17 of Psalm 103. They strike a most felicitous note of faith and comfort not quite provided by the other two selections.

The phrase "by some standing by" is omitted from the following rubric as unnecessary. In the committal prayer, the phrase "the soul of" has been omitted, as implying a division of the soul and the body. Likewise, in the prayer following the Lord's Prayer, the same phrase is omitted. Similarly, the phrase in the committal prayer, "the earth and the sea shall give up their dead," is omitted, since to some it implies the resurrection of the earthly, physical body.

The transfer of the revised anthem to the beginning of the service has already been noted. Provision is made here, by revision of the rubric, for the omission of the Versicles, the Lord's Prayer, and the prayer beginning "O God, whose mercies cannot be numbered," if a Requiem has been said at the church.

The prayers that follow represent an attempt to broaden the base of comfort and faith offered to the mourners. The suggested additions are offered out of the experience of pastoral needs. The first of the additions, "Almighty and everlasting God," etc., is an old Roman Collect *Pro vivis et defunctis* with Bishop Lancelot Andrewes' ending (see F. E. Brightman's edition of the *Preces Privatae*, page 273). The text, "O Father of all," etc., is taken from the English 1928 Prayer Book, and occurs also in the Scottish and Indian Books. The third prayer, "O God, whose days are without end," is Jeremy Taylor's, and transferred here from its place in the Visitation of the Sick (Prayer Book, pages 316-17). "Grant, O Lord, to all who are bereaved," etc. is drawn from the Irish Prayer Book (and also occurs in the new Indian Book), but we have made a slight alteration in the ending. Finally, the prayer, "O heavenly Father," etc., is a slightly altered form of a prayer occurring in the English 1928, the South African, and the Indian Prayer Books. Before the Benediction, the versicle and response, long familiar in supplications for the dead, are inserted as being appropriate.

All these prayers are placed before the Benediction in order that they may be convenient for the Minister and duly recognized as part of the service. The Commission feels strongly that the addition of prayers not provided by the Prayer Book in this way, or of passages from literature, either great, or as often happens inferior, not only is often sentimental and in poor taste, but is likely to be theologically unsound.

In keeping with the feeling that pertinent services should be together in the Prayer Book, we have moved the Collect, Epistle and Gospel from their present position on pages 268-69, to follow immediately after the prayer for the Burial of the Dead at Sea. In like manner, after the service for the Burial of a Child, we have supplied Propers for a Communion if it is desired.

At the Burial of a Child

The same principles have been followed in revising this service as for the preceding one. Only relatively slight changes are suggested. One has already been mentioned — the omission of the last sentence in the Lesson to avoid the mistaken interpretation sometimes given to the passage, that the souls of children become angels. The first prayer after the Lord's Prayer is a revision of the first in the present Office; the second is brought forward from the prayers at the grave. A new Blessing is provided from page 332 of the Prayer Book. A new prayer, "O Father of all," etc., replaces the one moved forward; we have noted its source in the English 1928 Prayer Book.

Since the Collect and Epistle for an adult are not appropriate for a child, we have used as Collect the prayer presently in the body of the service (page 340), and supplied as Epistle the passage from 1 John 2:28 ff. The Propers are put with the service for the convenience of both Minister and people.

One or two general comments may be added. From time to time it is suggested that a special form of the Office be provided for a service of cremation. It is the considered judgment of the Commission that the present service is completely adequate to such a situation and that no special provision need be made.

It has also been suggested from time to time that since burial is not always in consecrated ground, there should be some provision for blessing the grave. The tradition of the Prayer Book is one of blessing persons, not blessing things, except in Baptism and the Eucharist. A form for blessing a grave might better appear in the supplemental Book of Offices for Special Occasions.

Finally, the Commission feels strongly that departures from the service by the inclusion of extraneous materials are neither wise nor justifiable. The present draft attempts through Psalms and prayers to make provision for those ideas essential to the purposes of the service outlined at the beginning of this Introduction. Suggestions as to omissions or as to supplements will be welcomed by the Commission. But we believe that the free and easy departure from the stated service so often heard should be discouraged.

The Order for the Burial of the Dead

¶ The Minister shall from time to time advise the people that members of the Church are properly buried from the Church, except for urgent cause.

¶ Before the service begins, the coffin shall be closed and covered with a pall or some other proper covering.

¶ The Minister, meeting the Body, and going before it, either into the Church or towards the Grave, shall say or sing,

I AM the resurrection and the life, saith the Lord: he that believeth in me, though he were dead, yet shall he live: and whosoever liveth and believeth in me, shall never die.

I know that my redeemer liveth, and that he shall stand at the latter day upon the earth: and though this body be destroyed, yet shall I see God: whom I shall see for myself, and mine eyes shall behold, and not as a stranger.

For none of us liveth to himself, and no man dieth to himself. For whether we live, we live unto the Lord; and whether we die, we die unto the Lord: whether we live therefore, or die, we are the Lord's.

The Order for the Burial of the Dead   173

Blessed are the dead who die in the Lord; even so saith the Spirit; for they rest from their labours, and their works do follow them.

¶ *After they are come into the Church, shall be said one or more of the following Selections, taken from the Psalms. The Gloria Patri may be omitted except at the end of the whole portion or selection from the Psalter.*

Psalm 23

THE LORD is my shepherd; * therefore can I lack nothing.

He shall feed me in a green pasture, * and lead me forth beside the waters of comfort.

He shall convert my soul, * and bring me forth in the paths of righteousness for his Name's sake.

Yea, though I walk through the valley of the shadow of death, I will fear no evil; * for thou art with me; thy rod and thy staff comfort me.

Thou shalt prepare a table before me in the presence of them that trouble me; * thou hast anointed my head with oil, and my cup shall be full.

Surely thy loving-kindness and mercy shall follow me all the days of my life; * and I will dwell in the house of the LORD for ever.

Psalm 27

THE LORD is my light and my salvation; whom then shall I fear? * the LORD is the strength of my life; of whom then shall I be afraid?

One thing have I desired of the LORD, which I will require; * even that I may dwell in the house of the LORD all the days of my life, to behold the fair beauty of the LORD, and to visit his temple.

For in the time of trouble he shall hide me in his tabernacle; * yea, in the secret place of his dwelling shall he hide me, and set me up upon a rock of stone.

And now shall he lift up mine head * above mine enemies round about me.

Therefore will I offer in his dwelling an oblation, with great gladness: * I will sing and speak praises unto the LORD.

Hearken unto my voice, O LORD, when I cry unto thee; * have mercy upon me, and hear me.

My heart hath talked of thee, Seek ye my face: * Thy face, LORD, will I seek.

O hide not thou thy face from me, * nor cast thy servant away in displeasure.

Thou hast been my succour; * leave me not, neither forsake me, O God of my salvation.

I should utterly have fainted, * but that I believe verily to see the goodness of the LORD in the land of the living.

O tarry thou the LORD'S leisure; * be strong, and he shall comfort thine heart; and put thou thy trust in the LORD.

Psalm 39

LORD, let me know mine end, and the number of my days; * that I may be certified how long I have to live.

Behold, thou hast made my days as it were a span long, and mine age is even as nothing in respect of thee; * and verily every man living is altogether vanity.

For man walketh in a vain shadow, and disquieteth himself in vain; * he heapeth up riches, and cannot tell who shall gather them.

And now, Lord, what is my hope? * truly my hope is even in thee.

Deliver me from all mine offences; * and make me not a rebuke unto the foolish.

When thou with rebukes dost chasten man for sin, thou makest his beauty to consume away, like as it were a moth fretting a garment: * every man therefore is but vanity.

Hear my prayer, O LORD, and with thine ears consider my calling; * hold not thy peace at my tears;

For I am a stranger with thee, and a sojourner, * as all my fathers were.

O spare me a little, that I may recover my strength, * before I go hence, and be no more seen.

Psalm 46

GOD is our hope and strength, * a very present help in trouble.

Therefore will we not fear, though the earth be moved, * and though the hills be carried into the midst of the sea;

Though the waters thereof rage and swell, * and though the mountains shake at the tempest of the same.

There is a river, the streams whereof make glad the city of God; * the holy place of the tabernacle of the Most Highest.

God is in the midst of her, therefore shall she not be removed; * God shall help her, and that right early.

Be still then, and know that I am God: I will be exalted among the nations, and I will be exalted in the earth.

The LORD of hosts is with us; * the God of Jacob is our refuge.

Psalm 90

LORD, thou has been our refuge, * from one generation to another.

Before the mountains were brought forth, or ever the earth and the world were made, * thou art God from everlasting, and the world without end.

Thou turnest man to destruction; * again thou sayest, Come again, ye children of men.

For a thousand years in thy sight are but as yesterday, when it is past, * and as a watch in the night.

As soon as thou scatterest them they are even as a sleep; * and fade away suddenly like the grass.

In the morning it is green, and groweth up; * but in the evening it is cut down, dried up, and withered.

For we consume away in thy displeasure, * and are afraid at thy wrathful indignation.

Thou hast set our misdeeds before thee; * and our secret sins in the light of thy countenance.

For when thou art angry all our days are gone: * we bring our years to an end, as it were a tale that is told.

The days of our age are threescore years and ten; and though men be so strong that they come to fourscore years, * yet is their strength then but labour and sorrow; so soon passeth it away, and we are gone.

So teach us to number our days, * that we may apply our hearts unto wisdom.

Psalm 121

I WILL lift up mine eyes unto the hills; * from whence cometh my help?

My help cometh even from the LORD, * who hath made heaven and earth.

He will not suffer thy foot to be moved; * and he that keepeth thee will not sleep.

Behold, he that keepeth Israel * shall neither slumber nor sleep.

The LORD himself is thy keeper; * the LORD is thy defence upon thy right hand;

So that the sun shall not burn thee by day, * neither the moon by night.

The LORD shall preserve thee from all evil; * yea, it is even he that shall keep thy soul.

The LORD shall preserve thy going out, and thy coming in, * from this time forth for evermore.

Psalm 130

OUT of the deep have I called unto thee, O LORD; * Lord, hear my voice. O let thine ears consider well * the voice of my complaint.

If thou, LORD, wilt be extreme to mark what is done amiss, * O Lord, who may abide it?

For there is mercy with thee; * therefore shalt thou be feared.

I look for the LORD; my soul doth wait for him; * in his word is my trust.

My soul fleeth unto the Lord before the morning watch; * I say, before the morning watch.

O Israel, trust in the LORD, for with the LORD there is mercy, * and with him is plenteous redemption.

And he shall redeem Israel * from all his sins.

¶ *Then shall follow the Lesson.*

¶ *But NOTE, that when this Office is used as a Memorial Service, and there is no Communion, the Epistle and Gospel for* At the Burial of the Dead *may be substituted for the Lesson.*

1 Corinthians xv

NOW is Christ risen from the dead, and become the firstfruits of them that slept. For since by man came death, by man came also the resurrection of the dead. For as in Adam all die, even so in Christ shall all be made alive. But every man in his own order: Christ the firstfruits; afterward they that are Christ's at his coming. Then cometh the end, when he shall have delivered up the kingdom to God, even the Father; when he shall have put down all rule and all authority and power. For he must reign, till he hath put all enemies under his feet. The last enemy that shall be destroyed is death.

But some man will say, How are the dead raised up? and with what body do they come? Thou foolish one, that which thou sowest is not quickened, except it die: and that which thou sowest, thou sowest not that body that shall be, but bare grain, it may chance of wheat, or of some other grain: but God giveth it a body as it hath pleased him, and to every seed its own body. All flesh is not the same flesh: but there is one kind of flesh of men, another flesh of beasts, another of fishes, and another of birds. There are also celestial bodies, and bodies terrestrial: but the glory of the celestial is one, and the glory of the terrestrial is another. There is one glory of the sun, and another glory of the moon, and another glory of the stars: for one star differeth from another star in glory. So also is the resurrection of the dead. It is sown in corruption; it is raised in incorruption: it is sown in dishonour; it is raised in glory: it is sown in weakness; it is raised in power: it is sown a natural body; it is raised a spiritual body. There is a natural body, and there is a spiritual body. And so it is written, The first man Adam was made a living soul; the last Adam was made a quickening spirit. Howbeit that was not first which is spiritual, but that which is natural; and afterward that which is spiritual. The first man is of the earth, earthy: the second man is the Lord from heaven. As is the earthy, such are they also that are earthy: and as is the heavenly, such are they also that are heavenly. And as we have borne the image of the earthy, we shall also bear the image of the heavenly.

Now this I say, brethren, that flesh and blood cannot inherit the kingdom of God; neither doth corruption inherit incorruption. Behold, I shew you a mystery; We shall not all sleep, but we shall all be changed, in a moment, in the twinkling of an eye, at the last trump: for the trumpet shall sound, and the dead shall be raised incorruptible, and we shall be changed. For this corruptible must put on incorruption, and this mortal must put on immortality. So when this corruptible shall have put on incorruption, and this mortal shall have put on immortality, then shall be brought to pass the saying that is written, Death is swallowed up in victory. O death, where is thy sting? O grave, where is thy victory? The sting of death is sin; and the strength of sin is the law. But thanks be to God, which giveth us the victory through our Lord Jesus Christ. Therefore, my beloved brethren, be ye stedfast, unmoveable, always abounding in the work of the Lord, forasmuch as ye know that your labour is not in vain in the Lord.

¶ *Or this.*

Romans viii

As many as are led by the Spirit of God, they are the sons of God. For ye have not received the spirit of bondage again to fear; but ye have received the Spirit of adoption, whereby we cry, Abba, Father. The Spirit himself beareth witness with our spirit, that we are the children of God: and if children, then heirs; heirs of God, and joint-heirs with Christ; if so be that we suffer with him, that we may be also glorified together. For I reckon that the sufferings of this present time are not worthy to be compared with the glory which shall be revealed in us. For the earnest expectation of the creation waiteth for the manifestation of the sons of God. We know that all things work together for good to them that love God, to them who are the called according to his purpose. What shall we then say to these things? If God be for us, who can be against us? He that spared not his own Son, but delivered him up for us all, how shall he not with him also freely give us all things? Who is he that condemneth? It is Christ that died, yea rather, that is risen again, who is even at the right hand of God, who also maketh intercession for us. Who shall separate us from the love of Christ? shall tribulation, or distress, or persecution, or famine, or nakedness, or peril, or sword? Nay, in all these things we are more than conquerors through him that loved us. For I am persuaded that neither death, nor life, nor angels, nor principalities, nor powers, nor things present, nor things to come, nor height, nor depth, nor any other creature, shall be able to separate us from the love of God, which is in Christ Jesus our Lord.

¶ *Or this.*

St. John xiv

JESUS said, Let not your heart be troubled: ye believe in God, believe also in me. In my Father's house are many mansions: if it were not so, I would have told you. I go to prepare a place for you. And if I go and prepare a place for you, I will come again, and receive you unto myself; that where I am, there ye may be also. And whither I go ye know, and the way ye know. Thomas saith unto him, Lord, we know not whither thou goest; and how can we know the way? Jesus saith unto him, I am the way, the truth, and the life: no man cometh unto the Father, but by me.

¶ *Here may be sung a Hymn or Anthem; and, at the discretion of the Minister, may be said the Creed following.*

I BELIEVE in God the Father Almighty, Maker of heaven and earth:

And in Jesus Christ his only Son our Lord: Who was conceived by the Holy Ghost, Born of the Virgin Mary: Suffered under Pontius Pilate, Was crucified, dead, and buried: He descended into hell; The third day he rose again from the dead: He ascended into heaven, And sitteth on the right hand of God the Father Almighty: From thence he shall come to judge the quick and the dead.

I believe in the Holy Ghost: The holy Catholic Church; The Communion of Saints: The Forgiveness of sins: The Resurrection of the body: And the Life everlasting. Amen.

¶ *Then shall be said the Prayers which follow, and such other fitting Prayers as are elsewhere provided in this Book, ending with the Blessing; the Minister first pronouncing,*

The Lord be with you.
Answer. And with thy spirit.
Let us pray.

Lord, have mercy upon us.
Christ, have mercy upon us.
Lord, have mercy upon us.

OUR Father, who art in heaven, Hallowed be thy Name. Thy kingdom come. Thy will be done, On earth as it is in heaven. Give us this day our daily bread. And forgive us our trespasses, As we forgive those who trespass against us. And lead us not into temptation, But deliver us from evil. Amen.

REMEMBER thy servant, O Lord, according to the favour which thou bearest unto thy people, and grant that, increasing in knowledge and love of thee, *he* may go from strength to strength, in the life of perfect service, in thy heavenly kingdom; through Jesus Christ our Lord, who liveth and reigneth with thee and the Holy Ghost ever, one God, world without end. *Amen.*

MOST merciful Father, who hast been pleased to take unto thyself the soul of this thy servant (*or* this thy child); Grant to us who are still in our pilgrimage, and who walk as yet by faith, that having served thee with constancy on earth, we may be joined hereafter with thy blessed saints in glory everlasting; through Jesus Christ our Lord. *Amen.*

ALMIGHTY God, Father of mercies and giver of all comfort; Deal graciously, we pray thee, with all those who mourn, that, casting every care on thee, they may know the consolation of thy love; through Jesus Christ our LORD. *Amen.*

A Thanksgiving

ALMIGHTY God, with whom do live the spirits of those who depart hence in the Lord, and with whom the souls of the faithful, after they are delivered from the burden of the flesh, are in joy and felicity; We give thee hearty thanks for the good examples of all those thy servants, who, having finished their course in faith, do now rest from their labours. And we beseech thee, that we, with all those who are departed in the true faith of thy holy Name, may have our perfect consummation and bliss, both in body and soul, in thy eternal and everlasting glory; through Jesus Christ our Lord. *Amen.*

¶ *Or this.*

ALMIGHTY and everliving God, we yield unto thee most high praise and hearty thanks, for the wonderful grace and virtue declared in all thy saints, who have been the choice vessels of thy grace, and the lights of the world in their several generations; most humbly beseeching thee to give us grace so to follow the example of their stedfastness in thy faith, and obedience to thy holy commandments, that at the day of the general Resurrection, we, with all those who are of the mystical body of thy Son, may be set on his right hand, and hear that his most joyful voice: Come, ye blessed of my Father, inherit the kingdom prepared for you from the foundation of the world. Grant this, O Father, for the sake of the same, thy Son Jesus Christ, our only Mediator and Advocate. *Amen.*

UNTO God's gracious mercy and protection we commit you. The LORD bless you and keep you. The LORD make his face to shine upon you, and be gracious unto you. The LORD lift up his countenance upon you, and give you peace, both now and evermore. *Amen.*

At the Grave

¶ When they come to the Grave, while the Body is made ready to be laid into the earth, shall be sung or said,

MAN, that is born of a woman, hath but a short time to live, and is full of misery. He cometh up, and is cut down, like a flower; he fleeth as it were a shadow, and never continueth in one stay.

In the midst of life we are in death; of whom may we seek for succour, but of thee, O Lord, who for our sins art justly displeased?

Yet, O Lord God most holy, O Lord most mighty, O holy and most merciful Saviour, deliver us not into the bitter pains of eternal death.

Thou knowest, Lord, the secrets of our hearts; shut not thy merciful ears to our prayer; but spare us, Lord most holy, O God most mighty, O holy and merciful Saviour, thou most worthy Judge eternal suffer us not, at our last hour, because of any pains of death, to fall from thee.

¶ Or this.

LIKE as a father pitieth his own children, even so is the Lord merciful unto them that fear him.

For he knoweth whereof we are made; he remembereth that we are but dust.

The days of man are but as grass; for he flourisheth as a flower of the field.

For as soon as the wind goeth over it, it is gone; and the place thereof shall know it no more.

But the merciful goodness of the Lord endureth for ever and ever upon them that fear him; and his righteousness upon children's children.

¶ Or this.

ALL that the Father giveth me shall come to me; and him that cometh to me I will in no wise cast out.

He that raised up Jesus from the dead will also quicken our mortal bodies, by his Spirit that dwelleth in us.

Wherefore my heart is glad, and my glory rejoiceth: my flesh also shall rest in hope.

Thou shalt show me the path of life; in thy presence is the fulness of joy, and at thy right hand there is pleasure for evermore.

¶ Then, while the earth shall be cast upon the Body, the Minister shall say,

The Order for the Burial of the Dead

UNTO Almighty God we commend our *brother* departed, and we commit *his* body to the ground; earth to earth, ashes to ashes, dust to dust; in sure and certain hope of the Resurrection unto eternal life, through our Lord Jesus Christ; at whose coming in glorious majesty to judge the world, the corruptible bodies of those who sleep in him shall be changed, and made like unto his own glorious body; according to the mighty working whereby he is able to subdue all things unto himself.

¶ *Then, if the Kyrie and Lord's Prayer have not already been said, the Minister shall say,*

The Lord be with you.
Answer. And with thy spirit.

Let us pray.

Lord, have mercy upon us.
Christ, have mercy upon us.
Lord, have mercy upon us.

OUR Father, who art in heaven, Hallowed be thy Name. Thy kingdom come. Thy will be done, On earth as it is in heaven. Give us this day our daily bread. And forgive us our trespasses, As we forgive those who trespass against us. And lead us not into temptation, But deliver us from evil. Amen.

O GOD, whose mercies cannot be numbered: Accept our prayers on behalf of the soul of thy servant departed, and grant him an entrance into the land of light and joy, in the fellowship of thy saints; through Jesus Christ our Lord. *Amen.*

¶ *Then the Minister may say one or more of the following Prayers, at his discretion.*

O MERCIFUL God, the Father of our Lord Jesus Christ, who is the Resurrection and the Life; in whom whosoever believeth, shall live, though he die; and whosoever liveth, and believeth in him, shall not die eternally; who also hath taught us, by his holy Apostle Saint Paul, not to be sorry, as men without hope, for those who sleep in him: We humbly beseech thee, O Father, to raise us from the death of sin unto the life of righteousness; that, when we shall depart this life, we may rest in him; and that, at the general Resurrection in the last day, we may be found acceptable in thy sight; and receive that blessing, which thy well-beloved Son shall then pronounce to all who love and fear thee, saying, Come, ye blessed children of my Father, receive the kingdom prepared for you from the beginning of the world. Grant this, we beseech thee, O merciful Father, through Jesus Christ, our Mediator and Redeemer. *Amen.*

O LORD Jesus Christ, who by thy death didst take away the sting of death: Grant unto us thy servants so to follow in faith where thou hast led the way, that we may at length fall asleep peacefully in thee, and awake up after thy likeness; through thy mercy, who livest with the Father and the Holy Ghost, one God, world without end. *Amen.*

ALMIGHTY and everlasting God, who art Lord alike of the living and the dead: Regard all those for whom we now pour out our supplications, whether the present world yet holdeth them in the flesh, or whether, released from the body, the world to come hath even now received them; Give to the living mercy and grace; to the dead, rest and light perpetual; Give to thy Church truth and peace; to us sinners, penitence and pardon; through Jesus Christ our Lord. *Amen.*

O FATHER of all, we pray to thee for those whom we love, but see no longer. Grant them thy peace; let light perpetual shine upon them; and in thy loving wisdom and almighty power, work in them the good purpose of thy perfect will; through Jesus Christ our Lord. *Amen.*

O GOD, whose days are without end, and whose mercies cannot be numbered: Make us, we beseech thee, deeply sensible of the shortness and uncertainty of human life; and let thy Holy Spirit lead us in holiness and righteousness, all our days: that, when we shall have served thee in our generation, we may be gathered unto our fathers, having the testimony of a good conscience; in the communion of the Catholic Church; in the confidence of a certain faith; in the comfort of a reasonable, religious, and holy hope; in favour with thee our God, and in perfect charity with the world. All which we ask through Jesus Christ our Lord. *Amen.*

GRANT, O Lord, to all who are bereaved the spirit of faith and courage, that they may have strength to meet the days to come with steadfastness and patience; not sorrowing as those without hope, but in thankful remembrance of all the manifestations of thy great goodness, and in the joyful certainty of eternal life with those they love. And this we ask in the Name of Jesus Christ our Saviour. Amen.

O HEAVENLY Father, who hast given us a true faith and a sure hope: Help us, we pray thee, amidst all the things that pass our understanding, to live as those who believe and trust in thy fatherly care, in the communion of saints, the forgiveness of sins, and the resurrection to life everlasting; and strengthen, we beseech thee, this faith and hope in us all the days of our life; through the love of thy Son, our Saviour Jesus Christ. *Amen.*

V. May the souls of the faithful departed through the mercy of God rest in peace.
R. And may light perpetual shine upon them.

THE God of peace, who brought again from the dead our Lord Jesus Christ, the great Shepherd of the sheep, through the blood of the everlasting covenant; Make you perfect in every good work to do his will, working in you that which is well pleasing in his sight; through Jesus Christ, to whom be glory for ever and ever. *Amen.*

> ¶ *Inasmuch as it may sometimes be expedient to say under shelter of the Church the whole or a part of the service appointed to be said at the Grave, the same is hereby allowed for weighty cause.*

> ¶ *It is to be noted that this Office is appropriate to be used only for the faithful departed in Christ, provided that in any other case the Minister may, at his discretion, use such part of this Office, or such devotions taken from other parts of this Book, as may be fitting.*

At the Burial of the Dead at Sea

> ¶ *The same Office may be used; but instead of the Sentence of Committal, the Minister shall say,*

UNTO Almighty God we commend our *brother* departed, and we commit *his* body to the deep; in sure and certain hope of the Resurrection unto eternal life, through our Lord Jesus Christ; at whose coming in glorious majesty to judge the world, the sea shall give up her dead; and the corruptible bodies of those who sleep in him shall be changed, and made like unto his glorious body; according to the mighty working whereby he is able to subdue all things unto himself.

At the Communion

> ¶ *When the Holy Communion is celebrated as a part of the Burial Office, the following Collect, Epistle, and Gospel shall be read:*

The Collect

ETERNAL Lord God, who holdest all souls in life: Vouchsafe, we beseech thee, to thy whole Church in paradise and on earth, thy light and thy peace; and grant that we, following the good examples of those who have served thee here and are now at rest, may at the last enter with them into thine unending joy; through Jesus Christ our Lord. *Amen.*

> ¶ *Or this.*

O GOD, whose mercies cannot be numbered: Accept our prayers on behalf of the soul of thy servant departed, and grant him an entrance into the land of light and joy, in the fellowship of thy saints; through Jesus Christ our Lord. *Amen.*

The Epistle. 2 Thessalonians iv. 13

I WOULD not have you to be ignorant, brethren, concerning them which are asleep, that ye sorrow not, even as others which have no hope. For if we believe that Jesus died and rose again, even so them also which sleep in Jesus will God bring with him. For this we say unto you by the word of the Lord, that we which are alive and remain unto the coming of the Lord shall not prevent them which are asleep. For the Lord himself shall descend from heaven with a shout, with the voice of the archangel, and with the trump of God: and the dead in Christ shall rise first: then we which are alive and remain shall be caught up together with them in the clouds, to meet the Lord in the air: and so shall we ever be with the Lord. Wherefore comfort one another with these words.

The Gospel. St. John vi.37

JESUS said unto them, All that the Father giveth me shall come to me; and him that cometh to me I will in no wise cast out. For I came down from heaven, not to do mine own will, but the will of him that sent me. And this is the Father's will which hath sent me, that of all which he hath given me I should lose nothing, but should raise it up again at the last, day. And this is the will of him that sent me, that every one which seeth the Son, and believeth on him, may have everlasting life: and I will raise him up at the last day.

At the Burial of a Child

¶ The Minister, meeting the Body, and going before it, either into the Church or towards the Grave, shall say,

I AM the resurrection and the life, saith the Lord: he that believeth in me, though he were dead, yet shall he live: and whosoever liveth and believeth in me, shall never die.

JESUS called them unto him and said, Suffer the little children to come unto me, and forbid them not: for of such is the kingdom of God.

HE shall feed his flock like a shepherd: he shall gather the lambs with his arms, and carry them in his bosom.

¶ *When they are come into the Church, shall be said the following Psalms; and at the end of each Psalm shall be said the Gloria Patri.*

Psalm 23

THE Lord is my shepherd; * therefore can I lack nothing.

He shall feed me in a green pasture, * and lead me forth beside the waters of comfort.

He shall convert my soul, * and bring me forth in the paths of righteousness for his Name's sake.

Yea, though I walk through the valley of the shadow of death, I will fear no evil; * for thou art with me; thy rod and thy staff comfort me.

Thou shalt prepare a table before me in the presence of them that trouble me; * thou hast anointed my head with oil, and my cup shall be full.

Surely thy loving-kindness and mercy shall follow me all the days of my life; * and I will dwell in the house of the LORD for ever.

Psalm 121

I WILL lift up mine eyes unto the hills; * from whence cometh my help?

My help cometh even from the LORD, * who hath made heaven and earth.

He will not suffer thy foot to be moved; * and he that keepeth thee will not sleep.

Behold, he that keepeth Israel * shall neither slumber nor sleep.

The LORD himself is thy keeper; * the LORD is thy defence upon thy right hand;

So that the sun shall not burn thee by day, * neither the moon by night.

The LORD shall preserve thee from all evil; * yea, it is even he that shall keep thy soul.

The LORD shall preserve thy going out, and thy coming in, * from this time forth for evermore.

¶ *Then shall follow the Lesson taken out of the eighteenth Chapter of the Gospel according to St. Matthew.*

AT the same time came the disciples unto Jesus, saying, Who is the greatest in the kingdom of heaven? And Jesus called a little child unto him, and set him in the midst of them, and said, Verily I say unto you, Except ye be converted, and become as little children, ye shall not enter into the kingdom of heaven. Whosoever therefore shall humble himself as this little child, the same is greatest in the kingdom of heaven. And whoso shall receive one such little child in my name receiveth me.

¶ Here may be sung a Hymn or an Anthem; then shall the Minister say,

The Lord be with you.
Answer. And with thy spirit.

Let us pray.

Lord, have mercy upon us.
Christ, have mercy upon us.
Lord, have mercy upon us.

¶ Then shall be said by the Minister and People,

OUR Father, who art in heaven, Hallowed be thy Name. Thy kingdom come. Thy will be done, On earth as it is in heaven. Give us this day our daily bread. And forgive us our trespasses, As we forgive those who trespass against us. And lead us not into temptation, But deliver us from evil. *Amen.*

Minister. Blessed are the pure in heart;
Answer. For they shall see God.
Minister. Blessed be the Name of the Lord;
Answer. Henceforth, world without end.
Minister. Lord, hear our prayer;
Answer. And let our cry come unto thee.

¶ Here shall be said the following Prayers, or other fitting Prayers from this Book.

O MERCIFUL Father, comfort us, we beseech thee, with the knowledge that this thy child hath been taken into the safe keeping of thine eternal love; through Jesus Christ our Lord. *Amen.*

ALMIGHTY God, Father of mercies and giver of all comfort: Deal graciously, we pray thee, with all those who mourn, that, casting every care on thee, they may know the consolation of thy love; through Jesus Christ our Lord. *Amen.*

UNTO God's gracious mercy and protection we commit you. The Lord bless you and keep you. The Lord make his face to shine upon you, and be gracious unto you. The Lord lift up his countenance upon you, and give you peace, both now and evermore. *Amen.*

¶ When they are come to the Grave shall be said or sung,

JESUS saith to his disciples, Ye now therefore have sorrow: but I will see you again, and your heart shall rejoice, and your joy no man taketh from you.

¶ *While the earth is being cast upon the Body, the Minister shall say,*

In sure and certain hope of the Resurrection to eternal life through our LORD Jesus Christ, we commit the body of this child to the ground. The LORD bless *him* and keep *him*, the LORD make his face to shine upon *him* and be gracious unto *him*, the LORD lift up his countenance upon *him*, and give *him* peace, both now and evermore.

¶ *Then shall be said or sung,*

THEREFORE are they before the throne of God, and serve him day and night in his temple: and he that sitteth on the throne shall dwell among them.

They shall hunger no more, neither thirst any more; neither shall the sun light on them, nor any heat.

For the Lamb which is in the midst of the throne shall feed them, and shall lead them unto living fountains of waters: and God shall wipe away all tears from their eyes.

¶ *Then shall the Minister say,*

The Lord be with you.
Answer. And with thy spirit.

Let us pray.

O God, whose most dear Son did take little children into his arms and bless them: Give us grace, we beseech thee, to entrust the soul of this child to thy never-failing care and love, and bring us all to thy heavenly kingdom; through the same thy Son, Jesus Christ our Lord. *Amen.*

O FATHER of all, we pray thee for those whom we love, but see no longer. Grant them thy peace; let light perpetual shine upon them; and in thy loving wisdom and almighty power, work in them the good purpose of thy perfect will; through Jesus Christ our Lord. *Amen.*

MAY Almighty God, the Father, the Son, and the Holy Ghost, bless you and keep you, now and for evermore. *Amen.*

¶ *When the Holy Communion is celebrated at the Burial of a Child, the following Collect, Epistle, and Gospel shall be used:*

The Collect

ALMIGHTY and merciful Father, who dost grant to children an abundant entrance into thy kingdom: Grant us grace so to conform our lives to their innocency and perfect faith, that at length, united with them, we may stand in thy presence in fulness of joy; through Jesus Christ our Lord. *Amen.*

The Epistle. 1 John ii

AND now, little children, abide in him; that, when he shall appear, we may have confidence, and not be ashamed before him at his coming. If ye know that he is righteous, ye know that every one that doeth righteousness is born of him. Behold, what manner of love the Father hath bestowed upon us, that we should be called the sons of God: therefore the world knoweth us not, because it knew him not. Beloved, now are we the sons of God, and it doth not yet appear what we shall be: but we know that, when he shall appear, we shall be like him; for we shall see him as he is. And every man that hath this hope in him purifieth himself, even as he is pure.

The Gospel. St. John vi

JESUS said unto them, All that the Father giveth me shall come to me; and him that cometh to me I will in no wise cast out. For I came down from heaven, not to do mine own will, but the will of him that sent me. And this is the Father's will which hath sent me, that of all which he hath given me I should lose nothing, but should raise it up again at the last day. And this is the will of him that sent me, that every one which seeth the Son, and believeth on him, may have everlasting life: and I will raise him up at the last day.

PRAYER BOOK STUDIES XIV: AN OFFICE OF INSTITUTION OF RECTORS INTO PARISHES

The Standing Liturgical Commission
of the Protestant Episcopal Church in the
United States of America

1959

PREFACE

The last revision of our Prayer Book was brought to a rather abrupt conclusion in 1928. Consideration of it had preoccupied the time of General Convention ever since 1913. Everyone was weary of the long and ponderous legislative process, and desired to make the new Prayer Book available as soon as possible for the use of the Church.

But the work of revision, which sometimes has seemed difficult to start, in this case proved hard to stop. The years of debate had aroused widespread interest in the whole subject: and the mind of the Church was more receptive of suggestions for revision when the work was brought to an end than when it began. Moreover, the revision was actually closed to new action in 1925, in order that it might receive final adoption in 1928: so that it was not possible to give due consideration to a number of very desirable features in the English and Scottish revisions, which appeared simultaneously with our own. It was further realized that there were some rough edges in what had been done, as well as an unsatisfied demand for still further alterations.

The problem of defects in detail was met by continuing the Revision Commission, and giving it rather large 'editorial' powers (subject only to review by General Convention) to correct obvious errors in the text as adopted, in the publication of the new Prayer Book. Then, to deal with the constructive proposals for other changes which continued to be brought up in every General Convention, the Revision Commission was reconstituted as a Standing Liturgical Commission. To this body all matters concerning the Prayer Book were to be referred, for preservation in permanent files, and for continuing consideration, until such time as the accumulated matter was sufficient in amount and importance to justify proposing another Revision.

The number of such referrals by General Convention, of Memorials from Dioceses, and of suggestions made directly to the Commission from all regions and schools and parties in the Church, has now reached such a total that it is evident that there is a widespread and insistent demand for a general revision of the Prayer Book.

The Standing Liturgical Commission is not, however, proposing any immediate revision. On the contrary, we believe that there ought to be a period of study and discussion, to acquaint the Church at large with the principles and issues involved, in order that the eventual action may be taken intelligently, and if possible without consuming so much of the time of our supreme legislative synod.

Accordingly, the General Convention of 1949 signalized the Fourth Centennial Year of the First Book of Common Prayer in English by authorizing the Liturgical Commission to publish its findings, in the form of a series of *Prayer Book Studies*.

It must be emphasized that the liturgical forms presented in these *Studies* are not — and under our Constitution, cannot be — sanctioned for public use. They are submitted for free discussion. The Commission will be grateful for copies or articles, resolutions, and direct comment, for its consideration, that the mind of the Church may be fully known to the body charged with reporting it.

In this undertaking, we have endeavored to be objective and impartial. It is not possible to avoid every matter which may be thought by some to be controversial. Ideas which seem to be constructively valuable will be brought to the attention of the Church, without too much regard as to whether they may ultimately be judged to be expedient. We cannot undertake to eliminate every proposal to which anyone might conceivably object: to do so would be to admit that any constructive progress is impossible. What we can do is to be alert not to alter the present *balance* of expressed or implied doctrine of the Church. We can seek to counterbalance every proposal which might seem to favor some one party of opinion by some other change in the opposite direction. The goal we have constantly had in mind — however imperfectly we may have succeeded in attaining it — is the shaping of a future Prayer Book which *every* party might embrace with the well-founded conviction that therein its own position had been strengthened, its witness enhanced, and its devotions enriched.

The objective we have pursued is the same as that expressed by the Commission for the Revision of 1892: "*Resolved*, That this Committee, in all its suggestions and acts, be guided by those principles of liturgical construction and ritual use which have guided the compilation and amendments of the Book of Common Prayer, and have made it what it is."

THE STANDING LITURGICAL COMMISSION:

GOODRICH R. FENNER, *Chairman*
ALBERT R. STUART
JOHN W. SUTER, *Custodian*
MASSEY H. SHEPHERD, JR., *Vice Chairman*
CHARLES W. F. SMITH
FRANCIS B. SAYRE, JR.
BERTRAM L. SMITH
SPENCER ERVIN, *Secretary*
JOHN W. ASHTON
FRANK STEPHEN CELLIER

Bishop Fenner has been in charge of the sub-committee on the Office of Institution.

MASSEY H. SHEPHERD, JR.
Editor, for the Commission

History

Origin and Development in Feudalism

The idea for the Institution of Ministers had its roots in the feudal system of the Kingdom of the Franks in the seventh and eighth centuries. When the Frankish conquerors of Gaul settled down, they readily adjusted to the feudal system they found there. It was not widely different from their own system where the chief of the tribe gathered about himself a band of chosen warriors who formed a kind of private military force.

The Church was brought into the system when the early Carolingian princes, and Charles Martel in particular, found that the royal domains had been exhausted and their individual holdings were not sufficient to support an army. Large estates had been given the Church and were under the control of the bishops and abbots. The princes reached for these as a solution to their problem and offered the attractive terms of definite tenure and protection. While bishops and abbots became vassals of overlords, they were ecclesiastical lords in their own right. They were not expected to take up arms themselves, but they parcelled out part of their lands to lay vassals who owed them military service, and this in turn they passed on to their lords.

The relations between the vassal and his lord were expressed in a contract that took the form of the ceremony of "Homage and Investiture." The vassal gave his lord "homage" by placing his hands between the hands of his lord and swearing to be his man and to be faithful to him. The lord then responded with the ceremony of "Investiture," presenting to the vassal a spear, flag, or some other symbol representing the fief. The ceremony was defined by custom and constituted a binding agreement.

As the failure of general government to give proper protection, order, and supervision gave rise to feudalism, so its decline was inevitable when, in the 13th century, government finally resumed these functions. Near the end of this century a group of men — (chiefly lawyers and judges) — interested themselves in crystalizing in fixed forms the customs and usages of feudalism and the ceremony of "Homage and Investiture" was one of these forms they preserved.

In England

English feudalism differed greatly from the Continental system, but with all its differences it was well-established in England before the arrival of William the Conqueror. He changed nothing radically except to enforce the essential feudal theory that the land was a gift from the king as the supreme landlord to the subject as tenant of the land. This again meant reaching out for the estates of the Church. The issue was not joined between the Church and the king, however, until the beginning of the 12th Century when Henry I came to the throne. Henry required that the Church give homage to the king — a layman, before it could receive investiture from him. Anselm, the Archbishop of Canterbury, carried on a controversy with Henry for several years before a compromise was reached which gave bishops and abbots their positions by virtue of election by the clergy, and the king was to receive homage for their lands. Henry was content when he was thus acknowledged as temporal lord.

In the Frankish kingdom, the parish priest was a man of his secular lord, but in the ecclesiastical aspect of feudalism as it developed in England after the Norman Conquest the parish priest became the bishop's man. The parish priest gave the bishop the promise of canonical obedience, and the bishop in turn inducted him into his cure. The ceremony was still entirely feudal, but the basis for it had shifted from the principle of the lord and man relationship to that of the bishop being the chief pastor and committing one of his parochial holdings to the priest. This was justified by reference to the actual situation as it existed in the early Church metropolitan parishes along the Mediterranean coast. With the growth in the number of parishes, the bishop of necessity delegated some of his ministry to men he had ordained to assist him.

This feudal relationship between bishop and priest as expressed by institution and induction continued in England until the middle of the 19th Century. The priest came to the bishop "at some convenient place" or to someone the bishop had nominated to stand surrogate for him, and after taking the oath of obedience in the presence of witnesses, he was inducted into the parish. The convenient place might be in the bishop's chapel in his manor house or some place along his route as he traveled from one of his houses to another. No uniformity of method prevailed as between bishops and dioceses. Except for royal chapels, however, the institutions to benefices were always in the control of the bishop, and uniformly also, he gave title in "institution" and in "induction" he added possession. The procedure was a legal formality entirely, as it had been from the time of early feudalism, and, moreover, nothing indicates that there was ever any liturgical accompaniment.

The nearest approach to a religious implication in institution and induction was in the procedure prescribed by Lancelot Andrewes in the early 17th Century. His ceremony was held in the porch of the church, with the church itself empty and the door locked. A minister, who had been designated by the bishop, read the bishop's mandate. That done, the priest was to take hold of the key to the church and the institutor read to him the formula that inducted him into the "real actual and corporal possession of this parish. . . ." The inducted priest then unlocked the door and went into the church alone. After locking the door behind him he performed certain prescribed particulars that related him to his parish. Other practices that arose at about this time prescribed that the priest should ring the church bell as a public signal that he was now the incumbent of the parish. This served also to give notice that the institution was not done clandestinely. It was not until Warren's *Synodalia* appeared in 1853 that any evidence is to be found that a desire existed for a religious ceremony. This book contains a "Service for the Induction of Ministers to Their Cures." It was composed of Psalms, Lessons, and Collect. No distinction was made between Institution and Induction.

Wilberforce, Bishop of Winchester, issued services for Institution and Induction in 1871, and Selwyn of Lichfield issued a form in 1873. These were followed in 1876 by Lincoln, Peterborough, and Oxford. When Earle was Archdeacon of Totnes, (later Bishop of Marlborough), he used a form that included perambulations. The ritual of perambulations both in Totnes and in later developments was derived from Lancelot Andrewes' Office for the Consecration of a Church. Stations were made at different places in the church and appropriate lections and prayers were said. Perambulations are also included in the office of the 1955 draft *Prayer Book of Canada*. In its form of service the Canadian book also makes a distinction between Institution and Induction. The Lower Houses of Canterbury and York appointed a committee which reported in 1873 on *The Manner of Instituting or Collating to a Benefice with Cure of Souls*. It provided that Institution should always take place in the parish church concerned in order that the laity might thereby be edified. It provides also that Induction shall follow "as soon after as conveniently may be."

The custom in the English Church varies at the present time. In predominantly rural dioceses the bishop institutes in his private chapel and the induction is done by the archdeacon or the rural dean in the parish church. In dioceses of smaller areas, the bishop usually visits the parish church for the institution and the archdeacon or rural dean conducts the service of induction immediately afterward. Where the two parts are combined the perambulation of the church is usually omitted.

Induction in the Colonial Church

In the Colonial Church, the manner of inducting a minister into his cure followed the English custom with necessary adaptations. Instead of the bishop or archdeacon, the induction was accomplished on the authority of the royal governor or the vestry. The Church was officially established in Carolina, Virginia, Maryland and in the four counties of New York, and the King gave to the governors the duty of appointing ministers to the parishes of the Anglican Churches and the authority to induct them.

Virginia was an exception to this general practice. While the governors demanded the right to appoint ministers to parishes, the vestries through many years consistently and strenuously opposed their assumption of such a right. The Rev. Dr. G. MacLaren Brydon, the Historiographer of the Diocese of Virginia, in a recent letter stated that the Virginia Code of Laws in 1642-43 gave vestries this right, but it was not until the Code of 1748 that vestries won complete and final victory. Dr. Brydon stated further that there is no evidence at all that the Church ever had any liturgical service of Institution and Induction.

The appointment and induction of a minister into a parish in Maryland was wholly within the gift of the royal governor or proprietor. The Rev. Dr. Nelson Rightmyer, the Historiographer of the Diocese of Maryland, states that induction consisted merely of a letter from the governor to the priest he selected giving him possession of the parish. There seems, also, to have been some resistance in Maryland to appointments by the royal governor. Dr. Rightmyer mentions two cases where the governor had appointed priests that were not acceptable to the people. The people nailed the doors and windows shut that they might prevent the priest from "taking possession" of the church. In one case where this was done the priest surreptitiously entered through a window with two of his friends and proceeded to read the service. When this was discovered, the people were most unhappy, but no one seems to have doubted that by this act he had become the legal incumbent.

In the situation, moreover, in which the Colonial Church was placed, there were no bishops or archdeacons to induct or institute a minister into a parish. The authority he had in a parish was that conveyed to him in his ordination to the priesthood and the appointment he had received from a vestry or a royal governor.

The American Office

At the annual Convention of the Diocese of Connecticut held at St. John's Church, Stratfield (now Bridgeport) in 1799 the Rev. Dr. William Smith, Rector of St. Paul's Church, Norwalk, was requested "to prepare an office for inducting and recognizing clergymen into vacant parishes and present the same for adoption to the next Convention of the Diocese." The Office submitted by Dr. Smith was first adopted by the Bishop and Clergy of the Diocese of Connecticut in convocation at Derby, November 20, 1799. At the Convention which met in Litchfield, June 6, 1804, The Office of Induction as agreed upon by the Bishop and Clergy in Convocation was adopted.

When the Rev. Dr. Smith undertook to prepare the office, he had only meager precedents of Institution and Induction in England and the Colonial Church, but as has been stated, these were documents of legal form entirely. It has been thought that Lancelot Andrewes' "Manner of Induction" was one resource he had, but except for invoking the Triune Name at the end of the document there is no religious reference in it at all. Services set forth in several dioceses in England in the last quarter of the 19th century were adaptations of Andrewes' "Office for the Consecration of a Church." In the Rev. Dr. Smith's Office, however, there does not appear to be any influence of Andrewes' "Consecration of a Church" upon his work.

The Convention of the Diocese of New York, meeting October 6, 1802, adopted with slight changes the Office approved by the Connecticut Convocation of 1799.

A comparison of the three forms of 1799, 1802, and 1804 shows that when the General Convention of 1804 adopted the Office, it undoubtedly had before it the New York text of 1802. Moreover, the text of the present Office follows the New York Office closer than the other two, and is therefore the proximate source of our present Office of Institution. A comparison also shows that the slight differences between the three forms are mostly verbal and confined largely to changes in the rubrics.

We are indebted therefore to the Rev. Dr. Smith and the Connecticut Convocation for the provision of this Office for the Church. Dr. Smith's prayer of self-dedication, said by the minister in the second part of the Office is one of great beauty in literary quality and is also most intimate in spiritual expression. The minister kneels before the altar and makes his supplication for humility, devotion, and gratitude in his ministry of prayer, sacrament, in preaching, and in teaching.

There are terms used in this Office that are not in any other Office in the Prayer Book. Such words as "Altar," "Holy Eucharist," and "Ministers of Apostolic Succession," reflect the influence of the Scottish Church upon Bishop Seabury and the clergy of his diocese.

The service adopted by General Convention in 1804 was usually conducted by a presbyter acting as deputy for the bishop. He read the letter of induction that had been transmitted to him by the bishop.

In 1808 the word "induction" was dropped from the Office and "institution" alone was used. The principle of institution and induction is combined in the American Office; but only a vestige of the thought of induction remains. This appears in the beginning of the third paragraph of the letter of institution — "So we authorize you to claim and enjoy all the accustomed temporalities appertaining to your cure." The presentation of the keys by the senior warden denotes only that the priest is to have free access to the building where he may perform acts of sacerdotal function among the people. "Induction" was dropped from the title in order that there might not be possible conflict with state laws and the rights of vestries. There must have been the thought also that "induction" was unsuitable for the Church in America, inasmuch as historically it meant induction into a living or benefice that could be bestowed by an individual.

When the Office was first adopted by the diocesan Convention of New York in 1804, a canon was also adopted that made its use obligatory. A priest could not vote in the Convention of the Diocese unless he had been inducted.

A canon of like force was adopted by General Convention in the same year, but it was repealed ten years later when it was found that it worked a hardship in special cases. In Maryland, as an instance, no clergyman had ever been inducted and when Bishop Claggett wanted an assistant bishop it was discovered that all his clergy had been disfranchised. In 1814, immediately after the canon was repealed, Maryland was able to elect James Kemp as Suffragan Bishop.

The Office fell into almost complete disuse after it was made optional, and it was not until the last decade of the 19th century that Henry Codman Potter, the Bishop of New York, used the Office in his diocese and largely promoted its revival in the Church. Although it is used more frequently, it is still not in general use in the Church. It might be assumed that the canonical provisions for the election of a rector with the approval of the bishop and the acceptance of Letters Dimissory to the diocese are regarded as sufficient; but this purely canonical procedure loses the excellent teaching values contained in the Office and the participation of the congregation in the event.

The rubrics now provide that the Office be used with one of the Daily Offices or separately, but it hints strongly in its first two and last two rubrics that the instituting minister should be the bishop and that the service should be the Holy Eucharist.

Proposed Revision

The changes proposed in this revision of the Office of Institution of Ministers are mainly those of rearrangement and shortening. The rearrangement here suggested makes for an easier following of the service; and in shortening, certain parts of the present service are omitted that, while edifying, are not strictly essential to the purpose of institution. By proposing a shorter Office it makes possible its use with the celebration of the Holy Eucharist and Sermon without the service being carried to undue length.

The rubrical requirement that the Office be used with the Holy Eucharist is derived from the fact that the public institution of a rector into his parish has sacramental character. It is a solemn engagement that is ratified by a rite. The significance of this engagement or mutual pledge between priest and people is thereby deepened by its being integrated with this highest act of corporate worship which they offer together. To this end a Collect, Epistle, and Gospel are supplied at the end of the Office.

The title to the proposed Office has been changed from "Institution of Ministers into Parishes or Churches" to "Institution of Rectors into Parishes." This is done in order that it might be brought into conformity with present-day American Church usage. The word "parish" is accepted by the Church to denominate a congregation that under the Canons has a measure of independence with respect to calling and installing a priest as its rector. What we term a "mission" is also a church, but it does not have the independence or the competence that is accorded a parish. The word "rector" is substituted for minister, because used in connection with "parish," the rector is always a priest. A deacon cannot be the rector of a parish. A bishop may be, of course, but he is also a priest and if he should be the rector of a parish, he functions in his priestly capacity.

The charge to the congregation is transferred to the beginning of the Office where it properly belongs. The present order is confusing inasmuch as the Letter of Institution which is quite generally read should follow the charge.

The reasons for omitting the third paragraph of the Letter are first, that it carries the idea of "inducting into a living" or the gift of a benefice at the hands of the bishop. Except for some situations in the Colonial Church, this has never obtained in the Church in the United States. The "temporalities" relationship is uniformly between the rector and the vestry. Secondly, the matter of "dissolution of all sacerdotal relation" is taken care of by canon, and it has no need to be obtruded in the service itself. It would seem inappropriate also to mention the dissolution of a relationship before it has well begun.

The versicles, the prayer beginning "Direct us, O Lord," and the Lord's Prayer are omitted. This is suggested in order that the presentation of the Keys and the Books might come together, and also because they interrupt the flow of the service towards its essential purpose. The prayer, "Direct us, O Lord," is too general in its application, and as the Lord's Prayer must be used in the Liturgy, the use of it here is unnecessary duplication.

The Psalms provided in the present Office following the presentation of the Books are omitted for the reason that the Epistle and Gospel in the Eucharist supply the necessary lections.

The first and second prayers said by the instituting minister are conflated in this Proposed Office. The prayers as they stand in the present Office overlap one another in thought. The conclusion of the second prayer, "May the words of his mouth, etc.," and drawn from Psalm 19:14, breaks the orderly progression of petition as developed in the prayers.

The third prayer, "O God, Holy Ghost, Sanctifier of the faithful," is removed from its present position and substituted for the priest's prayer for the congregation at the end of the Office. This last prayer in the present Office is a cento of quotations from eight different sources. It is uneven in expression and appears to recapitulate what has already been said and add other petitions in the event something has been omitted. The prayer that has been transferred is based on the Collect for the Seventh Sunday after Trinity, and in its original form is derived from *The Gelasian Sacramentary*.

A rubric is provided before the Benediction given by the instituting minister that makes it clear that such Benediction is for the priest who has been instituted.

After the concluding prayer has been offered provision is made for the instituted rector to say the precatory blessing found in Numbers 6:24-26.

An Office of Institution of Rectors into Parishes

¶ *The Bishop having received due Notice of the Election of a Rector into a Parish, as prescribed by Canon, and being satisfied that the Person chosen is a qualified Minister of this Church, may proceed to institute him into the Parish.*

¶ *The following Office shall be used with the Order for the Holy Communion.*

¶ *At the time designated for the new Incumbent's Institution, the Bishop, or the Institutor appointed by him, attended by the new Incumbent, and by the other Clergy present, shall enter the Chancel. Then all the Clergy present standing in the Chancel or Choir, except the Bishop, or the Priest who acts as Institutor, who shall go within the rails of the Altar; the Wardens (or, in case of their necessary absence, two members of the Vestry) standing on the right and left of the Altar, without the rails; the Senior Warden (or the member of the Vestry supplying his place) holding the keys of the Church in his hand, in open view, the Bishop, or the Priest who acts as the Institutor, shall say,*

DEARLY beloved in the Lord, we have assembled for the purpose of instituting the Rev. A. B. into this Parish, (*or* Church,) as Priest and Rector of the same; and we are possessed of your Vote that he has been so elected; as also of the prescribed Letter of Institution. But if any of you can show just cause why he may not be instituted, we proceed no further, because we would not that an unworthy person should minister among you.

¶ *If any objection be offered, the Bishop, or the Priest who acts as the Institutor, shall judge whether it afford just cause to suspend the Service.*

¶ *No objection being offered, or the Institutor choosing to go on with the Service, then shall be read the Letter of Institution, as followeth.*

¶ *To our well-beloved in Christ; A. B., Presbyter. Greeting.*

WE do by these Presents give and grant unto you, in whose Learning, Diligence, sound Doctrine, and Prudence, we do fully confide, our Licence and Authority to perform the Office of a Priest, in the Parish (*or* Church) of E. And also hereby do institute you into said Parish, (*or* Church,) possessed of full power to perform every Act of sacerdotal Function among the People of the same; you continuing in communion with us, and complying with the rubrics and canons of the Church, and with such lawful directions as you shall at any time receive from us.

And as a canonically instituted Priest into the Office of Rector of Parish, (*or* Church,) you are faithfully to feed that portion of the flock of Christ which is now intrusted to you; not as a man-pleaser, but as continually bearing in mind that you are accountable to us here, and to the Chief Bishop and Sovereign Judge of all, hereafter.

In witness whereof, we have hereunto affixed our episcopal seal and signature, *[Sigillum Signat.]* at —, this — day of —, A. D. —, and in the — year of our consecration.

¶ *And then shall the Senior Warden (or the member of the Vestry supplying his place) present the keys of the Church to the new Incumbent, saying,*

IN the name and behalf of _____ Parish (*or* Church) I do receive and acknowledge you, the Rev. A. B., as Priest and Rector of the same; and in token thereof, give into your hands the keys of this Church.

¶ *Then the new Incumbent shall say,*

I A. B., receive these keys of the House of God at your hands, as the pledges of my Institution, and of your parochial recognition, and promise to be a faithful shepherd over you; In the Name of the Father, and of the Son, and of the Holy Ghost.

¶ *Then shall the Institutor receive the Incumbent within the rails of the Altar, and present him the Bible, Book of Common Prayer, and Books of Canons of the General and Diocesan Convention, saying as follows.*

RECEIVE these Books; and let them be the rule of thy conduct in dispensing the divine Word, in leading the Devotions of the People, and in exercising the Discipline of the Church; and be thou in all things a pattern to the flock committed to thy care.

Minister. The Law was given by Moses;
People. But Grace and Truth came by Jesus Christ:
Minister and People. Who is God over all, blessed for evermore. Amen.

Let us pray.

ALMIGHTY Father, who by thy Son Jesus Christ hast purchased to thyself an universal Church, and hast promised to be with the Ministers of Apostolic Succession to the end of the world: Be graciously pleased to bless the ministry and service of him to whom the charge of this Congregation is now committed. So replenish him with the truth of thy doctrine, and endue him with innocency of life, that he may faithfully serve before thee, to the glory of thy great Name, and the benefit of thy holy Church; through the merits of the same Christ

Jesus our Saviour, who liveth and reigneth with thee in the unity of the Holy Spirit, one God, world without end. Amen.

¶ *Then shall the Rector, who has been instituted, kneel, and the Institutor shall bless him, saying thus:*

THE God of peace, who brought again from the dead our Lord Jesus Christ, the great Shepherd of the sheep, through the blood of the everlasting covenant; Make you perfect in every good work to do his will, working in you that which is well pleasing in his sight; through Jesus Christ, to whom be glory for ever and ever. Amen.

¶ *Then shall the Instituted Minister kneel at the Altar, to present his supplication for himself, in this form.*

O LORD my God I am not worthy that thou shouldest come under my roof; yet thou hast honoured thy servant with appointing him to stand in thy House, and to serve at thy holy Altar. To thee and to thy service I devote myself, body, soul, and spirit, with all their powers and faculties. Fill my memory with the words of thy Law; enlighten my understanding with the illumination of the Holy Ghost; and may all the wishes and desires of my will centre in what thou hast commanded. And, to make me instrumental in promoting the salvation of the people now committed to my charge, grant that I may faithfully administer thy holy Sacraments, and by my life and doctrine set forth thy true and lively Word. Be ever with me in the performance of all the duties of my ministry: in prayer, to quicken my devotion; in praises, to heighten my love and gratitude; and in preaching, to give a readiness of thought and expression suitable to the clearness and excellency of thy holy Word. Grant this for the sake of Jesus Christ thy Son our Saviour.

¶ *The Instituted Minister, standing up, shall say,*

The Lord be with you.
Answer. And with thy spirit.

Let us pray.

O GOD, Holy Ghost, Sanctifier of the faithful, visit, we pray thee, this Congregation with thy love and favour; enlighten their minds more and more with the light of the everlasting Gospel; graft in their hearts a love of the truth; increase in them true religion; nourish them with all goodness; and of thy great mercy keep them in the same, O blessed Spirit, whom, with the Father and the Son together, we worship and glorify as one God, world without end. *Amen.*

UNTO God's gracious mercy and protection we commit you. The Lord bless you and keep you. The Lord make his face to shine upon you, and be gracious unto you. The Lord lift up his countenance upon you, and give you peace, both now and evermore. *Amen.*

¶ *Here may be sung a Hymn or an Anthem.*

¶ *The Instituted Rector, if he has been so appointed by the Bishop, shall proceed to the celebration of the Eucharistic Liturgy, using the Collect, Epistle and Gospel here following:*

The Collect

ALMIGHTY God, who dost call thy Priests to be ministers of thy grace: Vouchsafe unto them, by the guidance of thy Holy Spirit, so to dispense thy Word and Sacraments to the people committed to their charge, that they may be accounted faithful stewards of thy holy Mysteries; through Jesus Christ our Lord. *Amen.*

The Epistle. Romans xii. 3

FOR I say, through the grace given unto me, to every man that is among you, not to think of himself more highly than he ought to think; but to think soberly, according as God hath dealt to every man the measure of faith. For as we have many members in one body, and all members have not the same office: So we, being many, are one body in Christ, and every one members one of another. Having then gifts differing according to the grace that is given to us, whether prophecy, let us prophesy according to the proportion of faith; or ministry, let us wait on our ministering: or he that teacheth, on teaching; or he that exhorteth, on exhortation: he that giveth, let him do it with simplicity; he that ruleth, with diligence; he that sheweth mercy, with cheerfulness. Let love be without dissimulation. Abhor that which is evil; cleave to that which is good. Be kindly affectioned one to another with brotherly love; in honour preferring one another; not slothful in business; fervent in spirit; serving the Lord.

The Gospel. St. Matthew x. 37

HE that loveth father or mother more than me is not worthy of me: and he that loveth son or daughter more than me is not worthy of me. And he that taketh not his cross, and followeth after me, is not worthy of me. He that findeth his life shall lose it: and he that loseth his life for my sake shall find it. He that receiveth you receiveth me, and he that receiveth me receiveth him that sent me. He that receiveth a prophet in the name of a prophet shall receive a prophet's reward; and he that receiveth a righteous man shall receive a righteous man's reward. And whosoever shall give to drink one of these little ones a cup of cold water only in the name of a disciple, verily I say unto you, he shall in no wise lose his reward.

PRAYER BOOK STUDIES XV: THE PROBLEM AND METHOD OF PRAYER BOOK REVISION

The Standing Liturgical Commission
of the Protestant Episcopal Church in the
United States of America

1961

FOREWORD

This brief paper is an effort to explain with greater fullness the thinking of the Standing Liturgical Commission with respect to certain recommendations it plans to make to the General Convention of 1961. In this way we hope to reach many more readers than those who may obtain our more formal canonical report to the Convention. We ask only that those who read this Study will lend to it the constructive help of a fair and unprejudiced consideration, whether or not they agree with its argument.

Since this Study was completed the Commission has received with great regret the resignation of its esteemed secretary, Mr. Spencer Ervin. His name, however, is signed to this Study as one who made very substantial contributions to the formulation of its several topics of discussion. The Commission can never express adequately its profound gratitude to Mr. Ervin for the many hours of faithful and painstaking service he has rendered to the work of the Commission, and its indebtedness to his ever fair, generous, and disciplined contribution.

THE STANDING LITURGICAL COMMISSION

GOODRICH R. FENNER, *Chairman*
ALBERT R. STUART
JOHN W. SUTER, *Custodian*
MASSEY H. SHEPHERD, JR., *Vice-Chairman*
CHARLES W. F. SMITH
FRANCIS B. SAYRE, JR.
BERTRAM L. SMITH, *Secretary pro tem*
SPENCER ERVIN
JOHN W. ASHTON
FRANK STEPHEN CELLIER

Copyright, 1961, by
THE CHURCH PENSION FUND

The Problem of Procedures

Prayer Book revision is a lively subject of interest throughout the Anglican Communion these days. It is stimulated by a variety of factors:

1. The revolutionary changes in our world in the generation since the revision movement of the 1920's;
2. The impact on an ecumenical scale of the contemporary Liturgical Movement;
3. The significant advances in liturgical knowledge, especially of the New Testament and Patristic periods;
4. The emphasis of the new Biblical theology, which has altered our perspectives upon the doctrinal issues of both the medieval and Reformation eras;
5. The needs of younger Churches of Asia and Africa, now largely self-governing, to adapt liturgical usages to their own cultures;
6. The cross currents of influence from one Christian tradition to another, which stem from the encounters and discussions of the Ecumenical Movement.

At the Lambeth Conference of 1958, the Bishops devoted a major portion of their Report to the problems and principles which these new factors create for the task of Prayer Book revision in the immediate years ahead. They recognized that the coming generation will be one of notable liturgical changes, that new liturgical knowledge makes it impossible to accept tacitly the English Prayer Book of 1662 as a definitive norm of liturgical unity in our Communion, and that several provinces of Anglicanism must be allowed freedom to adapt our common inheritance to local needs and circumstances.

Within the past decade, several Anglican provinces have completed major revisions of the Prayer Book; namely, South Africa, India, Japan, and Canada. The process is still at work in the West Indies and (so far as we know) in China, and it is being inaugurated in Wales and England. Doubtless some of the newer as well as older provinces of Africa and Asia will soon be launched on the same venture. In our American Church, there has been much informal talk of a new review of the 1928 Prayer Book, stimulated in part by the Studies of the Standing Liturgical Commission. At the General Convention of 1958, a resolution designed to initiate a formal revision of the Prayer Book was introduced and passed the House of Deputies, though it failed to receive a concurrent vote in the House of Bishops. (See *Journal of the General Convention*, 1958, pp. 292–94.)

It is not the purpose of this paper to argue the pros and cons of whether the American Church should at this time engage in a formal revision. We shall assume only that a large proportion of our clergy and laity, if not a majority of them, desire such a move in the near future. If we dare to assume such a sentiment on a widespread scale, a more immediate problem presents itself for consideration: namely, what is the best way to proceed in Prayer Book revision? How can the Church not only profit by the best liturgical scholarship, but also be satisfied that the results of such a large undertaking will be as beneficial as possible for us, under God and the guidance of His Holy Spirit?

Until recent years, the pattern of procedure for revision of the liturgy has been basically similar in all our Anglican provinces. A commission has been appointed, representative of varying points of view, to prepare concrete proposals of change. These proposals have then been published for study and debate, and finally, according to the constitutional processes of the several provinces, they have been voted upon seriatim by the supreme legislative bodies of the Church. Thus the decisions made, pro and con, respecting each proposal of change, have been definitive and irrevocable, and a "new" Prayer Book issued on a determined date has taken its place as the one and only liturgy authorized for use in public worship. Specifically in our American Church, this procedure, as is well known, requires that every single proposal to change the Prayer Book (including commas, semicolons, periods, italics, no less than words and order of parts) be approved by concurrent majorities in both Houses of the General Convention for two successive conventions. Should any mistake have been made, whether of a major or a minor nature, as a result of this procedure, the only legal way of correcting it would be by concurrent majority vote of the two Houses in two more successive conventions. The only exception is the provision for change of the lectionary of the Daily Offices by vote of one rather than of two conventions.

The advantages of this procedure, which we inherit from the Constitution established by the first General Convention of 1789, are obvious. It assures the Church that the liturgy cannot be recklessly altered by a passing whim and without due consideration over a period extending for at least three years, though usually for six years or more. It provides sufficient opportunity for any member of the Church to air his views and to seek support for his opinions. Thus the Church is insured against arbitrary and autocratic action. The procedure gives ample time for the ripening of judgment upon any proposal, and, as past experience has shown, it almost inevitably leads to preponderant majorities for or against specific proposals when the time of final voting arrives. Certainly the record of voting in the General Convention during the revisions of 1880–1892 and 1913–1928 reveals that no sizable minority could claim that any changes of major import were passed by narrow margins, or that its conscientious acceptance of what was finally adopted was threatened.

The disadvantages of such a procedure are equally obvious, however, especially if one considers the present size and program of the General Convention. Our constitutional provisions for Prayer Book revision were drawn up when the House of Bishops consisted of three members, and the House of Deputies could be comfortably accommodated in a relatively small room. By comparison with present day Conventions, those of our early years seem like two committees, where every member of Convention had ample opportunity to speak, discuss, argue, and treat one with another in intimate personal exchange. Now, however, the House of Deputies numbers over 650 members, and the House of Bishops over 150 members. The amount of overall business with which the Convention is concerned is so greatly increased that it is difficult to comprehend within the allotted time of meeting all the pressing issues that await attention. Moreover, the large increase in "extra-curricular" activities that take place concurrently alongside the formal sessions of the General Convention is very time- and energy-consuming, however worthwhile they may be in purpose.

The result is that much of the business of Convention has to be directed to smaller committees of each House. These committees work with the best of will, but always under pressure, and frequently they have but a few months at most, or a few days at least, to give consideration to reports that may have taken years to formulate. It is no exaggeration to say that many deputies, for reasons both excusable and not excusable, give little study to the reports circulated among them, but depend as in all large assemblies of this kind — upon the opinions of leaders or the recommendation of committees. In recent years also, there has been a notable problem connected with the procedures for intercommunication between the two Houses of Convention. It often happens — as it did frequently in the last revision of the Prayer Book — that matters which are considered and voted upon in one House never reach the floor of the other. Thus the business in hand is delayed for another three years. As the Church grows in membership, and new dioceses are formed, the difficulties of the General Convention as at present constituted are likely to increase.

The situation just described obtained in large degree a generation ago during the last revision of the Prayer Book. Instead of taking from three to six years' time, the work of two General Conventions, it spread out over fifteen years and five successive conventions. The Deputies, for example, had passed through two successive conventions a sizable portion of the Joint Commission's proposals, in 1916 and in 1919, but much of it the Bishops did not even begin to consider until 1922. Hence much of the work had to be started all over again. The work of revision would have lasted longer had not the General Convention of 1925 decided to cut off all further consideration of "new" business connected with revision, in order to complete the required constitutional procedure in 1928. Nor should it be overlooked that most of what was finally passed in 1928 added up to what has been called "the unfinished business" of the 1892 revision.

This long delay in completing what had been begun with enthusiastic purpose was certainly not due to lack of extraordinarily able leadership in the conventions. It was due precisely to the fact that the General Conventions from 1913 to 1928 were engaged in many other projects of tremendous and time-consuming import, among other things the whole reorganization of the national structure of the Church and its missionary enterprise. It is difficult to believe that in the foreseeable future the General Convention will have any more leisure, from lack of other pressing business, so that it may devote its attention with sufficient time and concentration to the revision of the liturgy.

Another disadvantage of our procedures revealed by the last revision was the piece-meal way in which it of necessity was conducted. There was never an opportunity to consider what the final results of a revised Prayer Book would be like as a whole. It is the more remarkable that the Book of 1928 came forth with the consistency of rubric and formulary such as it has, especially when one considers that most of the bishops and deputies who participated in the final voting in 1928 were not the same as those who voted upon the earlier stages of revision in 1916 and 1919. Fortunately, the leadership of the revision during the five conventions maintained a sufficient continuity. Even so, the two primary leaders in the Deputies in 1916 and 1919, Dr. Parsons and Dr. Slattery, were elevated to the episcopate by 1922; though happily in their case, the House of Bishops waived its traditional custom that "baby bishops" should be seen but not heard!

A New Method

A new method of approach to Prayer Book revision, called "trial use," has come to the fore in recent years and has been followed with considerable success by many of the Anglican provinces that have recently completed, or are now at work on revision. It has been used in South Africa, India and Ceylon, Japan, and Canada, and it is being pursued in Wales and the West Indies. The Church of England's Liturgical Commission is also seeking enabling legislation from Parliament to allow the same method.

It should also be noted that the same method has been followed in the past decade in the liturgical reforms initiated in the Roman Catholic Church, in the development of the liturgical rites of the Church of South India, and in the promulgation of a new liturgy by eight Lutheran Churches in America. The Methodist Church in the United States, at its 1960 General Conference, adopted the same procedure for the proposed revisions of *The Book of Worship for Church and Home*.

This new method of "trial use" involves the following procedure: A duly appointed commission is engaged to prepare proposals for liturgical revision. As always, such proposals when drawn up and published are circulated throughout the Church for constructive criticism by letter and in the church press. The proposals are then considered by the supreme governing body of the Church as a whole, with opportunity to make changes if need be or if desired. The proposals are then authorized for trial use for such a time and under such conditions as the governing body deems appropriate. That is to say, the proposed changes, under the conditions laid down, may be used experimentally for a period of time as an optional alternative to the established and authorized liturgy. At the conclusion of the appointed time, with the experience gained not only from discussion but also from actual use, the supreme governing body then proceeds to formal voting of whatever changes it considers to be feasible and fitting. Only after this experiment has been made and the testing ratified or annulled by such a vote is the authorized liturgy or service book revised and published in its new version, and the period of trial use brought to an end.

Two objections to this procedure will at once come to mind. The one, which is more serious, is that less care may be taken in authorizing experimental forms than is taken in final voting, so that formularies or practices that are theologically unsound may intrude their way into the worship of many congregations. This is a risk, certainly, but only a risk. It assumes a priori that any commission appointed to prepare formularies for trial use will be less conscientious and responsible about the integrity of the faith than is a commission appointed to prepare final revisions. This is to prejudge the question. Similarly, it ignores the fact that the General Convention, in the case of our own Church particularly, would still have control over whatever proposals were authorized for trial use. Trial use does not mean that any and every proposal of the revising commission should or would be acceptable for experimental use. The General Convention would not give up its constitutional right to a veto. Moreover, if the Convention had any fear that promiscuous use of the trial proposals would do damage, it could lay down the conditions of time and place when and where such experiments might be made.

But this objection still does not meet a more formidable circumstance: namely, there is no assurance that revision under our present procedures would necessarily preserve the Church from doctrinal error. We have as a Church never claimed infallibility for the doctrine of the Prayer Book. It is perfectly clear that many clergy and laity at the present time do not believe that every doctrinal expression or nuance in our Prayer Book is incapable of improvement. The range of doctrinal interpretation allowed by our present formularies is considerable, yet this does not necessarily weaken the unity which we now have in the faith. In fact, our Communion has by and large boasted of its comprehension within the same fold of doctrinal expressions and emphases that are maintained in a certain degree of tension.

Should inept or inexact phrases of doctrinal import occur in formularies issued for trial use, remedy of them could be made in a single session of Convention. Under our present constitutional procedures, should such a misfortune happen to a formulary that succeeded in passing two successive conventions, it would take two more conventions to correct it. And we all are aware that General Convention has always been very loath, and rightly so, to make changes in the Prayer Book by bits and pieces. For this would require a whole new printing of the Prayer Book and the difficult task of replacing the slightly altered Book in all parishes, missions, and chapels. The practical problems are almost insuperable.

But changes in experimental forms, since they have nothing final about them, can be made much more readily and easily.

A second objection to trial use has to do with the practical problem of having varying liturgies in use simultaneously in the Church, to the confusion of the laity, who move about quite a bit, if not of the clergy. This objection would be the more solid were it not for two circumstances that obtain at present. One is that we are already accustomed in the Episcopal Church to considerable variety in liturgical usage — and that, too, legally — because of the flexibility of rubrics in some of our services, and also because of the great variations in ceremonial from parish to parish. It is arguable that variation in ceremonial causes more consternation and confusion to many laity than does variation in text. Whether this is desirable is not a matter for discussion in this connection. But it is reasonable to suppose that the Church allows such variation to continue, with all the risks involved, because it considers this to be fitting in a Church that claims to be comprehensive.

Another circumstance that should be borne in mind is due to the recent growth of the Church itself, with the increase and mobility of our American population. More and more parishes and missions now find themselves ministering to people who have no background either in the Episcopal Church or in any other Church with a fixed liturgical tradition. One of our greatest problems today is to mold these new people in the spirit of liturgical worship itself. They have no presuppositions about it and very few prejudices. It is very doubtful if they would be put off by liturgical variables. This is the more true if one considers the fact that any commission appointed to provide forms for experimental use is not likely to be so radical — and least of all is General Convention likely to be so — as to produce forms of unrecognizable relationship to the familiar patterns. An American churchman travelling abroad — and there are more and more of them — who attends the Daily Offices or the Holy Communion in churches of other provinces of Anglicanism is seldom disturbed by the variations from his familiar American Prayer Book which he encounters. And the amount of variation, as between the English and the American Prayer Books respectively in their orders of Holy Communion, is not inconsiderable.

There is one advantage to trial use that possibly outweighs all objections. It removes the task of liturgical revision from the realm of purely theoretical discussion and provides a basis of judgment on proposed forms from concrete experience. It has been aptly said that when the disciples asked the Lord to teach them to pray, He did not give them a lecture or a pamphlet to study, but He gave them a prayer to be said. One learns to worship and pray by doing it far more than by considering and discussing it. For the Spirit helps our infirmities in and through the act of worship itself. The whole purpose of trial use is summed up in the consideration that we cannot really tell what we ought to say and to do until we try it out under the provident assistance of the Spirit of God working in us.

Under our present arrangements for Prayer Book revision, we cannot know until it is too late whether what we think is good and proper is actually as effective and helpful as we suppose. Often this involves seemingly minor matters — directions of posture, syntax and punctuation, the difference of "may" and "shall" rubrics, the rhythm of Collects, the sequential arrangement of forms and ceremonies, the beginning and ending of lections. But it may also affect matters of major importance — the length of intercessions and consecratory prayers, the dramatic build-up of a rite, and the more subtle nuances of meaning that accrue from the order of words. The shift of position of a whole section of the Communion rite, for example — such as the intercession or the penitential devotions — might affect the whole movement and action of the service. Similarly, a Prayer of Consecration quite as long as our present one might be devised, but at the same time be made to seem less long and tedious because of a differing order of contents or of rhythmic relation of phrases.

It is possible, of course, that the principle of trial use might lend itself to a piece-meal revision. But if so, this would not have the disadvantage of such a method of revision as we have under our present procedures. We have noted that at present the slow and piece-meal process of revision makes it almost impossible to make an overall review of the Prayer Book as a whole. Under trial use, however, no final decisions would be made until the entire liturgy proposed had been subjected to experiment. Hence loose ends and awkward or obscure phrasing can be caught and corrected at the end of the process of revision before it is too late to deal with them. Such a procedure would also greatly enhance the likelihood of consistency of reference and coordination of rubrics in the final stages of revision.

Trial use has one inestimable advantage in the Church today, considering its present size and complexity and diversity of membership. It allows every member an opportunity to voice his or her reaction to proposed changes in the liturgy on the basis of actual experience. It would thus make the decisions of the General Convention more truly representative and responsive to broad sentiment within the Church. There would be less likelihood that a relatively small number of revising "experts" on the one hand or of powerful committee leaders on the other would dominate the course and results of revision. Of course, there would not be unanimity on every point and issue. Nor is there any way of predicting whether the opportunity afforded for a wider participation by the rank and file of church membership in the task of revision would lead to conservative, moderate, or radical changes. But this is not of great moment, compared to the prospect of creating a liturgical reformation that could witness to an informed and responsible public opinion throughout the Church based upon the broadest possible experience of actual participation in the task.

We must bear ever in mind today, in any process of liturgical revision, certain insights provided by the modern science of liturgical research and study with regard to the way in which the great rites of the historic Church have come into existence and exercise a living and creative influence upon the spiritual growth of the Church. As the late Dom Gregory Dix said so pointedly, "The good liturgies were not written; they grew." That is to say, a great liturgy is not merely an external, imposed law. It is a process welling up in continually fresh streams of devotion from the inner life of believing, practicing Christians. Law plays a very necessary part in liturgical revision, in that it preserves standards recognized and approved by the whole Church. But liturgies also develop through the emergence of unwritten customs responsive to needs of actual worshipping congregations. The recognition of this fact was a significant factor in the modern revisions of our Prayer Book in their ideals of "enrichment and flexibility" that modify in some degree the principle of a rigid uniformity.

A Specific Proposal

For the past three General Conventions (1952, 1955, and 1958) the Standing Liturgical Commission has offered with its report to the Convention a resolution seeking an amendment to Article X of the Constitution that would set up the possibility of trial use in any forthcoming revision of the Prayer Book. This resolution has been defeated in all three Conventions. The Commission is disturbed, not so much by its defeat, as by the fact that the proposal has not as yet been properly interpreted to the Convention. This circumstance has arisen in part from the peculiarity that the Commission has not been able to explain the proposal to the Convention except through mediate persons and groups. Though the Liturgical Commission is set up by Canon Law, it has no right to present its report and recommendations directly to the Houses of Convention, but its proposals are referred to committees which make such disposition of them as they please. In the House of Bishops, of course, an episcopal member of the Commission has the right of the floor to support, oppose, or elucidate the actions recommended by the committee of the House. In the House of Deputies, an amendment to the rules of procedure might well allow the Commission — and any other Joint Commission for that matter — to have the privilege of the floor of the Deputies to present and explain its report, especially in circumstances when no clerical or lay member of the Commission has been elected as a deputy.

The resolution offered in the 1958 Convention — one that will be offered again in the 1961 Convention — reads as follows:

> *Resolved,* The House of ... concurring, that the first proviso of Article X of the Constitution, be and it is hereby amended to read as follows:

> But notwithstanding anything hereinabove contained, the General Convention may at any one meeting, by a majority of the whole number

of Bishops entitled to vote in the House of Bishops and a majority of each order in the House of Deputies,
- a. Amend the Table of Lessons and all Tables and Rubrics relating to the Psalms;
- b. Authorize for trial use throughout the Church, as an alternative at any time or times to the established Book of Common Prayer or to any section or Office thereof, a proposed revision of the whole Book or of any portion thereof, duly undertaken by the General Convention.

It is section b) that primarily concerns us here. Contrary to opinions widely disseminated in the Church, this resolution is not intended to cover any and every proposal made by the Standing Liturgical Commission or by any other responsible group in the Church. It refers only to a proposed revision of the Prayer Book in whole or in part that has been *duly undertaken by the General Convention*. The prerogative of the General Convention is in no way altered by this resolution, since the Convention would still be the arbiter with respect to the when, the what, and the how of Prayer Book revision.

1. As to the *when*: The General Convention alone can decide at what time or times any revision may be undertaken and trial use permitted, and the length of time such trial use may be allowed. It does not give this authority to the Bishops alone, or to the Standing Liturgical Commission, or to any other body.
2. As to the *what*: The General Convention alone can decide whether the whole Prayer Book or any part of it may be brought under consideration for revision. It may, for example, decide to revise only one portion of the Prayer Book and determine, by the method of trial use, whether or not it wishes to proceed further along this line. But in no way does the amendment bind the General Convention to adopt the method of trial use for any and every proposed revision.
3. As to the *how*: The General Convention alone can decide what group or groups may be authorized to present proposed revisions. It is not bound to use the services of the Standing Liturgical Commission in this way. It is the more likely that it will follow precedent and call for the appointment of a Joint Commission on Revision, with such and so many representatives of clergy and laity as it sees fit.

It is therefore important to bear in mind that the proposed amendment to the Constitution is designed solely to provide the Church with the flexible resource of trial use for such time and under such circumstances only as the General Convention sees fit to employ it in the course of Prayer Book revision.

It is inevitable that this proposed amendment offered by the Standing Liturgical Commission will be linked to another proposal made by the Commission at the General Convention of 1958: namely, the resolution asking the General Convention to authorize for optional use a number of additional propers of the Holy Communion on the Lesser Feasts and Fasts. But the two resolutions are not necessarily linked together. But this second proposal may well be used to illustrate the first.

Under the present constitutional directives, the Convention in 1958 decided that it could only authorize the propers of the lesser holy days as a formal revision of the Prayer Book. Hence, if the Convention of 1961 ratifies the action taken in 1958, these propers will have exactly the same authority as the material of the Prayer Book itself — even though they are for optional use only and will not be printed within the Prayer Book itself. Furthermore, under the same canonical regulations, these propers of the lesser holy days cannot be changed without the vote of two successive conventions.

If, however, the Convention of 1958 had been able to operate under a constitutional provision allowing trial use, the propers of the lesser holy days could have been authorized by the vote of a single convention — and changed by the vote of a single convention — and a period for their experimental use could have been determined if so desired. Since these propers are certainly in the nature of an experiment — and no one can know at the present time how many of them will prove to be acceptable and regularly used — it would seem that trial use would have been a much better way of dealing with them. After a period of availability and use in the Church, it would be possible to determine how much of this material should ultimately be incorporated in a formal revision of the Prayer Book.

Furthermore, if these propers should prove to be inadequate to the need which they are designed to supply, trial use would make it easy for the Church to make such supplements to them as might from time to time appear desirable, and these supplements would in turn undergo a testing from trial use. Through this whole process of sifting a fairly sizable body of new material, the Prayer Book would remain unaltered and free from constant encumbrance with what might turn out to be of ephemeral interest.

Nor would the problem of doctrinal orthodoxy be so serious under a trial use as some suppose. Priests who found any of the material theologically defective or offensive would not be under any obligation to use them. If there should be widespread dissatisfaction on these or other grounds (such as literary style) with the material in use, the matter could be readily remedied by vote of General Convention. The offending material would be withdrawn, without jeopardizing the rest of the material. The Prayer Book would still remain unaffected, as our primary standard of doctrine, and nothing would be ultimately admitted within its covers except what the Church over a period of use and familiarity had come to believe was appropriate to its contents.

The Standing Liturgical Commission believes that the Church acting through the General Convention should have an honest confrontation with this proposal of constitutional amendment to permit trial use as a revision method. It believes that this method offers the best means whereby a future revision of the Prayer Book can be made to the satisfaction of the vast majority of the Church, and with the least burden of partisan tension. It believes also that it is only fair to offer to the Church a method of procedure that many other provinces in the Anglican Communion, as well as other distinguished bodies of Christian people, have found and are continuing to find effective. We believe that the present size of our Church and of its supreme legislative organ suggests that the method of trial use is the best we can devise to ensure that the whole Church — that is to say, all its members — may have an opportunity to participate and express themselves in the development of our common liturgical life.

www.ingramcontent.com/pod-product-compliance
Lightning Source LLC
Chambersburg PA
CBHW061347300426
44116CB00011B/2026